DISCOVERY ROAD

"The power comes from the excellence of writing."
The Independent

"Truely Inspirational reading 10/10"
Cycling Plus

"Readers will find themselves reassessing their lives
and be inspired"
Sir Ranulph Fiennes

"This book doesn't set out to change your life, but
don't be surprised if it does."
Roger Greenaway

"Once in a while you come across a book that's a
sheer delight to read. I'd recomend Discovery Road
to anyone in possesion of, or in search of the spirit
of adventure"
Al Humphries

DISCOVERY ROAD

Andy Brown & Tim Garratt

Published by Eye Books

Foreword Sir Ranulph Fiennes

Discovery Road
4th Edition
April Date 2005

Published by Eye Books Ltd
51 Boscombe Rd
London
W12 9HT
Tel/fax: +44 (0) 20 8743 3276
website: www.eye-books.com

Set in Frutiger and Garamond
ISBN: 0953057534

British Library Cataloguing in Publication Data
A catalogue record for this book is available from the British Library

Printed and bound in Great Britain by Creative Print & Design (Wales) Ltd

Contents

Dedication

Acknowledgments

Foreword

1   Something Happened   1

Australia

2   A flying wombat called Ethel   15

3   Cruising the Great Ocean Road   31

4   Beyond the back O'Bourke   42

5   Roo-shooters and roadrains   55

Africa

6   Beside the Jade Sea   75

7   Rikki-Tikki-Tonga and the Bongo Bongo Man   86

8   Crossing the Massai Steppe   110

9   Ladies who are not gentleman   137

10   Halfway around The world   159

11   Too much close encounters   176

12   Much further by bicycle   191

13   The heart of the matter   205

14   Sauerkrout and Cream Cakes   225

South America

15	Hottest spot north of Havana	237
16	Two scabby dogs on the road to Iguacu	247
17	The Lost Jungle	272
18	A little Argie bargie	279
19	Over the Pampas	298
20	Appointment at the end of the world	311

| Postscript | 328 |
| Equipment List | 330 |

Also by Eye Books
About Eye Books
Eye Books Club

For the proud people
of Turkana.
Against all the odds
may you prosper

Acknowledgements

The following people have contributed either their magic, faith, energy, vision, passion, support, money, skill, friendship or beer in an important way and we greatly appreciate all of them:

His Royal Highness Prince Charles.

Sir Ranulph Fiennes, adventurer and author.

Sir Bob Horton, former chairman of BP.

Dick Crane, adventurer and writer.

Mary and Petre Withall for the cottage, encouragement, kindness and wine (read Mary's novels published by Hodder and Stoughton).

John Brown, sorry you didn't get to read it Dad.

Ruth and Roy Garratt for a lifetime of love and support.

Simon Garratt for invaluable advice on equipment and those endless faxes.

Phyl for waiting and always being there when it mattered most.

Gordon, Trish, Colin, Lisa, Claire and all the kids for advice, space and a real home.

Suzanne and the Taplin family.

Cassie.

The people of Easdale Island for your welcome.

Bianca Pik Yiu Lam for your love, wisdom, kindness and gerunds.

Miriam Hurley for being there.

Steve 'Silver Back' Hodnett for your letters which followed us all around the world.

Sue Ryrie for love and endless support.

Simon Beames and Al Inglis for friendship, encouragement, advice and laughing in the right places.

Captain Greg Tonnison for smart ideas.

Paola, Kate, Piggy and Monty for the old days.

Phil Andrews and Carina for artwork and support.

Anne Maloney, Macy DeCarrie and Alistair 'Offshore' Westell for your friendship.

Jenny Hayward of Macmillans, Hong Kong, for artwork and advice.

The people at BP Polygon for helping the people of Turkana.

Debbie Smith at IT.

The people of Poulshot and Telford for contributing to fund raising events.

The staff and students of Bridgnorth Endowed School for support and inspiration.

Ken Heywood for the use of your workshop to tinker about with the bikes.

Anne Marie De Godoy and family and the friendly people of Féderal.

The staff and students of the Outward Bound Schools in Scotland and Hong Kong.

Huw Parsons for advice.

Saracen for bikes.

Kodak for film.

Karrimor for panniers.

Phoenix for tents.

Cotswold for camping gear.

On Your Bike, London Bridge for bike bits.

John Munyes and the staff of I.T., Nairobi, Kenya.

Thank you all

A word from Practical Action

Practical Action is absolutely delighted with the results of Andy and Tim's tremendous efforts in making this challenging journey, and achieving such a fund-raising success.
Tim and Andy showed an incredible amount of personal effort and dedication. Their skills of organisation, persuasion and creative thinking were used to the full. They had tremendous energy, not only initiating the voucher support system, and in raising the profile of their venture, but also setting up a pre-departure sponsored bike ride!

With over £35,500 Practical Action was able to support training programmes for farmers and pastoralists in the Turkana region of Kenya. To supplement their traditional knowledge, communities learned new skills to help them in coping with adverse conditions like drought and poor soil. A Practical Action study showed that new technologies, such as improved ways of harvesting rain water for sorghum crop growing, continues to be adopted.

This increased security enables women to restock their goat herds, buy household goods and contribute to school fees.

Epic journeys change lives forever. For Tim and Andy, life has a new perspective. For families in Turkana, life has an increased chance of security.

On behalf of Practical Action here and in Kenya, thank you.
Nick Burn
International Director,

Practical Action is the working name of Intermediate Technology Development Group Ltd.
The Schumacher Centre for Technology and Development, Bourton on Dunsmore, Rugby, Warks CV23 9QZ
UK. Registered Charity no. 247257

Foreword

I know little about bicycles but to attempt to cycle fifteen thousand kilometres, without back-up, through some of the most demanding terrain on earth is clearly no mean undertaking.

There are all too few young people like Tim Garratt and Andy Brown who, in this money aware age, are driven by a spirit of adventure and are willing to give up comfortable, safe lives for the hardship and danger of arduous venture.

This fascinating account is a kaleidoscope of sharp observation, humour and revealing introspection. We are taken on a voyage of self-discovery and are confronted with some of the crucial issues facing everyone living in the world today.

Readers will surely find themselves reassessing their lives and be inspired to reach out and follow their own dreams.

Sir Ranulph Fiennes
Explorer

1 Something happened – Andy

A delicate essence of human excrement, finely blended with rotting fruit, followed me down the station platform. An ageing brown cow with a hunched back nuzzled through a waste bin and contentedly chewed on a portion of crumpled newspaper. Beyond the cow, in half-light, lay a human corpse. A man in his thirties, lying to attention, feet slightly splayed and eyes staring up at the vaulted wooden roof. It was midnight in Agra, northern India. The air was still; the stench and the heat oppressive.

Ahead, in the dim fluorescent light of the platform, a scabby dog staggered around going nowhere, shaking violently and frothing at the mouth. He used to be a greyhound. Now, his rear leg was broken and gleaming white bone jutted through skin and black gunk. Odd tufts of ginger hair hung to purulent, pink flesh. I skirted him and climbed aboard the train.

The engineer was stoking up the boiler, ready for the off. Squeezing my way along the narrow corridors in the dark, I stumbled over sleeping bodies, a mother cuddling a child, a wrinkly man two hundred years old, several families on the move with their pots and pans, chickens and bulging white bundles. Using my lighter, I located the numbers painted on the ends of bunks and found my way, eventually, to my reserved bed.

Sitting smoking clay pipes on the opposite bunk were two white guys. 'Wild place eh?' I said as I lit a candle and introduced myself. Their names were Wink and Tim. 'Did you see the dog?' I asked. 'He's hoping to find someone who will be kind enough to shoot him in the head,' said Tim. They were English like myself.

Wink wore a flying helmet, but his resemblance to Biggles ended there. They both wore lightweight cotton, bought for a penny or two in some local market. In dim, flickering light we chatted amicably for a while about diarrhoea. A small boy came down the gangway selling chai. He waited patiently while we drank the sweet brew from fragile clay cups.

An open hand appeared at the window, resting on the ledge. We ignored it for a minute. Tim eventually looked out. 'Christ, look at this,' he said. 'We'll have to give this guy something.'

I moved over and looked down on the beggar and was shocked at the sight. His face was horribly contorted; skin seemed to drip off his skull like melted chocolate. Dark, empty eyes stared back from beneath folds of skin. He just stood there, not speaking, hand out. We each gave a few rupees to ease our consciences.

At last the train lurched into action and we lay back and tried to rest. Sleep was impossible with the banging of the carriage couplings and the rolling of the old beast, instead we recounted adventures long into the night.

'How about a little poetry Watson?' said Tim in time, looking to his friend.

In the dark, swaying train, Winker Watson recited Coleridge's *Kubla Khan*, from beginning to end. It sounded fantastic, although he probably made half of it up. I responded by reciting *If*, by Rudyard Kipling and certainly made half of it up!

Wink, the poet, worked in a scrap metal yard, melting down beer barrels; Tim was a teacher of English and Physical Education and they both lived and played rugby in Telford in Shropshire.

The three of us hit it off and went, eventually, up to Nepal, where we trekked, laughed and philosophised for a few weeks in the Himalayas. At about sixteen thousand feet, on the well worn trail to Everest Base Camp, I got sick and headed down, while they got sick and headed up.

I had met Cassie a short time before I went to India and when I got back to London we moved in together. I was really ill, amoebic dysentery, giardia, campylobacter and fish flukes were all drawing lots for my food before I could get to it. When Cassie eventually got tired of the smell, she pushed me into The Hospital for Tropical Diseases in St. Pancras, where I was fed nothing but cream crackers and after dinner mints; not because they were any good for me, it was just that these were the only foods the nurses could slide under the door!

For most of the next four years I behaved like an ambitious, suburban career boy, while Cassie and I toddled along quite happily. I devoted myself to the petroleum industry and made respectable, safe progress through the corporate ranks. The pension fund was building up nicely, I had a few shares, the cottage was stylish; stripped pine, Monet prints, mandolin on the mantelpiece and magnetic messages on the fridge.

Every morning a pile of paper an inch thick dropped on my desk and needed attention. I pushed and tweaked the business relentlessly; for this my staff used to call me the electric ferret. I travelled the country spending two or three nights a week in hotels trying to avoid ball-bearing salesmen at the bar. I persuaded people to believe in company policies in which I did not believe myself. The company squeezed every possible hour out of me; they owned my soul and my passing youth. Every month I paid a thousand quid to the mortgage company and every month the value of the cottage went down by the same amount and I worked harder and harder. I seldom slept peacefully, or found time to walk in the hills, watch the sunset, play with my nieces or see my friends. The more successful I became the harder it became for Cassie to put up with my unpredictable mood swings and my miserable face.

Meanwhile Tim, Wink and I only met up a handful of times. I dragged them down to London for one or two wild parties and they, being good old rugby playing Midlanders, thought me rather yuppyish; though compared to real yuppies I was a yokel! When everything started to change for me I had not seen them for nearly two years. Tim had even lived in London for six months but I had always been too busy to see him.

On a dazzling, blue January day I was invited to a business lunch in the private dining room of a country pub. It was a jovial, mutual back-slapping affair for the key management.

When the meal was finished the Director held the floor, '... and most of all', he said, ' I have to thank the Sector Managers, Andrew and Bernie, who have each made around a million pounds net profit over and above their targets this year. Without their innovation and persistence we would not have turned this company around or achieved these tremendous results.' He paused dramatically. 'Outstanding performance guys.' There was real emotion, his voice even cracked on the word 'outstanding.' Now it could have been the Chateauneuf du Pape talking or perhaps his jubilation at his imminent promotion and return to Aussieland on the back of our success, but he seemed to mean it.

'Christ,' I thought, nodding my head in thanks, 'this job's done then'. The job and the figures were not important to me; being successful and collecting the recognition was all that mattered. I had now achieved what I had wanted. Another thing struck me; 'Outstanding achievement' he had said, but where exactly was it? I could not see it or touch it, it was just a set of figures on paper. There would always be more petrol and more figures stretching on forever. My pioneering spirit would not allow me to plod on into middle age with more of the same, so what could I do now?

Perhaps reading my mind, the Director pulled me aside a few days after the lunch and said he was trying to sort me out a secondment in Europe or the States to 'keep me interested' and 'moving forward', 'No promises though.'

'Yeeee Haaa!!' I thought, 'Now that'll be a challenge.'

I soon attended a five day assessment programme, where twenty assessors analyze every move of the twelve candidates. The prize at the end of countless tests and presentations was a place on the fast track to oil stardom. When the fifty page report arrived a month later the summary read, 'While Andy is certainly able to operate at grade eleven (the grade of the posts mentioned in the US and Sweden) it is the view of the panel that Andy is too entrepreneurial and too innovative to become a senior manager in this organisation.' This was worth rereading a few times. It wasn't that I wasn't entrepreneurial enough or innovative enough, but too much so. For five years I had been under the impression that I was working for a business, I had clearly got it wrong, it must have been a government I was working for, perhaps in the Eastern bloc. It also struck me that no senior managers apart from my immediate boss had made any mention of the fact that I had produced an extra million pounds profit from the seventy businesses under my control, no 'well done', no 'how did you manage that?' no 'I bet you sacrificed a lot to do that!' in fact they didn't seem to care whether I made ten million or lost ten million. They seemed to be playing chess while I was playing world cup football.

Alone one night, flicking around for a late night movie, I was assaulted by images. The usual thing, you know: starving babies, injustice, apathy and greed.

'... 250,000 children die each week from easily preventable diseases...' the presenter informed me.

Not wanting to witness such misery I reached for the ON/OFF button, but was stopped, '... $2.5 billion per year, the amount spent on cigarette advertising in America, would prevent most child deaths in the developing world ...', the presenter went on, '... the quarter of the planet's population which live in the north consume three-quarters of the planet's resources...', on and on she went. I could not switch off.

The head of Oxfam came on, '... What is living? What is life?' he asked, speaking slowly. 'Living is discovering your intellect and using it ...', he was forceful and angry, '... for hundreds of millions of children there is no possibility of living in the true sense ...' More pictures of deformed, miserable, homeless children.

My cheeks were wet with tears. I felt embarrassed to be a European; ashamed that I was healthy, that I was capable of anything and doing nothing. I cried for the children starved of opportunity and I cried for my life, full of opportunity yet unfulfilling.

Another Friday evening, dark and drizzly. Windscreen wipers slid in time to Roy Orbison singing Mystery Girl. I joined Roy in the good bits, '...Darkness falls and I, I take her by the hand, take her to my twilight land ...'. We were not bad together Roy and I, we could have been great, except that when I went up he went down. The powerful car felt like a cheetah zipping up the motorway.

My phone rang. This would be my own mystery girl, Cassie. It was her first day back. Roy Orbison was cut off in mid flow. Pushing a button, I spoke to the microphone above my head. In case it was not her I said a formal, 'Andrew Brown'.

'Drasvadure!!' said the voice. It was her, bursting with enthusiasm. That word, some sort of Russian greeting, sounded like, 'Does your arse fit you?'

'Yes, thank you,' I said and we both chuckled as always. 'Hello, it's lovely to hear your voice, are you OK?'

'Yes. Come home, I want to see you.' She had been filming in the Soviet Union for five weeks. Too long, much too long!

After the call I turned the music up and sang on happily. Ahead, brake lights banged on across three carriageways. We all stopped, sat and waited. No movement. Must be an accident, I thought. Why do people have to have accidents on Friday evenings? Why can't they wait until Monday morning? It's so damned selfish. Eventually we started moving again, a metre at a time. Flickering jets floated down across the night sky. Where had they been?

I was so looking forward to seeing her tonight. Cassie had been twenty-one when we met. I was twenty-six then. She had lifted me up when my marriage had ended and taught me to enjoy living. Cassie was a beautiful girl, marvellous in lots of ways; bright, artistic, mischievous and passionate. I felt I would never find anyone better. Through her I had discovered the theatre, great art, foreign movies, toe sucking and taramasalata. I confess that, before Cassie, I had even eaten white bread.

The traffic crawled forward. We had moved half a mile in thirty minutes. I switched the tape off and listened to the radio. After a while the announcer said, '… and London's traffic this Friday night … There are long delays on the M25, anti-clockwise, approaching Heathrow Airport.' I could have told him that.

Things, though, had changed between Cassie and me over the last few months. It just happens. Work had got in the way, my electric ferret trips all over the country and her filming trips to the Soviet Union were starting to tell. We had started to form our own separate lives.

A large dark shape loomed up gradually on the left hand side of the motorway. As I edged forward, I could make out a crane, forty feet high. Ten minutes later I was level with the mighty praying mantis of a machine as it stood deserted on the hard shoulder. I inched past and was confused to see the cars in front zooming off into clear road. There had been no pile-up after all.

I exploded, 'You mean I've sat in a queue for half an hour,

while you lot have taken your turn to stop and look at a crane? A crane!! You stupid bastards!!' This was the last straw.

Had they no awareness of how their actions affected anyone else? Or was it that they were aware, but did not care?

Who were they, these motorway loonies, these crane spotters? People driving expensive company cars; they had power and position. They were off to warm, comfortable homes in the suburbs. All this talent, education, ingenuity, drive and skill being wasted on trivia; making and selling things that we do not need, while the world is crumbling about our ears. Their lives so dull that a crane was interesting. People LIKE ME!!

I realised I had always wanted to be in their gang and bit by bit, over the last years, I had joined. I was one of them, self absorbed, inward looking, unproductive and I despised myself for it. I was, after all, making my living by selling the earth's resources, polluting, using and consuming. My life was almost void of giving.

I pulled the car over onto the hard shoulder beyond the crane and turned the whole thing over in my mind. It just hit me, sitting there in the car: I did not want to be one of these people any more, or more accurately I did not want to be me any more.

It is a shocking experience finding that all you have worked for is worthless. I just sat, oblivious. There had been something else I had wanted to do, once. That might be a way out. What was that? I had a vague memory of studying maps and jotting notes on weather. I could give up the job, satisfy my stupid ego and my lust for adventure, drop the millstone of the mortgage, leave this poisoned air far behind, and maybe do someone a little good at the same time. There had been an idea; I had left it tucked away in a dark place at the back of my mind, safely out of view for two or three years.

Had I been in a movie, I would have jumped out of the car right there. Leaving door open and engine running, I would have kicked off my sensible, shiny shoes, discarded the white shirt and paisley tie and crossed those muddy fields to the roar and bright lights of the airport and caught the first flight out. But no. Too straight. Too stiff.

I kept my own council for a week while I mulled over my life. Work suffered, my head was full of distraction. I took long walks along the Thames towpath in the evenings, while a battle of conscience raged in my head. Wait for the job in Europe. No, break out and find new ground. Think of the dangers. You are thirty years old, grow up will you? You're still young, in your prime, you should be out hunting, it's a natural instinct. Knuckle down. No, make your life extraordinary. You've got it made, don't chuck it all away now. Stay with Cassie, get married, have kids. No, no, you fool, live your life as if your life depends on it. There was no easy solution, the price was going to be high whatever I decided.

'I have something to tell you', I said to Cassie at last. We were in the sitting room, reading and drinking a cheap Safeway Rioja.

There was a worried silence, then 'What is it?' She was more than beautiful, she was elegant and offbeat. She leant forward, supporting her chin gracefully with the back of her hand. I did not want to lose her. Her cheek bones statuesque. The dark silky hair was high on the forehead and severely short at the back, an image of cool efficiency.

'I'm going to cycle round the world.' For something so major for us both the words came out surprisingly easily.

More silence. 'Oh yes?' she said at last, flatly, not believing, 'Er ...Why?', even a hint of mockery. Her mahogany eyes were piercing and unyielding, missing nothing. She was weighing me up.

'Come with me Cassie, this life is no good for us. These jobs and the expense of living are destroying us.'

'Why, AB?' she said calmly putting down her book.

'Time's ticking away, I have to do something before my spirit is sucked out of me entirely. We can do it together.'

She held my gaze, 'AB, this life happens to be good for me, and anyway the furthest I've ever cycled is to the shops to buy sherbet dips when I was twelve. It's just not my thing.' Her face showed concern and strain but she was too strong and too proud to cry in front of me, even if her emotions pushed her. She would not give herself away.

'Cassie, I love you. I don't want to leave you, but I have to do something real. It's too painful and too wasteful playing by the rules all the time. I'm tired of being a suburban money grabber. There has to be a better way to live, that's all.'

'And what about the house?' she said.

'We'd need to sell it if you come – if you don't come I don't know, I'll need my share to finance the journey. We don't really own it anyway, the mortgage company owns it. It's just an illusion.'

'Well listen AB, I can't come with you. I don't share your need to escape from life.'

'No, no, you've missed the point,' I enthused, 'I'm not escaping from life, I'm escaping to life. Life is calling and asking more from me.'

'Well maybe.'

We sat silently for a few minutes. Cassie refilled the wine glasses and said, 'I can see that you must go or you'll just drift with your dreams and be a misery for ever.' I was to be released. She paused for a moment, 'Don't expect me to wait for you though,' she said coolly, 'I have my own things to do.'

So there it was, the ultimate price. Love. To find happiness I had to give up what I loved best.

After some months, I kissed Cassie goodbye, handed her my key and walked down the crazy paving path which I had laid myself a year earlier. I had proudly left my initials in the wet cement on the step by the front door. I reached the gate, turned to look at Cassie and the cottage, my life. This was the point of no return. I had managed to rescue half of the last dribble of equity in the house before the plummeting economy swallowed it, barely enough though for the trip, and nothing compared to the effort I had put in over the years to pay the goddammed mortgage. Though laden with a box of books, I waved, turned and walked out into the world. At that precise moment my life changed irrevocably, but it was not the joyous release I had expected. Never have I felt more sad, more lonely or more frightened.

I reckoned I still needed a year to plan the project. I rented a room in a house nearby and left Cassie to carry on with her life in peace.

There would be nothing to stop me now but my own lack of will. No means of transport but cycling had even crossed my mind; nothing else offered such self reliance, speed, cleanliness and simplicity. There is something pure and natural about revolving, repeating and rolling forwards under your own power.

There was much to figure out: Where to go? Which route? Who would come with me? For which charity could we raise money, and how? How much would it cost? What equipment would be needed? How do you fix a puncture? Would some bastard stick a knife in my back in some unknown backstreet? What about the wild animals and diseases? Was I just having a nervous breakdown? This last question kept popping up with alarming regularity.

I had not adjusted a set of brakes since I was eleven and I would not have known a bottom bracket if it had fallen out of my bottom so I took the first positive step in all this planning by deciding to take two weeks off work to cycle from John O'Groats to Land's End. The top of Britain to the foot. After all the upheaval I had caused so far, it was also about time I discovered whether or not I was actually up to cycling long distances.

As the train glided north across the green and pleasant Scottish lowlands, I could not help thinking, 'This is a bloomin' long way from Land's End. What have I done?' Somehow it did not matter that it all seemed too difficult. A microchip in my head had taken over my life. Once it was switched on it could not be switched off; like sex, once you have started you cannot stop, you are not really in control. Somehow I would do this thing.

At Thurso Station I met a girl. I lifted her bike off the train and fate did the rest. She too was doing the End to End ride, with a relay of friends to keep her company.

Suzanne Taplin was a bubbly character, short and strong with a pretty, rounded face, bright eyes, straight brown hair and was a dedicated, verbal communicator, if you know what I mean.

She was a primary school teacher, frustrated with the new compulsory testing. 'People are leaving the profession in droves,' she said. 'It's not the same any more, this Government's trying to control everything we do. Too many rules and forms.'

As we sat in the pub at John O'Groats, it was hard to get a word in once she had started. We made each other laugh though, and connected. Suzanne had done some travelling and was very active with swimming, cycling, rowing and horse riding. I could see that behind the chatter she had a special strength.

'Do you think you'll do any more travelling?' I asked.

'Maybe. I suppose now is the right time whilst I'm still single. If I meet someone special I probably won't have the chance again.'

My faithful, yellow mountain bike was accustomed to the

Thames towpath. It liked the flatness, the ducks and the pub by Hampton Court Bridge. Leaving John O'Groats, I was alarmed at the effort needed to persuade the bike to move at all. It was in a sulk over the panniers I had asked it to carry; stuffed with a tent, stove, too many clothes, food spares. I had to talk very gently to let it know that I was, indeed, its friend.

I cycled with Suzanne and her friend, Bridget, for a few days along the Scottish coast and through the mountains.

While scooting past fields of freshly rolled wheat, I divulged my vague plan.

Suzanne visualised me struggling along mud roads in Asia, in unbearable heat and dismissed it, 'You are NUTS! It's not possible ... Is it?'

'Haven't you heard Suzanne,' I said, quoting one of my beloved motivation tapes 'the choicest fruit is always to be found on the highest and most precarious branches. You just have to reach out further and take a risk to win it.'

'Nuts'.

On the way south towards Land's End, having left Suzanne and Bridget in Edinburgh, I asked the bike how it felt about a teensy-weensy detour to Telford to see the boys. You should have heard the language!

I turned up on Tim's doorstep unannounced, hungry, dirty and particularly smelly. He took me in without a word, fed me and later whisked me off to the Red Lion in Wrockwardine Wood.

Tim is an uncompromising rugby centre, with hard features and solid build. He has sparkling blue eyes and short curly hair. Ladies find him good looking.

'How's Wink these days?' I asked as we sat down to our first pint.

'He's great. He found he didn't have enough time to read poetry at the scrappy, so he left and joined the Fire Brigade instead. He got married recently. You remember Maggie don't you?'

'Yes, of course, that's great. Marriage is further away than ever for me.'

'How's Cassie?'

'Ahh, don't ask. She's picked up with a new man, and she seems really happy. It's hard to handle. Anyway, what's happening with you?'

> **Tim recalls:** 'I remember Andy sitting there looking lean and mean. The cycling was obviously doing him good. His blond hair and round glasses made him look like a cross between John Lennon and a Surfer's Paradise beach bum. It was surprising to have him pop up out of the blue after two years.'

'Hm I'm in a bit of a rut really,' said Tim. 'I'm not attached at the moment, so I've been thinking I might do some more travelling; go off to South-East Asia for a while. Life's a bit too easy here you know. Don't you think we hear so much bad news all the time from everywhere else? I have an idea to go travelling again to see if the world is as shitty as it's made out. How about you, what are you up to?'

'Ah ha,' I thought.

I asked Tim, 'How do you feel about risking everything, to find out if you can cycle round the world?'

This very nearly put him off his pint, and that is no mean feat.

'WHAT, TONIGHT?' he chuckled.

'No, next year, a twelve month journey,' I said. 'I haven't worked out the details yet, but it's got to be different and difficult; none of this catching buses and pushing bikes up hills rubbish; a proper expedition.'

I gave him ample time to think it over. After five seconds I said, 'What do you reckon then?'

Tim protested, 'I haven't ridden a bike since I was a kid! And anyway, what would be the point?'

'That's just it, I've been missing the point. I got caught up in the trap of suburban life; collecting things and chasing comfort. I'm tired of it all, it's meaningless. Now I want discomfort, to reconnect with myself and with real things like hills, forests, wind and rain. I need more purpose to my life. We take food, water and shelter for granted, but for over half the world's population the attainment of those most basic needs is an impossible dream, while we all live like kings at their expense. I'd like to think that there's a way of balancing things out so that we have less and they have what they need to live real lives.'

'Oh yeah?' scoffed Tim, 'How?'

'I have absolutely no idea, but I want to try to find out. You have to start somewhere. We have to go and take a look. We only have one chance of life in this world and this world has only one chance of us. We should try to contribute more. Anyway whatever happens it'll be a great adventure eh?'

Tim recalls: 'The idea seemed totally absurd to me, how could anyone possibly cycle around the world in twelve months? And as for Andy's ideas on balancing the supplies to human needs, well it seemed a bit far fetched. Over the following weeks, however, I began to see what he meant and became more aware of my need for some kind of fulfilment. The prospect of continuing year after year, treading the same waters, was suffocating and the thought of going off to South-East Asia just for the hell of it seemed empty. Andy's idea was a lifeline that could save me from drowning in a sea of security. If I had the guts to join him.'

The next day I left Tim to think and pushed on to eventually reach Lands End, overflowing with hope for a new life and dreams of adventure.

A few months later I announced my plans to give it all up to try to cycle round the world. The company was very understanding, 'Poor chap', they thought and humoured me, probably not believing I would pull it off. They allowed me to set up an in-house charity fund raising scheme and even left a door open for me to return to work for them, (on the off chance that I come back alive). Through the winter and spring I assembled the team, gained commitment to the plans, and ploughed through a mass of logistical issues and the dream slowly became a solid entity.

A year after the Land's End journey, on a sweltering August morning, stuck in the typical traffic jam on the M25 were three people not on their way to work, but on a journey of discovery.

At Heathrow Airport, a television reporter asked Tim, 'What do you expect to be the hardest part of the journey?'

'Well', he said, 'the deserts, mountains and jungles.'

'So, all of it really.'

'Yes. All of it.'

AUSTRALIA

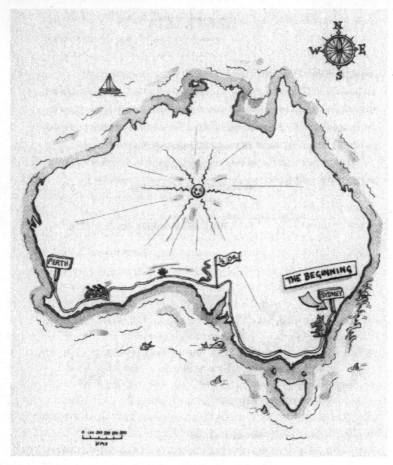

'We must all hang together,
or, most assuredly,
we shall all hang separately.'

Benjamin Franklin   4th July 1776

2 A Flying wombat Called Ethel – Tim

'Will Mr. Ray Johnson please report to the information booth immediately,' a woman's shrill voice boomed over the tannoy. 'Mrs. Johnson has been waiting for him for over two hours.'

A loud cheer went up from the crowd into the clear morning sunshine.

'He's in the bloody pub missus,' someone shouted.

'Piss off and leave him in peace!' called another.

The crowd roared its laughter, high on the camaraderie of people having fun.

Suzanne, Andy and I had chosen Bondi Beach as the starting point of our journey. Unfortunately, so had the *City to Surf* half marathon and we found ourselves competing for space with several thousand runners, back up teams, spectators and hot dog vans. The race had started at Sydney Opera House two hours before and was finishing here on the grassy esplanade overlooking the beach.

A clown, complete with red plastic nose, baggy yellow trousers and red braces, jogged past juggling multi-coloured balls. Minutes later a large, black gorilla loped towards me. I clapped him on his way.

'G'day,' came a grunted greeting as he passed.

I stripped down to black cycling shorts for a ceremonial dip and Suzanne paddled amongst the white breakers of the Pacific Ocean to fill a miniature plastic gin bottle with water.

'It's symbolic,' she explained with a smile. 'Coast to coast, east to west. This water will travel with me all the way to Perth where I'll set it free in the Indian Ocean'.

I was impressed, I would never have thought of something like that, but then girls are different aren't they.

Exhausted runners were still collapsing under the finishing clock as we lined up our bikes to start. This was the last time we would look so smart, if a little pasty-faced from too much British sunshine! Crisply ironed white T-shirts boldly stated our mission – *'CYCLE FOR I.T.* – *Biking Across 3 Continents for Intermediate Technology'*. On the back of the shirts were green outline maps of Australia, Africa and South America and a dotted line indicating our intended route. Were these absurdly simple statements the product of supreme confidence or just foolish arrogance? I had a feeling we were soon to find out.

'This is weird,' said Andy. 'All these people are finishing their journeys and we're just beginning ours.'

We sat astride the bikes and held hands, Suzanne in the middle. Andy blessed the trip, 'Here's to success and friendship.'

'To success and friendship,' we chanted, shook hands and took our first pedal.

Three hundred metres down the road we stopped for lunch!

Saracen, a British bike company, had kindly provided us with three gleaming, black mountain bikes which meant Andy and Suzanne did not have to bring their veteran steeds out of retirement. It also meant I had something to ride, as I had not previously owned a bike. Each bike was fully loaded with twenty kilograms of kit. We had decided to be totally self sufficient, which added a lot of weight to the panniers, but allowed flexibility. We were carrying tents, sleeping bags and stoves. Our route would be a world's first and we were planning on three hundred and sixty-five days to get the job done – fast enough with all that gear.

I was new to the cycling game. Andy had repeatedly advised me back in England to go out and get a couple of 'fifty-milers' under my belt, carrying full kit. But the weeks before we flew to Australia were pure mayhem, too hectic to spare the time. Final planning and emotional goodbyes to families and friends we were not to see over the next twelve months had left us drained. It had been difficult to leave my girlfriend, Phyl, at the station. I had met her three months before we were due to leave. She had known from the beginning that I had been fully committed to the expedition, but this did not make parting any easier. I boarded the plane with more pints of Guinness than cycling miles under my belt after our warm-up trip to Ireland.

'I prefer to hold with the true traditions of the great British amateur.

Too much preparation smacks of vulgarity,' I told Andy when he had last enquired about my state of readiness. In reality I was not feeling nearly as confident as these words of bravado suggested. I knew I was physically fit from a hard season of rugby and the demands of my job, but I had my doubts about the coming challenge. Would I be able to pedal a fully laden bike up to a hundred kilometres, day after day, week after week? Would my knees seize up in the middle of a desert? What if I got sick and had to give up? What would I do if I got bitten by a snake or knocked off my bike by a truck? The sun would be too hot, the Aboriginals too fierce, the beer too cold. The list of doubts went on and on and on …

Over the previous nine months we had set up fund raising schemes which involved organising a major collection of petrol gift vouchers, sponsored bike rides, selling hundreds of T-shirts and pestering our families, friends and local businesses for donations. All the money would be going direct to charity as we were funding ourselves.

Six months after their first meeting at Thurso Station, Suzanne and Andy had started a relationship. It was intense and passionate. Periods of deep affection were punctuated by great eruptions of anger and misunderstanding. At these times words and heavy objects flew around hitting any unsuspecting bystander!

The excitement of planning and preparation further fuelled the bond between Andy and Suzanne but also their explosions. They had realised this was not a sustainable set-up for the trip, too unbalanced and too emotionally charged. Three months before the off they agreed to split, but it was a bitter split. You can't just snap your fingers and switch from passionate lovers to friends without a little confusion.

The pill had stuck in Andy's throat when, three weeks before departure, Suzanne had declared she was in love. In love with a new guy called Richard. We all sensed a rocky road lay ahead.

Once away from the urban sprawl of Sydney we found ourselves heading south into the great open spaces of New South Wales. It slowly dawned on me that no one was going to bring us food, water would not appear at the turn of a tap and no one would show us the best camping spots or the safest routes. The wilderness offered a unique sense of freedom but it also came without safeguards or guarantees.

It was strange, but I had never really thought about hills before. In a car they are effortless. On a big heavy bicycle they are murder! Another realisation dawned – seventy kilometres is less than an hour's drive, but using pedal power it is a whole day of hard work. My concept of distance was changing.

During these first few days it was a novel experience to be alone, with only myself for company, for many hours each day. It seemed, for as far back as I could remember, that there had always been people around; noisy school kids, friends, family. There had rarely been a chance to escape, to find time to reflect on the hectic path of my life. At times I had felt as if I had no control over what was happening. It was all like a bob sleigh ride that had gone out of control. More than once in recent months I had thought, 'Stop the world, I want to get off!' Now I had the glorious luxury of all the time and space in the world to clear my mind, reflect on the past, live the moment and make plans for the future.

We stopped by one of the small streams that regularly crossed the road. They all had names like *Murphy's* or *O'Sullivan's Creek*. As I gulped down the cold, clear water and refilled my bottles I considered the names and the history behind them. Back on the bike, pedalling away in a steady rhythm, my mind began to drift – I bet Murphy was a bank robber out of the Ned Kelly mould of Australian outlaw. Vivid, colourful images formed in my head. I could see Murphy, complete with iron helmet, long brown overcoat and pistol in hand as he blasted his way out of a bank with a big bag of cash. O'Sullivan, on the other hand, had a droopy moustache, thin greasy black hair and a mournful face. He was the lawman who gave the orders to gun Murphy down. I saw O'Sullivan's dark brooding eyes and cruel mouth as he stood over the outlaw lying bleeding in the dirt.

At this point my attention was jerked back to reality by the piercing shriek of a klaxon, as a huge truck hammered past threatening to suck me under its massive screaming wheels. Where had I been for the last few kilometres? I shook myself out of the day dream and wondered whether I was going to be able to cope with all this time living inside my own head during the coming months.

After two days on the road the whole expedition looked like falling apart. We stopped for lunch in an idyllic spot under a shady tree, on the bank of a creek. You could have cut the tension between Andy and Suzanne with a Swiss Army Knife. I had been cycling ahead all morning. I had no way of knowing what it was all about.

We pushed the bikes back on to the road and started pedalling again. Suzanne soon started to lag behind and we stopped to wait for her. 'Are you okay Suzanne?' Andy asked as she pulled up.

'No,' she replied.

'What's up?'

'I feel so alone. This land is so empty and I don't feel as if you and Tim are really with me.'

'Suzanne, don't you think I feel lonely as well?' Andy told her. 'I think about Cassie and my friends and miss them just as much.'

'Andy, you're nuts, you left Cassie ages ago. She's happy with someone else now. There's no comparison. I just find myself wishing I could be with Richard the whole time.'

'But you've only known him three weeks, Suzanne,' said Andy rather bemused. 'It's early days yet. You need to get your head down, forget about him and it'll pass.'

She rounded on him angrily, 'You're just impossible Andrew. I want to be with someone who understands me!'

'You're right Suzanne', he said, 'I don't understand you. You have this incredible opportunity but your heart and mind seem to be back in England with Richard, not here with the team.'

Suzanne glared at him and snapped, 'How dare you say that to me. You know very well how much time and effort I've put into this project. Don't question my commitment and don't blame anything on Richard. He has nothing to do with it. If you were a real friend you would understand that it's just not possible to forget about somebody you care for very deeply!'

'That's great, seeing as you hardly know the guy.'

This really did the trick.

'Right! That's it!' Suzanne blazed, 'I've had enough – I'm quitting! I knew this was all a mistake!'

From the grim, determined look on her face it seemed as if she had made up her mind. She turned her bike around and started to pedal north.

Andy let her go, continuing to pedal south. I sat stunned, going nowhere.

Andy recalls: 'I was beginning to see all the months of hard work being pulled apart and a dream start to fade almost before it had begun. After a few hundred metres I turned around and pedalled after her. I always knew I would; there was too much at stake. I couldn't understand, after all the commitment she had shown towards the project, how she had let herself fall in love a few weeks before leaving to cycle around the world. But then I'm just a man. What do I know about the female mind? I felt a very strong sense of responsibility towards Suzanne. It was, after all, because of my influence that she had become involved in the first place. We had pledged to look after each other come what may. It was not on for anyone to cycle off and quit after only a couple of days, no matter what the provocation.'

After five minutes they reappeared and nodded to each other unsmiling and without a word we carried on as a threesome.

We rode through vast, lonely eucalyptus forests, the three of us spaced out hundreds of metres apart, following a smooth grey ribbon of road undulating into infinity, and then past great open areas of grassland untainted by man's machinery or artificial boundaries. I felt small and insignificant amongst the grandeur and scale of it all; an ant crawling on the underside of the world.

I had a tendency to ride off ahead, frustrated at having to slow my pace to suit the team. I was feeling strong and felt the urge to put my head down and burn up a few kilometres. Inevitably, I found myself waiting and brewing tea in the bush by the side of the road. When the other two eventually caught up they were chatting away happily and from their accusing glances I assumed that I was now the villain.

Andy recalls: 'Suzanne and I had been letting off steam. Once we had calmed down, we felt we understood each other a little better and were back on an even keel yet the underlying problems and my depression deepened.'

The way we pitched the tents that night was a study in body language. Andy's tent faced towards the road, Suzanne's faced in the exact opposite direction, towards the forest and mine was somewhere in between, facing the campfire. Things were obviously not right between us and I stared into the glowing embers of the fire deep into the night, reflecting on the situation. None of us really understood exactly what was happening, only that it was threatening the future of the expedition.

We had realised, well before flying out from London, that we were three very different characters. We each had our own ideas on how things should be done, which rarely seemed to match up with the other two views. Each of us had our own quirks but, most of all, our independence. This fierce independence which we all treasured so much in our lives back home made it difficult for us to behave other than as three individuals.

Andy had always been the most committed to the project. It had been his concept and he had thrown himself tirelessly into the planning and organisation from the outset. I had nicknamed him 'Joe Admin'. He was always so well organised, planning everything down to the last detail, covering all angles, leaving nothing to chance. It had been Andy's dynamic energy that had kept the project going. He had set up the petrol voucher scheme with BP which was bringing in thousands of pounds for Intermediate Technology back home. He had been a dog worrying a bone, never letting go, never accepting defeat, always optimistic and dedicated to the cause. He did not believe in the word 'cannot'. This single-minded drive in search of perfection was Andy's strength, and was to help carry us through many problems.

Suzanne shared Andy's single-minded pursuit of personal targets and was also quite a perfectionist. If a job was to be done then it had to be done correctly, no half-measures, no corners cut. We had all been very impressed with the way she had organised her charity bike ride earlier in the summer, back in Wiltshire. It had been planned with the military precision of a budding Napoleon and brilliantly executed. We were certainly not in any doubt as to our job responsibilities on that Sunday morning! Always full of energy, she could be great fun and the life and soul of any party. At the same time she could also be headstrong and unwilling to compromise in the interests of the team.

We had read that less than a dozen women had ever cycled from Sydney to Perth. I knew Suzanne was determined to add to the number.

I was the laid back member of the group with a more easy going approach to life. I was not going to get stressed out by the bad feeling, nor would I become involved in petty arguments. It annoyed the others intensely that I did not consider the situation to be of earth shattering importance.

I had a feeling that night in New South Wales, that with such an interesting triangle of characters we would, indeed, be in for more fun and games long before we had pedalled the five and a half thousand kilometres across Australia!

On the road the three of us rode apart, just close enough to see the person in front. I felt my body gradually hardening, slowly adapting to this new form of exercise. I was now able to maintain a steady pace, hour after hour, rhythmically turning the pedals, conserving energy, leaning into hills, sitting up in the saddle to free wheel into a breeze on downhill gradients.

I was beginning to relax and sink into the rhythm of our new existence. Life had taken on a different slant now that our time was no longer dictated by the restrictions and responsibilities of work. Waking in the morning these days was a different experience. There was no school to go to, demanding kids to teach, bills to pay or people breathing down my neck. That morning I felt like a child again, in those long ago days when I had woken without a single worry to cloud the horizon. I had no idea what was going to happen each day. I decided to let everything take its natural course and to enjoy this new found feeling of freedom.

I was, of course, fooling myself. We had given ourselves a tight schedule of twelve weeks to cover over five thousand kilometres. To achieve this we would need to pedal an average of eighty kilometres per day, five days a week.

On the morning of the eighth day I stuck my head out of the tent to find myself surrounded by kangaroos in the small forest clearing. They reminded me of huge tame, grey rabbits nibbling contentedly in a back garden. It was difficult to believe they were in fact wild animals. The 'roos were everywhere, bounding in between the tents, munching the grass and lounging sleepily in the early morning sun. I was intrigued by these gentle animals with their light brown fur, huge flat feet and tiny arms. I had a desire to get close enough to stroke their fur, and was surprised to find that a female let me walk up to her and touch her long furry ears. A tiny black nose and a small, clawed foot, poked out from her pouch. I reached tentatively in and was surprised that Mum carried on munching grass, trusting and unworried. The pouch was blood warm and velvet soft, a really cosy place to hide from the world whilst you got things sorted out. I touched warm silky hair and floppy ears before the little *joey* struggled, as if to say, *'You've woken me up. Go away and leave me to sleep.'*

It was still very early and there was no sign of the other two stirring. I decided to explore our camping place. The grassy clearing in which we had pitched the tents the previous night was a couple of hundred metres wide and led down from dense forest to the sea. We were surrounded by spindly gum trees with peeling, silver trunks and bushy tops. The pale, cropped grass of this natural park gave way to the shale and sun bleached pebbles of the beach. We were in a bay with wooded promontories, jutting into pale blue sea on either side.

I sauntered along the beach, firing smooth stones into the noisy surf and laughing at my friends the 'roos, basking in the sun like lazy holiday makers.

The whole bay was teeming with wildlife. Noisy Rosella parrots squabbled in thick bushes, their crimson and metallic blue feathers glinting in the sunshine. I listened to the strange, melodic, chuckling song of a kookaburra somewhere deep within the forest and tried to picture the bird which sang so beautifully. It was a perfect retreat, there would be no cycling for the next couple of days.

Later that morning we met an Aussie couple walking on the

beach. Brad was in his late thirties; a big man whose body was starting to put on the bulk of middle age. He wore an old baggy sweater with red nylon windproof trousers and had the soft white hands of a businessman. His three day stubble suggested he had few cares. Alison was a quiet, petite woman a few years younger than her husband. I was struck by the mass of red hair which she wore tied up. She was dressed in a comfortable old sweater and the type of training shoes normally reserved for gardening. We chatted for a while and Suzanne invited them to a tea party at 'our place'.

That afternoon there followed a bizarre party which Andy later described in a letter to his two young nieces:

'Along with our two Australian friends, about sixteen kangaroos turned up for the tea party. It is difficult to be exact about the number of furry guests as none of them was actually invited or even sat down. Most of the kangaroos sampled the tea but were not too keen. A parrot watched the proceedings perched on the kettle and one guest put a big clawed foot in the mango juice. Everyone seemed to like the special cheese with fruit in it but someone ate all the chocolate chip cookies. The liquorice disappeared and the sticky buns were a real treat. After a while the guests decided to dance. Kangaroos are very good dancers with big back legs especially designed for the job and small front paws to hold their partners. We did have one small problem – there were only five of us humans and too many roos, which meant some of us had to dance with four or five lively partners. The parrots sat on shoulders playfully nibbling ears or swooped noisily to capture tasty crumbs. Suzanne even had to run into the sea to escape her furry admirers.

After a while the sticky buns ran out and the party gradually started to break up. Everyone agreed it had been a lovely afternoon, and we must all do it again sometime ...'

That evening we squashed into Brad and Alison's caravan for roast dinner. I was impressed that Alison could produce such a marvellous feast, using a portable barbecue, in the middle of nowhere.

'So how are you Pommies finding good old Oz?' Brad asked over dinner.

'Well so far so good,' replied Suzanne. 'The hills have been really hard work but we love the sunshine and the Australian way of life.'

Brad laughed, 'You mean barbies and drinking the piss!'

'That's one way of putting it,' Andy smiled. 'But we haven't seen the real Australia yet.'

Brad sounded surprised, 'What do you mean, the real Australia? Look around, isn't this real enough for you?'

'I think what he means is the rough stuff, the outback,' I chipped in.

'Oh you mean the Back Of Bourke. I wouldn't bother. It's full of bulldust and flies, leave it to the Abos.'

'I'd love to meet some Aboriginals,' said Suzanne.

Brad raised an eyebrow at this, 'I'd steer clear of the Abos if I were you, darlin'. As far as I'm concerned they're a dirty, degenerate race, good for absolutely nothing. The state has tried to swamp the problem with dollars. Saw it myself up in the Northern Territories. Cash handouts, building expensive settlements and giving the Abos fancy four-wheel drives. The whole thing has been a bloody disaster! They waste the cash on cheap grog, the houses are broken up for fire wood and the vehicles abandoned as soon as they run out of gas!'

A seething resentment poured from his lips. 'What the government should do with the Abos, for their own good, is stick 'em all in a reservation up north somewhere and charge the tourists ten bucks a time to see 'em. At least the lazy bastards would be bringing some money into the country instead of sponging off the state. They're paid for being black. Listen, I'm not a racist – I just don't like Boongs.'

Suzanne was incensed 'If they're so useless, how come they've survived here for forty thousand years? They just have a different way of life to the whites. It's not wrong, just different.'

'What do you know about it?' snapped Brad. 'You've only been here five minutes!' It was disappointing to have travelled to the other side of the globe in search of enlightening new philosophies and cultures only to find the same old prejudices, racism and bigotry I could have heard back home. Perhaps the depressing message was that these are an integral part of man's nature to be found wherever you travel.

I knew none of us agreed with Brad's views but as we were guests in his caravan, eating his food and drinking his beer, I felt this was not the best moment to start an argument. I changed the subject in the cause of peaceful relations.

'How long are you and Alison going to be travelling for?'

'Jeez, I don't really know mate. I had a horticultural business back in Adelaide, got pissed off with all the bullshit flying around so I sold up, married this little girl,' he put an arm around Alison's slim waist, 'and headed off into the sunset. So, we'll be on the road as long as it takes I reckon.'

This seemed to be a popular dream – to jack everything in, hitch up a caravan and satisfy the nomadic spirit that seems to be in Ozzies of all ages.

After Pebbly Beach the weather turned and we found ourselves pedalling through torrential rain storms, hail stones and high winds. Six feet of snow had fallen in the Snowy Mountains just to the north-west and skiing conditions were perfect. A few days previously we had been sunning ourselves on the beach. Andy had suffered badly from asthma for many years, a condition aggravated by polluted London air. He had a few difficult days, coughing and wheezing in the wet and cold of the Victorian winter, stopping regularly for a puff on a Ventolin inhaler.

Slowly getting stronger, fitter, harder, we pedalled up to eighty kilometres each day through the picturesque coastal towns of Narooma, Bega and Eden. Each one clean and tidy, full of civic pride. Neat rows of whitewashed wooden bungalows reminded me of sleepy, small town America. Some perched bravely on the edges of grassy cliffs, overlooking a breezy blue Pacific.

We stopped late one night and pitched the tents amongst great silver gum trees, having battled for eight hours in the wind and rain, up and down steep hills. The rain was hammering off the fly sheets as Andy and I locked the bikes to a tree.

'This's what it's all about mate,' I said.

'Yeah, it's great isn't it. We're right out in the middle of it now,' said Andy.

Overhearing this, Suzanne said testily, 'Don't think it's only you boys who can enjoy a bit of hardship.'

Andy and I crawled into our tents and were soon snuggled into our sleeping bags whilst Suzanne heroically stayed out, in the pouring rain, to cook the meal. It took her five minutes to fetch water from the creek and another ten to light the two damp kerosene stoves. First of all she produced two steaming mugs of tea with ginger nuts. Next came billy cans full of macaroni cheese with added mustard. The feast was completed with semolina and a dollop of raspberry jam.

'You're a complete hero Suzanne,' I said, handing back the empty can to be washed up.

'I second that,' came Andy's voice from his tent. It certainly made a change from Andy's *'Pasta Surprise'*, famous throughout the world (the surprise being that there was nothing but pasta in it). His porridge with added apple was something else entirely! Food had become an obsession. I often caught myself dreaming about it whilst pedalling along. Big steaming stews, juicy steaks, liver and onions, all floated in front of my eyes at some stage during the day. We were burning up massive amounts of calories. Regular, dedicated eating was the only solution.

After doing the washing up, Suzanne handed us cups of coffee and disappeared into the forest. Andy peeked out of his tent and glimpsed a quite astonishing sight through the torrential rain.

'Here Tim, you're not going to believe this; she's taken off all her clothes and she's out there in the creek having a bath.'

'Cor, she really is a hero,' I said, pulling my stinky sleeping bag over my head.

The following morning I woke to the steady rhythm of rain falling on my tent. Six thirty, still early yet. I'll just give it ten more minutes to stop and then I'll get moving. It is funny how easy it is to convince yourself of anything if you really try. What I should have been thinking was *'Great, a little drop of rain won't hurt anyone. Come on Garratt get yer boots on and get out there!'* Instead, I continued to lie there in a comfortable stupor and talked myself into *'another ten minutes, just in case the rain stops.'*

At seven I had a fit of guilt and dived out of my cocoon into cold driving rain. 'Wakey wakey, up and at 'em!' I called to the other two tents. I was greeted by deafening silence, not a stir. Obviously I was not alone in my weakness this morning. After a few moments Andy's head appeared.

'What time is it?' he asked. This was a question which always bugged me. Andy had decided before the trip he was sick of his life being ruled by the constrictions of time and had decided not to have a watch. This was all well and good but he must have asked me the time on ten occasions each day.

'It's gone seven,' I told him. 'We should make a move.'

There was still no sign of life from the other tent as we lit the stove for a brew and started to pack up the kit. Andy approached Suzanne's tent.

'Hey Rip Van Winkle, shake a leg, we've got a continent to pedal across.'

'I'm thinking,' came the reply.

'Oh great,' said Andy, raising his arms helplessly to the heavens. 'We've only been on the road twelve days, we're already two days behind schedule and she's thinking,' We all knew, whatever else happened today, we were in for a soaking. Andy and I wanted to get on with it.

I made porridge and tea for everyone and handed Suzanne's to her through her tent flap. By the time we had packed up all our gear there was still no sign of movement from the third tent.

Andy tried again. 'Come on Suzanne, we need to get going. You can't lie there all day.'

'I'm still thinking,' was the only response.

'Okay. How about if we meet you in the next place twenty kilometres down the road?'

'Alright, I'll see you later,' she called.

The *Bell Boy Hotel* appeared, after an hour's gruelling effort, through a shroud of heavy rain, at Bemm River. The hotel was the only building in Bemm River. Andy and I leaned our bikes against a white, peeling wooden wall and walked in. It was a strange, run down place which, judging by the broken windows and bandaged furniture, was home to the serious drinkers of the area. It reeked of masculinity. The head of a crocodile stared, glassy-eyed, from the wall beside faded, black and white pictures of bearded men hell-raising in the bar. I sat on a sagging brown settee which seeped yellow foam from a dozen wounds. The only welcoming thing about the whole place was a roaring log fire. An ancient radio-set sat over the fire, spurting Aussie Rules Football. The place was seedy and unkempt, full of discarded boots and hats waiting for the return of their owners. A chainsaw hung from a nail behind the bar. Was this for decoration or was it a lethal weapon in the barman's armoury, kept for occasions when the drinking games really went over the top? Who were these wild men who drank in this run down shack, sixty kilometres from the nearest town? Did they appear magically from the forest at opening time?

I approached the big, bearded barman. He was barefoot, wearing tatty denim shorts and a grimy blue T-shirt which read, *'I don't have a drink problem, I drink, I get drunk, I fall down – no problem!'*

'Hello,' Andy greeted him.

'Uhhh,' he grunted. 'Pommies.'

'Yeah, we're cycling.'

'On bikes are yer? People think they can cycle in Oz, but when they get here they find out how big she is. Where yer goin', Melbourne?'

'Yeah and then we're going to try and cross the Nullarbor to Perth,' I told him.

'Nullarbor eh? You Pommies won't get past the snakes and Abos.'

'Well we'll give it a go,' I said, 'and if by any chance we should make it, then we're going to try to cycle across Africa and South America.'

'Oh yeah', he snorted, 'and my mother's a flying wombat called Ethel!'

We all laughed.

'Do you have anything we can eat?' Andy asked.

'Nope.'

'Okay, anything to drink?'

'Beer.'

I could tell this guy had won trophies for outstanding conversational ability.

'We were thinking about something a bit warmer. What about coffee?' I asked hopefully.

'Folks round here don't drink coffee.'

'Well we drink coffee, so what's the chance of getting some?' I persisted.

'Suppose I might,' he grunted and ambled off into another room.

'Friendly guy,' Andy observed.

'Yeah, a real barrel of laughs.'

We waited half an hour for Beard-Face to reappear with the coffee. It was luke warm with a nasty white skin floating on top.

'If the coffee's not hot enough I could give it a blast,' he grunted to nobody in particular. I thought, *What? Why not just boil it in the first place?* Just what had this guy been doing for the last thirty minutes?

At this moment Suzanne walked into the bar having completed her meditations. She looked damp but happy.

'Watch out for the barman', Andy advised her, 'he's a real comedian.'

I decided to skip the coffee and make the most of the fire to dry out a little. Pulling off a sodden boot I found a squashed spider with definite red markings on its back. I approached our friend the barman for the benefit of his local knowledge.

'Excuse me,' I said, placing the spider gingerly on the counter with the aid of a long fire poker. 'Could you tell me what this is?'

The big barman studied it carefully from all angles before replying gravely, 'Yep, I reckon that's a spider.'

3 Cruising the Great Ocean Road – Tim

'You blokes are not Greens are yer?' an aggressive red-faced man challenged. 'Coz if yers are, we'll have to beat the shit outta ya and ask yers to leave!'

I had just walked into the gloomy spit and sawdust bar of the *Gum Tree Hotel* in timber town, Orbost, closely followed by Andy and Suzanne. After two weeks on the road we had just crossed the Great Dividing Range which runs for two and a half thousand kilometres from the northeast tip of Australia all the way down to Victoria in the southeast. This range divides the fertile eastern coastal strip from the barren desert lands of the interior. Early convicts believed to the west of the range lay China.

We had camped in a gum tree forest the previous night and crossed from New South Wales into Victoria early that morning. It had been another day of sodden pedalling in heavy rain. A warm, friendly bar had seemed a good idea. I was beginning to think we may just have picked the wrong one. I quickly realised we looked out of place in our green and blue Goretex jackets. The rugged looking men at the counter were dressed in an assortment of jeans, T-shirts and donkey jackets. The atmosphere was not friendly. We were a welcome distraction for these locals and they obviously sensed the chance of some entertainment at our expense. My new found buddy thrust his beery face within inches of mine, giving me the full pleasure of his buffalo breath.

'And another thing mate, we have two rules in this here bar – no poofters, no sheilas and no greens!' He leered at Suzanne then turned to wink at his mates, propping each other up at the end of the bar. 'What do you blokes say?' He looked for support.

'That's three rules Wal,' one of his mates corrected him.

'No poofters yeah, but we don't mind sheilas Wal,' another added.

Before long there was a full scale debate going on concerning the rules of the bar. We were soon forgotten; left to sup our beers.

The local lads loosened up a little when they found out we were cyclists.

'Why didn't you say you were Pommie cyclists when you came in?

We thought you was greens in those fancy rain jackets.'

My red faced friend was all hospitality now. 'So we won't have to beat the shit outta yers after all!'

We agreed this was jolly decent of them and we all became instant buddies. It turned out 'greens' were environmentalists who had been putting great pressure on the government to reduce logging operations in this part of Victoria.

'Thing is Orbost is a timber town, always has been,' one of the drinkers told me. 'We depend on the timber to put grub in our kids' bellies. Then these bloody city slickers, arsehole Greens stick their noses in where they don't belong and before yer know it the bastard government has cut the bloody quotas!'

It was easy to see why these men were so hostile. Their livelihoods were on the line. The drinker took a large sup from his glass, wiped froth from his mouth with the back of his hand before continuing. 'Timber quotas have been cut to shit over the last ten years. Most of the yards round here are dead. All the blokes who worked the trees are shit outta luck. No timber, no job – it's a real pisser!'

We stood at the bar with these rugged timber men and discussed their woes long into the night. It was clear that Orbost, along with many of the surrounding towns, was dying a slow, inevitable death. We could see both sides of the problem. On the one hand I was with the so called 'greens', after all the forests had taken hundreds of years to grow and were being decimated to produce wood-chip for Japan. It must surely be in everyone's interest to look after the natural resources of the planet for the well-being of the present population and the future of generations to come. What we had here, however, was the practical reality of implementing an effective long term environmental policy. In theory, it is fine. With careful management and a reduction in timber quotas deforestation can be drastically reduced and, eventually, turned around. Unfortunately, if you happen to depend on the timber trade for your livelihood then the reality of these policies is unemployment, poverty and the destruction of whole communities.

The Great Ocean Road hugs the southwest coast of Victoria. It is a thin, grey ribbon winding west from Melbourne for three hundred kilometres to the beaches of Warnambool. The project, completed in 1932, was devised by the government to provide work for demobbed soldiers, back home after the Great War.

During the second week of September the weather improved as we pedalled west, past white surfing beaches, climbed steep cliffs and dropped down again to cross gushing creeks which flowed out of dense forest.

The road was made for cycling, never flat, always twisting and turning, climbing and falling through lush forest. We dropped down to deserted beaches, some of grey pebble, others of clean, white sand. There was a constant rumble and crash of the sea. At times it was difficult to make out the road ahead as surf-spray mingled with mist rolling off the forest. This was a time of pleasant cycling, we felt slightly disappointed that it was not a little more physically demanding, but it was a good warm-up for the rigours of the Nullarbor Plain to come.

In Apollo Bay we came across Keith, a burly triathlete, who had just finished a fifty kilometre training run. He was in his mid-twenties with a youthful tanned face, a gringo moustache and cropped black hair. He sported a pair of star-spangled running shorts and was pulling on a clean, white sweat shirt that read, *'Wind surfers do it standing up.'* We chatted for a while and told him about our trip.

'Good on yer blokes,' he said, his face dripping sweat. 'So you're going to pedal across the Nullarbor?'

'That's right. We hear it's going to be tough.' Suzanne answered.

He nodded. 'Could be. There was a girl who ran the Nullarbor last year. She was doing about forty km a day with a back-up vehicle and it took her five weeks.'

'That takes some doing,' said Suzanne. 'What about yourself, you're lucky to have such a lovely place to do your training.'

'Yeah, but if you want to see the most beautiful place in Victoria,' he said, 'take a detour from here up Wild Dog Road onto Turton's Track.'

'Thanks for the advice,' said Suzanne.

'No worries.'

'Where are you going now?' I asked.

'I think I'll go home, pick up the bike do a few k's and maybe get a bit of swimming in later. See yer around.'

'Yeah, nice meeting you,' said Andy. 'Good luck with your training.'

We got back on the bikes and rode off. Andy looked at me, 'Jeez, who was that guy?'

We took Keith's advice and followed Wild Dog Road inland. We soon found ourselves in a different world, a hidden green valley with steep sides. The road took us up the side of the valley and soon became a rough track covered in loose stones. I stopped the bike to rest and looked down into what could have been a typical Welsh scene, a meandering river with sheep dotted amongst green pastures. We ignored a 'Road Closed' sign – *Surely they can't mean us,'* I thought, *'We're on mountain bikes!'*

I muscled the bike up and up in a low gear, under the warm morning sun and rounded a bend to find Andy off his bike, standing in front of what looked like orange quicksand. We were faced with a landslide. The sandy hillside, waterlogged by days of continuous rain, had finally given up, depositing many tons of sand and mud across the road for a distance of one hundred metres.

'It's alright,' Andy assured us, ever the optimist. 'Only a bit of sand, we'll be across this in no time.' He stepped out positively and sank up to his knees in sucking orange mud. 'Ah, well maybe there is another way around.'

Even Andy knew when he was licked! We retraced the road back down the valley and, eventually, strained and panted our way up a small side road, climbing even more steeply than before. The landslide was soon skirted and we continued to climb gently through thick gum tree forest for the rest of the morning. The track levelled out, enabling us to cruise along easily. I was in the middle of a pleasant day dream about a big, juicy sirloin steak, with pepper sauce, washed down with a couple of ice cold beers when the dog struck. He had been waiting for us all morning. The great black brute launched himself from behind a wooden shack.

'I suppose that's why it's called Wild Dog Road.' I quipped after my heart had restarted.

We eventually Picked up Turton's Track, and entered a copper and emerald forest, pierced by shafts of white sunlight. Huge ferns and vines pressed in on us as we turned the pedals in the cool darkness of the forest floor.

In the late afternoon we emerged from the forest on to tarmac and rode into the hamlet of Beech Forest, nestling on the edge of the woodland. Andy was a few minutes ahead. He had stopped his bike in the road as a short tomboy, dressed in old blue dungarees, appeared from the pub.

Lyn was in her early thirties with close cropped, spiky hair and a cheeky grin. She started to chat to Andy, obviously attracted by his matinée idol looks. Mind you, she'd had a few.

'I did some bike touring a few years back,' she told him. 'Rode from Sydney to Brisbane once. Come on, I'll buy you a drink.'

Suzanne and I spotted Andy's bike leaning up against a post outside the pub. We joined him for 'a couple of quiet ones.' Andy introduced us to Lyn, and after sharing a few midis (medium glasses of beer) with her, she invited us all back to her place to meet her friend Louise. We followed her clapped-out Renault down the road.

Lyn introduced us to Louise, a motherly, mountain of a girl with Italian ancestry. The two of them, standing side by side, looked like Laurel and Hardy.

'We met a few years back whilst working with a road mending gang in New South Wales,' Louise explained. 'When the job was finished, we decided to stick together, bought this old wooden cabin with a bit of land and a few chooks and we've bin goin' strong ever since.'

Lyn proudly showed us around their small holding and introduced us to Cecil and Gerty, two healthy looking brown milk cows. They also had ducks, geese, chickens and a goat called Bert.

'I used to have a job in Melbourne but all the rushing around stressed me out. Now all I've got to worry about is remembering to milk Cecil and Gerty, pick up the eggs, and water the vegetables. I just love it here.' I could see that Lyn and Louise were thriving on their version of Old MacDonald's Farm.

Louise wore the trousers in this relationship, but Lyn seemed happy enough to be bossed about. Louise was wary of us at first but soon warmed to our light-hearted banter.

'Listen Louise. How about if Andy and I cook us all a meal?' I suggested. 'We have all the stuff we need in our panniers.'

'Not on your life mate,' came the answer. 'If you think I'm going to let two ham-fisted blokes loose in my kitchen you can think again.'

Suzanne was allowed to stay but Andy and I were ushered out and placed in comfortable old armchairs by a wood burning stove in the front room, cold tubes of lager in our hands.

Louise soon appeared with a delicious pasta dish with a thick tomato sauce topped with Parmesan cheese.

'Andy, I think this is what Pasta Surprise is supposed to taste like,' I teased him. A thunderous black scowl was the only response! We chatted away late into the night, comfortable in the warmth and friendliness that radiated from these two. Eventually we three cyclists bedded down on lumpy mattresses in a dusty spare room.

In the morning we breakfasted on fresh scrambled duck eggs, followed by pancakes and honey. We said our goodbyes and were sad to have to pedal away from this happy little place. These two seemed to have found a perfect little niche for themselves; free from the pressures of career, bringing up a family or material possessions. I wondered whether this was the type of life I could settle into. One reason for my being here in the first place was to take a look at how people in other places cope with life. I wanted answers to some questions that had been bugging me for some time. Was I expected to spend the next thirty years chasing some elusive notion of career advancement? Should I really be selling my soul to the Company Store? Maybe I should be slogging away back home to pay off a big mortgage and a bank loan on a fancy car, video and hi-fi. Or should I be up to my elbows in nappies, talc and Farley's Rusks?

I smiled to myself. There's no rush. I think I'll stay out here, pedalling along under an endless sky, pondering the mysteries of life a little while longer. Other people can worry about the bank manager just now. For the first time on the expedition I felt I was beginning to understand what I was doing out here. I had a deep and real contentment within myself. Back home I had felt few people really understood why I had to make this trip. Some thought it was self indulgent and that I would have been better employed sticking at my career and climbing the ladder. In truth, I had always questioned that philosophy of life. The thought of working year after year, in the same place, with the same people, doing the same things had never appealed.

Later that day our wheels rejoined the Great Ocean Road. Conditions were perfect for cycling, bright sunshine and a fresh sea breeze at our backs. We gazed, in awe, at the natural rock formations known as the *Twelve Apostles*. These are huge pillars of rock soaring out of pounding surf. Over thousands of years they have been battered relentlessly and crafted into beautiful natural sea sculptures. In an orange sunset it was all quite stunning. The next morning we stopped at a formation called *London Bridge* which had, until recently, been a huge natural stone bridge jutting out into the sea. Thousands of tourists have walked across it over the years. Not long before we were there, a group of Americans walked across the fragile piece of stone and became stranded on the far side, as the middle of the bridge collapsed into the sea. After several hours they were all plucked to safety by helicopter.

Twenty-four hours cooped up together in a tiny, wooden chalet in Warnambool at the western end of the Great Ocean Road, waiting out a heavy storm, was the perfect recipe for another bust up. This time Andy stormed off after another shouting match with Suzanne over breakfast. This was starting to resemble a soap opera.

It was not until much later in the morning that we caught up with Andy, at Port Fairy. The three of us had one of our open discussions in which we all aired grievances and tried to get everything out in the open. I had realised, from the early days in New South Wales, that our biggest challenge would be to get along with each other for a whole year. People rarely spend so much time together in such claustrophobic and difficult conditions as Suzanne, Andy and I were in. Here we were living in each other's pockets; getting away for any length of time was just not possible. Inevitably, something had to blow. Once again steam was let off and frustrations voiced. The team pedalled on together a little happier.

By mid-September we had crossed from Victoria into South

Australia. We now found ourselves pedalling our way north west along the Coorong, a lonely strip of marshland curving along the coast for one hundred and fifty kilometres, south of Adelaide. We rode by the side of a long, narrow lagoon and a complex series of salt pans which are separated from the ocean by the huge sand dunes of the Younghusband Peninsular.

At the southern end of the Coorong we had ridden into the small port and holiday town of Robe. I could not believe my eyes – there, amongst the yachts and dinghies in the harbour, was an eighteen metre Southern Right Whale spouting white plumes of spray high into the air.

Even for the locals this was a special event. The whole town had stopped to watch. We spent the afternoon with school children, plumbers and policemen, following the progress of this gentle creature of the deep as it ploughed majestically across the bay. At one point it was so close I could make out grey callosites encrusted on the broad black bonnet.

These whales live in shallow, coastal waters, usually in small family herds of up to six, but our whale appeared to be alone. We watched it lift a great black tail out of the water and bring it crashing down onto the surface. A local teacher called to his group of children, 'That's known as lob-tailing, he'll dive now, watch!'

I introduced myself to the teacher, who was a mine of information.

'These whales are very rare,' he told me. 'We've not seen one here in Robe for eleven years. There are only about four thousand left in the world which means they're an endangered species.'

'Are they still hunted?' I asked.

'They used to be, for their oil but they've been protected since the 1930's.'

Not all the wildlife of the Coorong was as peaceful. On a lonely stretch of road a shadow materialised in front of my bike. Looking up, I was surprised to see a large magpie hovering threateningly, several metres above my head. The black and white plumage was unmistakable. It was screeching loudly and was clearly agitated. I put my head down and kept pedalling as it made a series of swoops. The bird gained height and plunged into a dive-bombing descent. It crashed into the side of my head and pecked viciously at my scalp with a stiletto beak. The impact was sufficient to knock me off the bike. When I picked myself up, I felt a trickle of blood run down my forehead; just like a bit part player from Alfred Hitchcock's movie *The Birds*.

Later I learned it was the nesting season. At this time magpies become very aggressive in defence of their territory. I needed no further evidence of this and wore my cycling helmet for the rest of the ride through Magpie Mafia territory.

Leaving the small town of Wellington on the Murray River, some hundred kilometres Southeast of Adelaide, a raw westerly wind hit us right between the eyes. As any cyclist will agree, the one thing we all really hate is a head wind. Hills, rain and punctures can be tolerated, but a strong head wind is a killer. This one was a monster. It felt as though a giant hand was pushing the bike back. I was cycling through thick 'glue', my eyes slitted against the blast. Progress was desperately slow, down to a walking pace of five kilometres per hour. Being lighter, Suzanne was having most problems with the wind, which at times brought her to a standstill. Andy and I tried to form a human shield, riding two abreast in front of her to provide some form of protection. In this way we slogged along for the next two hours, covering less than ten kilometres.

'This is crazy,' I shouted over the roaring wind. 'We can't ride in this. Let's stop for a brew.'

The others were only too relieved to take a break from the unrelenting grind. We found a wooden shed full of farm machinery and sat on large white bags of grain whilst I lit the stove. Suzanne made Vegemite sandwiches and Andy produced warming mugs of hot chocolate. We sat and chatted, all happy to be out of the elements for a while. It was a rare moment of solidarity between the three of us. No arguments, working as a true team.

'I've been doing some sums,' said Andy. 'We ought to be on the Nullarbor in three weeks and it should take another two weeks to cross it. If we meet these kind of headwinds out there, we're going to have real problems. The roadhouses are a minimum of a hundred kilometres apart with nothing in between but bush and sand. If the wind slows us to five k's an hour, it's going to take two or three days to get between roadhouses. Summer's coming and it's starting to warm up out there. If it gets above forty degrees we're going to need to drink ten litres of water each, per day. That means, for three days we'll need to carry a total of ninety litres to be safe.' 'Well, that's impossible,' I said. 'We have a maximum capacity of thirty-five litres, even that's going to be very heavy and will slow us down.'

'If we lose more than nine litres of body fluid in a day and don't replace it, we're dead very quickly,' Andy said, matter-of-factly.

Suzanne looked concerned, 'So what's the answer then?'

'The answer is, A: pray for favourable winds and B: pedal faster and further each day now to get across before it gets too hot.' This was the logical, problem-solving businessman in Andy talking.

After an hour there was no sign of the wind lessening in its ferocity.

'Well, we aren't going to get to Perth sitting around here. Shall we hit it again?' Andy was working hard to perk us all up.

The afternoon dragged on as we continued to make desperately slow progress. Was it my imagination or had the wind got even stronger? I suspected I was simply getting tired. Late in the afternoon the landscape changed from untidy dairy farms to row upon row of neat, orderly vineyards, stretching as far as I could see on either side of the road. We were now entering the wine-making region of South Australia. From here in the Bleasdale region, it stretches two hundred kilometres north through the Clare and Barossa valleys.

We struggled into the town of Langhorne Creek and Suzanne spotted a sign:

'Bleasdale Winery – Free Wine Tasting'

It had been a rough day on the road. We had taken all day to pedal just thirty kilometres, and we were in need of some form of distraction. A little wine-tasting could be the answer! We followed the signs and came to an old converted barn tucked away behind a large grey stone farmhouse with a number of smaller stone buildings. Leaning our bikes against the wall, we went inside.

'You're a bit late if you've come to taste the wines,' an elderly silver-haired lady told me inside the barn. 'We're just about to shut up shop.'

'Oh please, don't shut just yet,' said Suzanne in her most persuasive voice. 'We've cycled two thousand kilometres to taste your wine.'

Aunt Mickey turned out to be a very friendly and accommodating lady and an hour later we had sampled just about everything in the barn – Chardonay, Cabernet, dark port, light port, you name it, we swigged it.

After another half hour we were having difficulty reading the labels and Suzanne had started to sway dangerously. We slurred our goodbyes to Aunt Mickey, who took it all in good spirit. She even gave us a free bottle of sherry to take with us.

The strong, cold wind made me feel light-headed but it had an even more dramatic effect on Suzanne. She managed to weave her bike up the road for fifty metres, giggling to herself, before veering off and disappearing into a tangle of vines. All Andy and I could see were her legs sticking out of a squashed, green bush. This was enough to send the three of us into a fit of hysterical laughter. It was a good ten minutes before we could pedal on.

We rode into Adelaide towards the end of September, six weeks and more than two thousand kilometres after leaving Sydney. We were a worrying nine days behind schedule and very tired, our minds and bodies run down by the relentless physical effort. It was time to enjoy a rest, a shower, clean sheets and a roof over our heads for the first time in ten days. Suzanne had retained that magical female quality of being able to keep clean and tidy no matter what conditions we found ourselves in. By this stage Andy and I had begun to hum.

Over the next couple of days we picked up mail from the Post Office, developed photos to send home, serviced the bikes and washed clothes in a launderette.

Suzanne picked up several letters from Richard and made long phone calls to him. She appeared distant and distracted once again but chose not to share her thoughts as we made preparations to move on. We were all aware that the next stage of the journey would test us to the limit. Silently, I hoped she was in the right frame of mind to tackle the feared Nullarbor Plain. The second night out of Adelaide brought the most furious explosion yet between Andy and Suzanne. Suzanne kicked a burning stove and pan full of boiling water all over the Andy's tent. They hardly exchanged a word for days.

4 Beyond the back O'Bourke – Tim

At the end of September, seven weeks after leaving Sydney, we pedalled across the Flinders Range through Horrock's Pass. Immediately, we experienced a change in climate and landscape. Gone were the lush meadows and neat rows of green vineyards. In their place were parched brown scrub and bush.

Dead snakes plastered the road, others were definitely alive and well. A sleek, black snake writhed across the asphalt in front of my bike and disappeared quickly into the bush. Andy provided us all with a very close view of a deadly brown snake which was curled up in the middle of the road. He pulled up sharply in front of it; I piled into the back of him, Suzanne followed into the back of me. We all finished up standing around the serpent which, fortunately, was not alarmed by all the commotion.

These snakes lie in the sun absorbing energy from the sun. When they appear to be sleeping they are often at their most powerful and dangerous. After this encounter we all became terrified of the prospect of treading on one of them in the bush.

We pedalled slowly through the colourless desert scrub, in strength-sapping heat, to the curiously named town of Iron Knob. The town was carelessly scattered around a massive open quarry. We watched colossal yellow dumper trucks and diggers buzz back and forth, intent upon their mission – to tear iron ore from the earth.

We left Iron Knob before dawn the next morning to avoid the worst of the heat. I was pleasantly surprised to see the scrub and bush turn to wheat fields. We had expected the desert to stretch, unbroken, all the way to Norseman, sixteen hundred kilometres to the west.

On reaching Kimba we danced a quick jig to celebrate the half-way point across Australia – only another two thousand eight hundred kilometres to go! We celebrated with cold beers and thick rump steaks. After buying the second round of beers I returned to our table to find Suzanne chatting away to a guy called Rick.

'So you're a Pommie sheila eh?' Rick asked in the typically brusque manner of the Australian male.

He was a good-looking lad in his early twenties with a clean cut, tanned face, dressed in tight blue jeans and white T-shirt, the uniform of cool young men the world over. He had the sly look of a predator.

'And which of these two blokes are you with?' he asked her smoothly.

'Both of them,' she told him with a smile.

'Shit mate! Ain't that something.' I could almost hear Rick's mind turning over the possibilities.

'I'm actually with both of them and with neither of them. I'm really with another guy back home in England.'

This really did interest him.

'Ah, shit mate! Well, if you're not with these blokes and the other bloke is back in Pommie land, you're with me tonight.'

It was more statement than question. I could see from the look on Suzanne's face she was not sure if he was joking. As far as I could tell he was deadly serious.

Suzanne quickly changed tack. 'What do you do for work Rick?'

'Well I can do anything' he replied confidently.

'What do you mean, anything?' she asked.

'Ah, shit mate, I mean anything. I'm free to do anything I choose.'

She persisted, 'But what *do* you do?'

'Er ... nothing.'

All four of us laughed, but I wondered how many of us have the freedom and ability to do anything we choose, but are constrained by our own fears and inhibitions. Most of us dream, at some time or other, of doing wonderful, challenging things but take the easier option, the one to plod along and do nothing.

After a while we caught onto his catch phrase and he would not let us go until all three of us could say 'Ah, shit mate!' in perfect Aussie twang.

We pedalled on through the occasional agricultural settlement, Kyancutter, Wudinna and Poochera, all with identical massive grain silos, railway tracks and gas stations. Ahead of us lay the lonely Eyre Highway, one thousand three hundred kilometres of straight, flat road that runs along the edge of the vast Nullarbor Plain.

Temperatures can soar to over fifty degrees Celsius in summer. For the next two weeks we planned to cycle through this inhospitable and barren landscape.

The Eyre Highway takes its name from John Edward Eyre, an English colonial administrator and explorer who, at the age of twenty-five, made the first east to west crossing of Australia. Eyre set out from Adelaide in South Australia on 18th June, 1840, accompanied by an overseer, John Baxter.

The expedition was re-supplied by a South Australian Government ship in Fowler's Bay, near the present day town of Ceduna. On February 25th, 1841, they set off once more with three Aboriginals, nine pack horses, a pony with foal and six sheep. Eyre hoped he had sufficient provisions, as both food and water were virtually non-existent in this harsh land. After two months hard walking, his companion, John Baxter, was killed by two of the Aboriginal guides.

Eyre recounts the death of Baxter on 28th April, 1841:

'It was now half past ten, and I headed the horses back, in the direction in which I thought the camp lay, that I might be ready to call the overseer to relieve me at eleven. 1 was startled by a sudden flash, followed by the report of a gun, not a quarter of mile from me ... I immediately called out, but as no answer was returned, I got alarmed, and leaving the horses, hurried up towards the camp as rapidly as I could. About a hundred yards from it, I met the King George's Sound native (Wylie), running towards me, and in great alarm, crying out, 'oh Massa, oh Massa come here,'... Upon reaching the encampment, which I did in about five minutes after the shot was fired, I was horror-struck to find my poor overseer lying on the ground, weltering in his blood, and in the last agonies of death. Glancing hastily around the camp I found it deserted by the two younger native boys, whilst the scattered fragments of our baggage lay thrown about in wild disorder, and at once revealed the cause of the harrowing scene before me.

Upon raising the body of my faithful, but ill-fated follower, I found that he was beyond all human aid; he had been shot through the left breast with a ball, the last convulsions of death were upon him, and he expired almost immediately after our arrival. The frightful, the appalling truth, now burst upon me, that I was alone in the desert... The horrors of my situation glared upon me in such startling reality, as for an instant almost to paralyse the mind. At the dead hour of night, in the wildest and most inhospitable wastes of Australia, with the fierce wind raging in unison with the scene of violence before me, I was left, with a single native, whose fidelity I could not rely upon, and who for aught I knew might be in league with the other two, who perhaps were even now, lurking about with the view of taking away my life as they had done that of the overseer.'

After Baxter's death, Eyre and Wylie, the one remaining Aboriginal, struggled on westward, along the Great Australian Bight, until they reached Albany on the south west coast of Western Australia on 7th July 1841. It had been an epic journey of nightmare hardship in the wilderness, covering approximately two thousand kilometres and lasting more than twelve months.

By 1877 a telegraph line had been laid across the Nullarbor, roughly delineating the route that the first road would take. Later in the century miners, en route to the gold fields of Western Australia, followed the same telegraph line across the empty plains.

I was especially interested to learn that the first crossing by bicycle was made in 1896 – sixteen years before the first car was driven across. Up The Peddlers!

In 1941 the war inspired the building of a transcontinental highway. It was little more than a rough track when completed in the 1950's and only a few vehicles made the crossing each day. Finally, in 1976, the last stretch from the South Australian border was surfaced, making the Nullarbor crossing possible for ordinary mortals. The journey is still only attempted by a handful of cyclists each year.

In the Aboriginal language Ceduna means *'a place to sit down and rest'*. We decided to heed this advice to recharge batteries and service equipment before setting out on our journey across the Nullarbor Plain. Part of our routine was to clean and check the bikes each week. They had so far been excellent, strong and reliable in all conditions. The only problem had been with spokes snapping under the weight of all the kit we were carrying. This was solved by re-building the wheels with heavy duty steel spokes.

Now the bikes were ready for anything; I hoped the riders would prove as strong!

There was evidence in Ceduna of a problem that weighs heavily on the Australian conscience. All around the town were vagrant Aboriginals. Most of them drunk. They stood in dark silent clusters, in the shade of gum trees; no more than waif-like shadows. All had the very black skin and broad, flat noses, characteristic of their race. Some lay in gutters or dingy corners, others staggered, belligerently, down the middle of the street, shouting angrily at passers-by, their clothes ill fitting, ragged and dirty. They were odd shapes, some with spindly match stick legs, others almost grotesque in their fatness.

Australia is the land of the drinker. It seemed rare to see white males without a 'tinnie' in their hands and the whole culture revolves around booze. The difference for Aboriginals is that they drink to get drunk, to fall over and to lose themselves in oblivion. They drink with a fierce desperation, not for fun. It is not uncommon to see an Aboriginal polish off a four litre carton of wine, then start on meths or turpentine to achieve the required effect.

The Aboriginal problems date back to the first arrival of white colonists in the 1770's. During the following two hundred years their lands were taken from them by white settlers and many were killed off by exotic diseases. Their culture has been eroded by tobacco, alcohol and narcotics, all introduced by the white man. A highly sophisticated society, based on family groups with an egalitarian political system, has been gradually destroyed. An advanced culture, with its own religion, history, laws and a highly developed sense of art, is in a state of terminal decay.

A disturbing trend has been the number of Aboriginal deaths in custody. Many imprisoned for petty crimes, have been found dead in their cells. They are essentially a nomadic people who cannot comprehend loss of liberty. They will often hang themselves rather than endure the living hell of captivity.

Over the last thirty years successive governments have tried to tackle the problems. A proportion of land, owned by their ancestors, has been returned. In the Northern Territories they have been granted title to large areas of marginal land (mainly unproductive desert). The granting of land rights has been delayed in other states as most of the land is privately owned, some of it containing rich mineral deposits. Some Aboriginal communities, however, do receive substantial incomes from companies mining on their land.

These modern day Aboriginals have drifted into a state of limbo and it is difficult to see how they can escape from their plight. Having lost the traditional skills and values of their tribes, many are unable to make the transition to life in a modern, highly developed Australia.

On our second day out from Ceduna, we reached Nundroo Roadhouse and the eastern edge of the Nullarbor plain, where the road passes through the Yalata Aboriginal Reserve.

We would have to rely on roadhouses for food and water. They are spaced out along the highway up to two hundred kilometres apart – perhaps two full days of hard pedalling between each (wind permitting). A roadhouse supports a tiny, isolated community where travellers can stop for fuel, food and rest on their long journey across the empty plain. We knew that, apart from these occasional havens, we would be dependant upon each other, and upon the equipment we carried. The first thing I noticed, as we pedalled further into the reserve, were the bottles. Thousands of them, littering the bush on either side of the highway. Beer bottles, wine bottles and the occasional gin or vodka bottle, all lying dusty and dead in the sand.

'Looks like quite a party,' I said.

'Yeah,' Andy replied, 'I hope they don't decide to use us for target practice.'

The Aboriginal Community Roadhouse at Yalata was a depressing, run down place. The petrol station was shabby, newspapers and beer cans littering the forecourt. The public toilet was smashed up and smeared with excrement. The restaurant building was cleaner, although the off-white paint was peeling and the windows cracked.

Small groups of Aboriginals sat about under bushes or in shady corners, swigging from dark brown bottles. Most of them wore cheap acrylic trousers and T-shirts streaked with grime. All were barefoot. It was the same hopelessness and despair we had seen in Ceduna. A white policeman wandered across the forecourt towards us.

'How's it goin' blokes?' he greeted us. 'We don't see many cyclists out here.'

We sat drinking tea with Greg and his wife Helen in the small pre-fabricated bungalow that served as the Yalata Reserve Police Post.

'These people really do have problems,' Helen told us.

She was a nurse at the clinic in the reserve, a plain, well-built woman in her mid twenties with long, straight brown hair.

'Alcohol is the biggest killer out here,' she said. 'Aboriginals have a different metabolism to whites. Their bodies have become very finely tuned over thousands of years to cope with conservation of water in hot desert conditions. This means alcohol affects them much more than it does us. Many die from liver and kidney dysfunction.'

Greg had been policing the Yalata Reserve for over a year, 'The booze causes all sorts of other problems,' he told us.

'What sort of things do you have to deal with?' Suzanne asked.

'Mainly domestic violence. Husband and wife get smashed out of their minds on cheap grog and start attacking each other, sometimes with knives or bottles – whatever they can lay their hands on.'

'We get a lot of family neglect as well,' explained Helen. 'Because the parents are drunk a lot of the time, the youngsters often get neglected. I see many children suffering from malnutrition and vitamin deficiency.'

Sit & Rest

It was starting to get dark so I went off to find somewhere for us to sleep, leaving the others to chat. On the forecourt I asked an Aboriginal boy where we could camp. He took me to the back of the roadhouse, past a baby camel tied to a tree and a couple of burned-out trucks. He pointed into the bush, 'All this area is full of snakes. Don't go too far from the building big fellah.'

We slept fitfully that night, no one daring to venture out for a pee.

The two lane highway cut through thick bush, the concrete smooth and well maintained. An unbroken white line marked a wide hard shoulder, sanctuary from thundering road trains. The sandy earth did not appear capable of sustaining life. Beyond a broad gravel apron withered trees with bushy green tops provided a canopy over dry, scrubby grass. We pedalled past a large sign which read: NEXT 92 KM. Above this, three yellow diamonds displayed silhouettes of a camel, a wombat and a kangaroo. The bush stretched out on all sides, monotonous and unrelenting. I felt vulnerable and insignificant, swallowed up by the vastness. Dread of the coming days washed over me. No birds sang. The only sound was the gentle whirr of the gears. When I stopped there was total silence, the air clear and still. A wisp of cirrus cloud lay, like a white brush stroke, against deep blue sky. Now that I was motionless, the fierce heat bore down on me. Apart from a handful of trucks, the sign was the only man-made object we had seen for two days.

Nullarbor is bad Latin for *'no trees'* and a good description of this stretch of the journey. We were three days and three hundred kilometres west of Ceduna when the dense bush gave way to open plain. Looking to all points of the compass, I could see nothing but ankle high, brown scrub extending to the horizon. The very nothingness was a feature in its own right; not a tree, a hill, nor even a bush. The only sound now was the wind in my ears, blowing hot off the desert. If I were to walk north, the wilderness would engulf me within hours. The first sign of man would be many weeks walk, hundreds of kilometres distant, at Ayre's Rock in the centre of the continent. It was all quite incomprehensible, an agoraphobic nightmare. Inexplicably, I loved it.

We set up camp on the sand behind Nullarbor Roadhouse as

the thin swirl of a dust devil swept across the plain. It was our fifty-ninth day out from Sydney.

In the blessed relief of the air-conditioned restaurant we drank ice-cold Coke and planned the next stage of the journey.

'It's two hundred kilometres between us and the next roadhouse at Border village,' I said. 'That's two hard days pedalling.'

'Yes, two good days as long as the wind holds off,' Suzanne added.

'It's going to be really hot out there. We'll have to carry as much water as possible,' said Andy.

'Let's drink as much liquid as we can tonight and tomorrow morning,' said Suzanne. 'All we can do then is carry our thirty-five litres and hope the water tank at the half-way point hasn't been shot full of holes by Red Necks.'

We had stocked up with supplies in Ceduna: batteries, candles, chain oil and some dried food. We saved our provisions for the coming days in the bush and tucked into expensive T-bone steaks.

The following morning we were favoured with a cool tail-wind, blowing steadily from the south east, off the ocean. The temperature was a bearable thirty-two degrees Celsius and the bikes cruised across the open plain at a pace that would enable us to cover one hundred and twenty kilometres before dark.

In the distance a *'road train'* made its way towards us, a thin spiral of black smoke leaking from a gleaming, vertical exhaust pipe. The cab was protected by thick steel *'Roo-Bars'*. Instinctively, I looked over my shoulder and saw another huge truck bearing down from the other direction. The silence of the desert was shattered by deep, mournful, wails as the two trucks bellowed warnings. We pulled the bikes off the highway as the metal monsters closed in, greeting each other with a blink of lights and more hoots. The beasts crossed in front of us in a thundering explosion of sound, enveloping us in choking, white dust. Both had double trailers, stretching back thirty metres. One carried sheep, hundreds of them, crammed together on six different levels. The smell of ammonia, excrement and misery lingered long after the trucks had been swallowed by the desert.

Late that afternoon, I stopped to fix a puncture which put

me behind the others. I rode on, alone, under a limitless sky awash with reds and pinks, as a burnt orange sun sank over the long, straight road. This was a special moment of freedom. I remembered a poster I had seen years ago in a friend's house.

'Each man must choose his own path', it had stated.

'YAAAAAAAAAHOOOOO!' I shouted into the still air and began laughing hysterically. I knew now why I was here.

When I caught up with the others they were setting up camp, amongst a clump of dull grey salt bushes, beside the Great Australian Bight. Here land meets sea in sheer, hundred metre cliffs; the ocean pounding furiously against a crumbling sandstone rockface far below.

Andy cooked up soya mince curry before we slumped into our tents. As I lay exhausted an image formed in my mind. It was Friday night and my old mate Ken was leaning against the corner of the bar of the Malt Shovel, pint in hand. I knew, when I returned after twelve months away, Ken would still be standing in the same corner with the same pint. He would say, 'Oh, hi Tim! Haven't seen you around for a couple of weeks. Have you been away?'

I fell into a deep, dreamless sleep. Out here time meant little, our days regulated only by the rising and setting of the sun. Even Andy had stopped asking me the time.

We rose at dawn and I prepared a simple breakfast of muesli washed down with sweet, black coffee. No one spoke as we broke camp; we were all still weary and felt this was going to be a tough day. Now, out in the middle of the Nullarbor, each of us needed to prepare in our own way.

Suzanne bent over her bike, packing her panniers, when a hornet, who had fallen out with his missus earlier that morning, stung her on the bum. She spent the next few minutes running about the campsite, clutching the offending part, in an Apache war dance. She chose to apply the ointment, discreetly, behind a large bush.

Ahead were eighty kilometres to the Western Australia border and the sanctuary of the Border Village. We soon found the pedalling hard. A strong scorching, north-westerly wind blew off the desert into our faces as we battled westwards. To make matters worse, by noon the temperature had risen to forty-six degrees Celsius (117 degrees F). It was like riding into the open doors of a blast furnace. Andy and I wore wide-brimmed khaki bush hats pulled low over our eyes, long-sleeved cotton T-shirts and dark mountain glasses. Suzanne was similarly dressed but, for some reason, despite our advice, she had refused to wear her sun hat all morning.

We stopped at the water tank on the edge of the Bight and were immediately enveloped in black, buzzing clouds of bush flies. Thousands of the loathsome creatures crawled into my eyes and ears and got right up my nose and the water tank was empty!

It was impossible to rest; we just had to keep pushing on or be eaten alive by voracious insects. Progress was painfully slow into the wind, only eight kilometres per hour. At this rate we would be out here, under the blistering sun, for ten hours. To add to my misery I was still smothered with flies.

There was a brief respite in the wind. I read from the cyclometre that my speed had risen to twenty kilometres per hour. I had a thought, *'I wonder how fast these flies can move?'* I put my head down and pedalled harder – 21 – 22 – 23 – 24 – 25 kilometres per hour. Suddenly the flies dropped away. I shook a fist at the vanquished enemy and shouted triumphantly, 'I've got you now, you little buggers!'

Andy looked up from his handlebars with interest. He shook his head sadly as he witnessed his old cycling pal slowly losing his mind under the fierce desert sun.

'Bad business – saw it happen to Carruthers back in '82 don't you know!'

It was mid-afternoon and we still had forty kilometres of pedalling to do before we reached the Border Village. The northwesterly and the flies returned to plague us and Suzanne started to suffer badly. She was finding riding into the hot wind very tough. For a while Andy and I rode in front to shield her from the worst of it but Suzanne was in no mood to accept any help.

I studied her carefully. Her movements were slow and laboured. She had withdrawn into her own little world of suffering. Her eyes looked straight ahead, pupils contracted to unseeing, staring points. Her lips had a bluish tinge and her tanned complexion had turned chalky. Suzanne was showing signs of sun stroke and dehydration.

We stopped for a rest and the three of us squashed into the meagre shade of a solitary bush.

Andy recalls: 'It was somewhat unpleasant. I lay under the bush with my hat pulled completely over my face. The heat and wind had sapped all energy. I watched with detached interest as flies tried to get at me through the eyelets of the hat. They were all too fat and as each gave up another took its place. I imagined the feel of the flies in my mouth, chewing them as they buzzed about in panic, breaking them into pulp, rolling their juices round my mouth and drinking them down.'

Things were not looking too good sitting by the side of the road in forty-six degree heat, blasted by the wind and covered in flies. Worst of all, we had drunk the last of the water. We were all becoming badly dehydrated, despite having already drunk seventeen litres between us that day.

The final thirty kilometres became a test of endurance, every muscle strained by fatigue, my nose burned a raw pink by the desert sun. We kept going with a grim determination, minds and bodies numbed by pain, bone-weary with exhaustion.

'How are you doing mate?' Andy asked.

'Fine old boy, how's it going with you?' I answered.

'Oh, I'm great. No problem.'

We were both acting as if we were out on a Sunday morning spin in the leafy lanes of Shropshire. I actually felt as if I was about to pass out and wondered if he was suffering as much pain as me. Suzanne kept going in grim, determined silence. I had the feeling she would rather have died in the saddle than admit defeat.

Suddenly, up ahead, I could make out the familiar green sign of a BP roadhouse. The ordeal was over and we soon found ourselves sitting in front of three large pots of tea. All three of us had immediately sat down at separate tables. It was clear we were all extremely hot and bothered and needed our own personal space.

I looked across at Andy. His face was drained to a pasty white, the eyes staring into space. His forehead dripped a puddle of sweat onto the table. Salt had crystallised on his face, giving him the look of a real adventurer. 'I hope I don't look as bad as you,' I told him.

'Well, you're no oil painting yourself,' he said. 'Christ, I'm totally knackered.'

'That was absolute bloody murder!' I had to agree.

'It was worse than that!' said Andy.

'Yeah, and we're only half-way across!' I replied.

Our eyes met and we began to laugh hysterically. I was totally exhausted, hurting all over, and feeling a very long way from home. I smiled to myself. At that moment there was nowhere in the world I would rather have been.

5 Roo-shooters and roadtrains – Tim

Many people had told us the Nullarbor was a boring, featureless desert.
- 'There's nothing out there,'
- 'It's mind numbing.'
- 'It'll take three months to pedal.'
- 'There's snakes all over the road.'
- 'You won't find any water.'
- 'Bloody tedious!'
- 'It'll boil yer brains out.'
- 'You can only do it in a four-wheel drive.'
- 'It's not possible.'
- 'The Abos will rob yer.'
- 'Watch out for them drop bears'

We discovered that not all of these were old wives' tales. Travelling for twelve hundred kilometres, from Ceduna to Norseman, in a car takes two or three days and is numbingly boring. On a bicycle it is totally mind blowing!

Suzanne, Andy and I pedalled on through limitless space for a hundred kilometres. We camped. We went to sleep. We got up. We pedalled on through limitless space for another hundred kilometres. We camped. We went to sleep. We got up ... Then, suddenly ....nothing happened!

Andy recalls: 'I passed the hours on the bike singing to myself, half-remembered songs; *Homeward Bound, It's a Long Way to Tipperary* and *The Long and Winding Road*. My repertoire was limited and repetitive so I tried singing the words of one song to the tune of another. I tried to recite the lyrics backwards, I made up my own lyrics, I made up my own tunes. Eventually I returned to the originals.'

'If you get bitten by a snake out here for God's sake don't panic.' I listened carefully to this advice, after all this guy should know, he was one of the famous Royal corps of Flying Doctors from the Eastern Gold Fields.

I was standing on the edge of a tiny grass air strip out in the bush, close to Madura Roadhouse, seven hundred and fifty kilometres and eight days riding to the west of Ceduna. Doctor Marty Kearns was waiting for his plane to taxi up. Dressed in dirty, beige cotton trousers, open necked red shirt and beaten up bush boots, he looked more like a hard up gold prospector than a doctor. Thinning strands of once black hair plastered a pink, balding pate. He was in that difficult to guess age, somewhere between forty and fifty, his complexion that of a man who had spent too much time in the sun. Dark brown, unhealthy blotches had already corrupted his face and arms.

'Snakes are normally shy critters and try to keep away from us blokes, but if you tread on one in the bush you can expect him to get a little riled and have a go at yer,' Marty explained. 'Some of them can be deadly, like the Taipans and tiger snakes, although you should also give death adders, copper-heads and red-bellied black snakes a miss if yer can.'

I used to be scared of snakes, now I was developing a morbid fascination for the creatures.

I asked Marty what we should do if we were bitten as we were all terrified of the prospect of a painful, lingering death out here in the bush.

'Trick is, mate, keep calm and keep still. Don't start running about like a roo on heat or the poison will get into yer blood stream much quicker. If that happens then you might as well put your head between your knees and kiss you're arse goodbye!' Marty chuckled at his own joke. 'If you're lucky you'll get to a radio or a phone. Give us a call and we'll come running.'

I thanked Marty for the information, watched his tiny plane climb into the pale blue sky and silently prayed we would not have to call upon his services as we hit the desert road once more.

We pedalled into Cocklebiddy Roadhouse in the dark the evening after leaving Madura. The first person I saw was Les, sitting on an old rusty oil drum, with a tin of beer in his hand. He studied the three of us for a while, listening to our conversation, then his ruddy face lit up with a huge grin.

'Well I've seen it all now – three crazy Pommie bastards on pushies out in the middle of the bloody Nullarbor. You're as mad as a nest full of cut snakes!' he declared delightedly.

'Why thank you,' replied Suzanne. 'You don't know where we could find a pot of tea do you?'

Les showed us into the roadhouse and magically produced three more tinnies.

'What are you doing out here in the middle of nowhere?' I asked.

'I'm a Petroleum Transfer Engineer,' he declared with a gleam in his eye. Suzanne laughed: 'Does that mean you work the petrol pumps?'

'You got it, I used to be the boss, but these days I pump gas and shovel shit.'

Les cut a comical figure with bushy grey beard, beer paunch and spindly white legs sticking out from a pair of old cotton shorts. He had twinkling blue eyes and a dry wit.

'What do you find to do in a place like this?' Andy asked.

'Drink piss and pump petrol – ain't a lot else a bloke can do!'

We pitched the tents on wasteland in front of the roadhouse, accompanied by the rusting bones of a decomposing truck. A huge brown cactus stood a lonely guard in the sand, its thick spiked arms pointing east and west. The ground was rock hard, impossible for tent pegs. We used rocks to secure the guy ropes in the freshening breeze. I was woken at two in the morning by the tent flapping dementedly around my ears. The wind was raging outside, tearing ferociously at the fly sheet. The guys had been torn free of the rocks and the tent had taken on a life of its own. We spent the rest of the night fighting our tents as they tried to carry us off into the desert. Andy reminded me of an old crone with his tent wrapped, shawl-like, around his head and shoulders. He grinned across at me, thumb up. I did worry about that lad sometimes – he actually seemed to be enjoying himself!

For the next two days we rented a cheap room at the back of Cocklebiddy Roadhouse and holed-up whilst a westerly gale raged. The wind stirred up great clouds of red sand and rolled thorny tumbleweeds across the desert. This ceaseless wind had a strange effect, making us restless and jumpy as it battered the flimsy wooden walls of our room.

Les offered to take us out into the bush in his battered old truck to find Cocklebiddy Cave. We turned off the highway onto a rough dirt track and were soon engulfed by the bush. The track ran through a sparse landscape dotted with withered trees and parched salt bushes. I was sitting in the front of the small truck, watching a plume of bull dust billowing out behind us, when I spotted a kangaroo; a big male, standing over six feet tall.

The long, brown ears had detected us long before we saw him. He stood perfectly still, watching us for several moments before turning and bounding away at astonishing speed. This was the panic signal. Suddenly the bush was alive with fleeing animals previously indistinguishable against the dull backdrop. There were hundreds, scattering in every direction.

'These are the first live kangaroos we've seen on the Nullarbor,' I told Les.

'There's thousands of the bastards out here,' he said. 'They breed like rabbits and do as much damage. They're vermin and need controlling. That's why we have the Roo-shooter.'

I looked across at him, 'Roo-shooter? What the hell's that?' 'He hunts at night; creeps up on the critters; fixes 'em in the spotlight so as they're blinded and can't move, and blows their brains out one by one.'

'Nice job!' I laughed.

'Don't knock it. I bet he makes more than you ever did as a teacher.'

This shut me up rather quickly. 'I'll show you his place. It's not far from here.'

We carried on down the rough, dusty track. The space was unnerving, the sky oppressive, the grey, flat scrub depressing. After a bone jarring twenty minutes we arrived in front of the Roo-shooter's home. It was a large wooden caravan showing signs of age. Pale green paint had long since blistered and peeled, leaving patches of bleached, grey wood beneath. Empty bottles were strewn around the caravan – gin, whisky and vodka. A small mountain of beer cans had erupted from a rusty dustbin and rolled restlessly about in the wind amongst the rotting remains of half-eaten meals. A generator chugged away in front of a small, prefabricated shed.

'That's his refrigeration plant. He stores the roos in there until he's ready to sell 'em off to the pet food people,' Les told us.

I spotted an open-back truck behind the refrigeration shed and walked over to take a look. Piled on the back were a dozen kangaroos, some staring with sightless, yellow eyes. The bush flies had already taken an interest, swarming busily over weeping scarlet wounds.

'Where's the Roo-shooter then, Les?' said Suzanne.

'Oh, he's around somewhere. I don't want to talk to him. Come on, let's go.'

'Okay,' I agreed. We had all seen enough of this outback abattoir. We drove deeper into the bush until we found Cocklebiddy Cave, hidden away in a small, shallow split in the land. The four of us entered the cave using an iron ladder which previous explorers had fixed to the rock. Inside the cave the temperature dropped immediately, the fierce heat outside replaced by cool, musty air. We lit the way with our small head-torches. It took half an hour to scramble over a previous rockfall before reaching the bottom of the cave. Here we found a large cavern with a pool of clear, still water. Les stripped down to a pair of army issue *Big Pants*.

'Last one in's a poofter!' he challenged and waded in.

Our torches sent ripples of reflected light across the ceiling of the cavern. The three of us stripped down to our Marks and Sparks undies and raced into the brackish water. The eerie blackness was broken only by the swinging beam of Les's waterproof torch. We swam, fearfully, into the dark recesses of the cave. After a hundred metres it narrowed into a low tunnel, like the entrance to a dragon's den. We half expected to be dragged beneath the surface by some hideous beast. Eventually we came up against an impenetrable rockface.

'These tunnels carry on for miles under the desert', said Les 'but unless you're a fish, this is as far as you go.'

Later that morning Les took us south of the roadhouse, once more into deep bush. He stopped the truck on the edge of a great hole some thirty metres across and twenty metres deep, like a plug-hole in the earth's crust.

A tunnel led away to the south from its base. We could make

out the bones of unknown animals far below.

'Can you blokes feel that cold air?' Les asked.

We leaned over the edge and felt a cool blast that lasted several seconds then stopped.

'That's travelled thirty kilometres, all the way from the coast. Every time a wave comes in it pushes cold air up the tunnel. Good place for a tinnie don't you think?' added Les with that familiar twinkle in his eye.

We met Barbara Brown at Cocklebiddy Roadhouse where she was doing some part-time cleaning. She was an attractive woman in her late thirties with thick black hair, intelligent dark eyes and a healthy outdoor sheen. She lived with her family on a sheep station which she invited us to visit. It was a forty kilometre drive, on a dirt track, from the highway at Cocklebiddy to the station house. I travelled with Barbara in her four-wheel drive pick-up whilst Andy and Suzanne followed in Les's truck. We stopped at the occasional metal gate which separated one massive paddock (field) from another. I opened and closed each gate as we passed through. The paddocks had a sparse covering of scorched, dusty salt bush a few centimetres high. I wondered how sheep could survive out here.

'We need to check a water tank on the way,' Barbara told me. 'We constantly worry about bore holes, windmills and water tanks. The main job on the station is to make sure that they're all working properly.'

We pulled up by the side of a bore hole serviced by a fifteen metre high windmill made of black painted iron. Nearby was a metal water tank.

'We must keep the bore holes going whatever happens. If one breaks down we can easily lose a lot of animals,' she explained. 'My husband and son use motor bikes to get around. It takes days to check them all out.'

The tank was about three metres tall and ten metres across. A pipe led to a drinking trough which was dry.

'Something is blocking the pipe,' Barbara told me. 'The sheep haven't had any water today. We'll have to try and clear it.'

I clambered up the side of the tank and peered over the top

and spotted the problem immediately.

'There's a bloody great black crow stuck in the water feed pipe,' I reported.

'Can you reach it?' Barbara asked.

I thought, *'Uugh, I don't know if I really want to'* but I did not want to appear a whinging Pom, so replied, 'I'll have a go'.

With Barbara holding onto my legs, I freed it with a long stick and the crow floated to the surface. I reached down, grabbed hold of a sodden wing and threw the carcass out of the tank.

'Thanks', said Barbara, 'that was an important job. I'd say you've earned your supper tonight.'

At the homestead Barbara introduced us to her husband, Peter, and their son, Simon. Peter was a big, untidy man about the same age as his wife, with a powerful physique and smiling green eyes He gripped my fingers in a handshake that made me wince.

Simon was a strapping fourteen-year-old who had inherited his father's strong build and his mother's features.

'I'm a Jackaroo,' he told us. 'Me and dad run the whole place together.'

He had taken naturally to the rugged life of a station hand and lived in a house separate from his parents. It had been the foreman's house before Peter had been forced to lay men off, due to difficult times in the wool industry. Barbara told us later that Simon still came over to the main house to get fed and have his washing done. He now considered himself to be foreman. He could already mend machinery, shear sheep and smoke cigarettes behind his father's back. Simon's girlfriend lived, 'just down the road', near Border Village. This was, in fact, over three hundred kilometres away; roughly the distance between London and Manchester.

'We have over eight hundred thousand acres and seventeen thousand sheep here, quite a spread to keep an eye on.'

Andy recalls: 'I was so overawed by the sheer magnitude that I later calculated it would be possible to put the whole of London and its suburbs, all the way to the M25, inside this sheep station. I found myself wondering what would happen if all the people inside the M25 area were suddenly lifted and magically plonked into this sheep station. Would they continue to rush about competing, consuming, selfishly ignoring each other's needs or would they adapt and learn to conserve and share precious resources? Neither, they'd probably hitch a lift to the nearest pub, get drunk and wonder what the hell they were suddenly doing in the middle of the Nullarbor.'

'We drive bore holes deep below the surface to reach the water-table,' said Peter. 'It's salty water out here on the Nullarbor, but these sheep are amazing critters and drink it anyway.'

Barbara Brown was a very resourceful lady. She had taken on the heavy responsibility of educating the three children.

'The nearest school is seven hundred kilometres away,' she explained, (the equivalent of Exeter to Edinburgh). 'We didn't want to send the children away to boarding school when they were little so I taught them here on the station.'

Barbara showed us the schoolhouse Peter had built. 'We don't use it any more, but I've kept it just as it was.'

Inside were a blackboard, three desks and a gleaming brass bell. On the walls were shelves crammed with books and a project on South America.

'We taught all three kids here with the help of radio broadcasts from the School of the Air.'

She had done a good job. Their other two children were now away studying in further education. Simon, however, was dyslexic and once away at boarding school, the main stream system had failed him.

'I shouldn't worry about Simon,' I said. 'He seems to be doing just fine here on the station. He's obviously practically minded and most of the skills he needs can't be taught in a classroom.'

We stayed for dinner (lamb chops of course) and spent the evening in lively discussion on topics ranging from the state of world wool markets to agricultural skills in desert conditions. Peter was a member of a committee concerned with rain catchment techniques in arid conditions. He had even heard of the project in Africa, run by Intermediate Technology, for which we were raising funds.

The following morning we made an early start, pedalling fifty kilometres to the roadhouse at Caiguna by lunchtime. Norseman now lay three hundred kilometres to the west. We stocked up with food and water for the next two day stretch to Balladonia.

This section of highway resembled a butcher's shop, hundreds of dead kangaroos littered the asphalt. Plenty of work here for the Roo-scraper. This is one of the straightest pieces of road in the world – one hundred and sixty kilometres, arrowing through the bush. It was disconcerting to see the road ahead disappear into infinity like the perspective drawings I had once practised at school. We knew it would be like this for the whole day, and the whole of the following day; pedalling hour after hour without the slightest change in either road or flat, sparse bushland. I felt I was standing still or even going backwards. Time became warped. Minutes could drag by and hours fly past, unnoticed.

The camp fire Andy built that night would have been described by an Aussie bushman as, 'a real beaut'. We had pitched the tents in a sandy clearing surrounded by grey, dusty bush. On the far side of the fire lay a pile of dry, dead wood, enough to keep us going well into the night.

Andy recalls: 'I spent a cautious hour pulling branches and twigs out of the undergrowth shouting, 'Come on you snakes!' at the top of my voice. A family of kangaroos studied me curiously from a safe distance of about twenty metres. I was deeply depressed at this time by the almost daily battles with Suzanne and liked to be busy.'

I sat cross-legged on my sleeping mat admiring Andy's handiwork. I was cook tonight. In front of me was a bed of glowing orange embers that he had scraped out of the fire, six inches wide and a couple of feet long. Using light from my head torch, I tended three billie-cans that sat bubbling away. On tonight's menu was hot chilli and rice with cobs of sweet corn, and lots of it. Supper would taste all the better for being carried all the way from Ceduna. Whilst eating, we chatted about the events of the day and planned the next, discussing head winds, distances, faulty spokes and our favourite subject – food.

After this culinary masterpiece I stretched out on my mat, replete. The sky was clear, the air still, the hot northerly wind of the day having been put to rest at sunset. The three of us sat in companionable silence under the southern stars. It was a source of satisfaction and wonder to me that we had reached this anonymous place, having propelled ourselves and all our possessions over four thousand kilometres from Sydney in the last ten weeks.

In the morning we pushed our bikes out of the bush, back onto the highway and had to think hard about which way we were going – one direction looked much the same as the other. In the afternoon we came to a bend, the first for three days. We all cheered and punched the air in triumph.

It is strange what effect a little bend can have on three brain-dead Pommies. On reaching the roadhouse at Balladonia I got into conversation with Mick, a truckie, who regularly crossed the Nullarbor in a roadtrain on his way to and from Perth. Mick was a big barrel-chested man with thick hairy arms. He was wearing a white Stetson, shiny brown cowboy boots and a blue denim shirt. Was this guy for real? His face reminded me of the boxer Joe Bugner who had emigrated to Australia from England a few years before. Perhaps it was the large owl-like eyes and small, petulant mouth, or maybe it was his boasting, arrogant manner.

'Those roos really splatter well on the bars on the front of my truck,' he declared gleefully. 'I usually manage to do about a dozen on a crossing.

They get dazzled in the lights, freeze then... splat, he chuckled, stuffing *'Hamburger-The-Lot'* into his mouth (an Australian delicacy of hamburger, cheese, egg, bacon, beetroot, pickles and anything else that happens to be lying around at the time.)

Mick continued talking through a mouthful of mush. 'It's pretty boring hauling a truck across the Nullarbor. Sometimes I read a book when I'm driving to keep awake.'

This did little for the confidence of three vulnerable cyclists.

Another man, who had been sitting at the next table, joined in the conversation. 'You blokes want to be real careful riding pushies on this highway,' he said. 'I picked up the bits of the last bloke who pedalled through here.'

'Was that the Jap who got splattered by one of my boys?' Mick asked him eagerly.

'Yeah, I was the guy who drove the ambulance. This Japanese bloke was out there pedalling away, listening to his Walkman. He pulled out to miss a dead roo, didn't hear the roadtrain 'coz his head was full of Bob bleedin' Marley. The poor sod got sucked under the back wheels. Driver couldn't do a thing about it. We were scraping bits of him off the road for half a mile.'

I left the restaurant feeling a little sick and was pumping up my tyres when I heard a question in thick Scots brogue.

'So you've cycled across the Nullarbor have ye?'

I turned to find a silver-haired gentleman, in a tweed jacket, staring questioningly at me.

'Yes, we're almost there now,' I replied.

'Well, what was it like?'

'I can't tell you, there is no way to explain what is was like. The only way you can know is to do it yourself.'

'I see,' he said, but clearly did not.

'And where are ye people goin' now?'

I gave him the standard answer, 'We're cycling from Sydney to Perth.'

'Are ye by God? And what'll ye do when ye get there?' he asked.

'Well, then we fly to Africa and cycle across Kenya, Uganda, Zaire, Central African Republic and Cameroon.'

'Will ye really? Then I s'pose ye'll fly home?'

'No, if we're still fit and strong after all that, we plan to fly to South America and cycle across Brazil, Paraguay, Bolivia and Peru.'

He looked at me, a little wild-eyed. 'Australia and Africa are fine lad, but Soooth America, that's where ye'll end yer days!'

After this pessimistic prediction, he turned and walked briskly into the roadhouse. He reminded me of Frazer, the dour Scotsman and prophet of doom in *Dad's Army!*

After another bush camp we awoke to our last day on the Nullarbor. I could feel a faint tail wind as we broke camp. The last seventy kilometres to Norseman were a real pleasure. I pedalled away smoothly, remembering the endless empty miles, flies and heat, we had endured during the last two weeks. I felt a real sense of achievement as we rode into the old gold mining town. The infamous Nullarbor Plain was behind us at last.

The town is named after a horse called 'Norseman', who had stumbled and thrown his rider at this spot towards the end of the last century. The horse had trodden on what, at that time, was the largest nugget of gold found in Western Australia. The rest is, as they say, history. Today Norseman is a large, modern gold-mining town surrounded by ugly flat-topped hills, carelessly fashioned from the waste of numerous gold processing plants.

We decided to celebrate our achievement in the *Railway Hotel*, a seedy looking Victorian building in the centre of town. We had a choice of two bars. The back bar for serious drinkers, Aboriginals and pool players, or the up-market front bar, with its shabby furniture, dull peeling wall paper and linoleum floor covered with cigarette butts. We opted for the front bar.

'Three very large and very cold beers please' I asked the huge lad behind the bar.

'Are ye celebrating tonight then?' asked Nessie, the landlady of the pub. She was a big Scotswoman wearing a billowing, flowered dress. Her hands were the size of dinner plates, her fingers like bunches of bananas.

'Yes, we're celebrating cycling across the Nullarbor,' Andy told her.

'Well that certainly deserves a drink. There aren't too many folk can say they've done that. Here you go, these are on the house,' she said, placing three beers on the counter.

I nipped out to the washroom for a couple of minutes and returned only to find Suzanne and Andy involved in a full blown argument once more. This time the subject was English football of all things!

'Oh, shut up Andy, what do you know about it, you wally.'

'You what!' Andy was incredulous.

'You know what I mean, Wally.'

The next few seconds passed in slow motion. I saw everything with the same clarity with which I had once witnessed a car accident. On impulse Andy threw the contents of his full glass of beer at Suzanne. I watched in fascination as the stream of golden liquid hit her square in the chest and exploded over her white T-shirt. For an instant there was a look of complete surprise on Suzanne's face which changed to one of fury. She reached for her glass and launched it at Andy. The beer hit him full in the face and he stood frozen, unable to see, his specs covered in white, frothy beer. Finally he took them off, muttered 'Good shot', turned and stormed out of the bar.

The whole pub had gone quiet, enjoying this unexpected entertainment. Nessie was unmoved by the whole episode.

'Strange way you English folk have of celebrating,' she commented, replacing Suzanne's empty glass with a full one. I wondered if they were still secretly in love.

The English Celebrating

For the next two days Suzanne and I rode the two hundred kilometres south to Esperance and the ocean. Andy decided to stay behind in Norseman for another day to recover from a stomach bug and a mysterious case of frothy spectacles.

A few days later the three of us were re-united in the hostel at Esperance. An under-current of bad feeling lingered, despite the time apart. We were bone-tired and decided to take a break from the bikes. This was a time for rest and reflection after the hard graft of the past two weeks. The three of us explored the coastline of Cape Le Grand National Park. We walked for mile upon mile on the most beautiful beaches I have ever seen, discovering secluded bays and swimming in a clear turquoise sea. The sand was a pure, white paste which squeaked as we walked on it.

It was whilst we were in Esperance that we read the news in the International Express that civil war had broken out in Zaire. The Foreign Office was strongly advising British nationals to leave the country and the borders had been sealed preventing anyone entering. This was a major problem for us, as our intended route across Africa was to have taken us through Zaire. It did not seem very wise to ride bikes through the middle of a civil war, so an alternative had to be found.

As ever, Andy was planning ahead and paid a visit to the town library.

'I think I've got it,' he declared on his return. 'If we can't go through Zaire then there may be a route that will take us across Africa through Tanzania, Malawi, Zambia, Zimbabwe, Botswana and Namibia.'

It always amazed me that Andy could be so organised and be constantly thinking ahead. As far as I was concerned each day was demanding enough without having to think weeks in advance.

I woke one morning in the youth hostel and lay thinking about our team problems. I was fed up with the constant running battle between Andy and Suzanne which always left me somewhere in the middle. The main challenge in Australia had now been met and, over the next couple of weeks, I had to decide whether I wanted to continue in such an unhappy atmosphere. I put these ideas onto a shelf in the back of my mind and decided to take a day-ride west, along the coast for some air, some exercise and to clear my thoughts.

I found Free Beach, famous for its nude bathers in summer time. A the beginning of November it was totally deserted. As I walked alone on the white sand I revelled in space and freedom. I stood on the edge of the ocean watching the white-topped breakers come crashing in. At that moment I found perspective, my worries seemed trivial and unimportant. I shouted my joy into the restless wind.

We left Esperance riding once more into a westerly wind past rich, wet fields of wheat. The land was still remote, with only the occasional farm house to signal human presence. Our objective for the day was to reach a stash of water our friend Lester had left on his way to Perth. He was a farmer we had met in the youth hostel who had offered to help us out. Our map showed no towns and no surface water for two hundred kilometres, which meant this water was of great importance.

Lester was as good as his word and we found a small, neat note under a piece of wood behind the sign to Stoke's Inlet. The note read:

'Dear Suzanne, Andy and Tim, you will find the precious, life-saving liquid you require four paces to the north – Lester.'

Strangely, before reading the note, we had scanned the undergrowth but had seen nothing. As soon as we had read the note the bulging, blue water bag seemed to peep out from beneath a bush.

We pitched the tents in a field shielded from the road by thick gorse bushes, and quickly took shelter as a heavy storm blew up sending large, black clouds scudding in from the west. The flexible tents were almost blown flat by the strength of the wind and rain during the night.

I woke at the usual time of seven am to hear rain hammering on the fly sheet. A strong westerly wind still tugged strongly at the guy ropes. There was not a whisper from the other two tents; none of us moved although we were all awake. I felt tired and run down, still recovering from the huge physical effort required to get across the Nullarbor. I assumed the others were feeling the same way. I was gasping for a mug of tea, but this meant movement and discomfort in these conditions. Instead, I snuggled up in my warm, down sleeping bag and went back to sleep. The first communication came at eleven am during a brief break in the storm.

'Is anyone alive out there?' Andy called.

'No', replied Suzanne, 'and I don't feel very well either.'

'What's the problem?' I asked.

'I just don't feel very well,' came the reply.

'Well, I can't see us doing any cycling in this weather,' I said, voicing what was on all our minds. 'We might as well write the rest of the day off and get some rest.'

'Suits me,' said Andy.

'I could do with a rest as well,' said Suzanne, sounding rather forlorn.

We had just enough food and water to last through the day if we were careful. As long as we found water first thing the following morning we would be safe.

Feeling a little guilty but relieved, we hibernated. Andy proved himself a stout Yeoman, supplying us regularly with food and tea. I did not move from my tent for over twenty four hours and, in between dozing off, read the whole of Bruce Chatwin's 'Songlines' and wrote a long overdue letter to Phyl back home. The last thought I had before dropping off into another dreamless sleep was that at least the day had not been a total waste of time.

We crossed the Sterling Ranges, three hundred and fifty kilometres west of Esperance, in the second week of November. The whole area was ablaze with the colourful blooms of a hundred species of wild flower. It was easy to see why the Australians had chosen green and gold for their national colours. It must have been in appreciation of the deep green leaves and bright yellow flowers of acacias that cover the countryside during late winter and early spring. Banksias, waratahs, bottlebrushes, paperbarks and many other flowers added shades of red and blue and gold – a kaleidoscope of natural colour.

A week after leaving Esperance we dropped down to the old whaling town of Albany, tucked away on the southern tip of Western Australia. It was here that John Eyre had finished his epic transcontinental journey, one hundred and fifty years before.

Things were still deteriorating between Andy and Suzanne. After another bust-up coming into the town, he decided to stay in the *Backpackers Hostel*. Suzanne and I stayed with her contacts, Syd and Daphne. There were letters and gifts from Richard waiting for Suzanne.

Syd was a life assurance salesman who had lived in the area all his life. He should have been retired but they could not stop him working. Syd stood a little over five feet tall, smartly dressed in sports jacket and plain brown tie, his snowy white hair carefully combed over a pink, balding head. As with many short men, he tried to make up for his lack of inches with an aggressive front. His first words to us were, 'I'm seventy four years old, I had open heart surgery a year ago and I'm one hundred and twenty percent fit for my age. What do you think of that then?'

'That's great Syd,' I told him, not really knowing what I thought about it.

'Marvellous Syd,' added Suzanne, 'and you certainly don't look a day over sixty.'

'Sixty!' I could see he was mortally offended. 'I have the body of a fifty year old!'

'What's your secret then, Syd?' I asked.

'I eat well, I don't smoke and I get plenty of exercise,' he told us proudly. 'Come on I'll show you my bike.' Syd took us to the garage behind the house and produced an immaculate, gleaming racing machine.

'What do you think? She's a beaut ain't she?' His face radiated boyish pride.

'Nice machine Syd,' I encouraged him. 'Do you get out on it much?'

'Bet your bloody life I do – every day. You blokes think you're cyclists, well come out with me and I'll show you what cycling is all about!'

'*Oh no*', I thought, '*that's all we need. We've come to Albany for a rest from bikes and this crazy, seventy four year old fitness fanatic wants to take us out racing. Let me out!*'

'I'd love to Syd', I said, 'but I've got to rest my bad knee.' Syd was disappointed. 'The trouble with you Pommies is that you just don't have the stamina!' he declared and roared off on his silver machine. Syd really looked after us over the next couple of days, driving us around the sights and setting up a local press interview. Underneath all the bluster there lurked a first rate guy.

The three of us set off, re-united, on the final four hundred kilometre leg, north-east to Perth, having negotiated a tenuous cease-fire. On 21st November, two weeks behind schedule, we pedalled into Freemantle harbour at the end of our five and a half thousand kilometre odyssey across Australia. I sat amongst the warm breakers of the Indian Ocean sipping from a bottle of chilled champagne, enjoying a few moments of quiet reflection. The last three and a half months had been a unique experience travelling slowly through a land of unimaginable emptiness, contrast and natural beauty. Above all it had been bloody hard work and one hell of a long way to pedal a bicycle. As I left the warm ocean I suspected the euphoria would be short lived. We had arrived in Perth – it was now time to decide the future of the expedition.

'Okay it's make your mind up time,' Andy opened the discussion.

'Do the three of us carry on as we are or do we go our own ways?'

We were sitting outside a cafe in Hay Street, a shopping precinct in the centre of Perth, trying to sort our lives out.

'What do you think Suzanne?' Andy asked quietly.

'It's going to be very difficult' said Suzanne, 'but I think we should try and stick together.'

'How about you, Tim?'

'As far as I can see', I stated, 'it's going to be impossible for us to carry on as we are. We've had nothing but rows most of the way across.

Let's face it, we just don't get on. I haven't finally decided, but I'll probably be going on alone.'

'What about the visit we've planned to the I.T. projects in Kenya?' Suzanne asked.

'I won't go,' I said. 'You and Andy can go together, it doesn't need three of us.'

By now I had had enough of the squabbling and the thought of the three of us spending a week together in a Landrover did not appeal. Andy was not happy with my attitude, 'What about all the fund raising we've done back home?' he said. 'You have to go, to fulfil your obligation to I.T. and all the people who have given money to the project.'

'I don't have to go anywhere Andy,' I glared at him.

'I see,' Suzanne joined in, 'so you're not bothered about the charity projects then? My mother always said you didn't do much fund raising work anyway.'

Ouch! This was too much even for my easy going nature. I got up from the table. 'Well, if that's the way you see it Suzanne then you and Andy are better off on your own.'

I got on my bike and stormed off into the throng of shoppers. For the first time on the trip I had really lost it. I was absolutely seething; blood boiling, bells ringing, steam coming out of ears, the full works. I had to stop pedalling. I could not see where I was going; my eyes full of the tears of rage, frustration and disappointment.

'I would like to change the date of my flight please,' I told the smart young girl seated behind the computer terminal. I was standing in the Quantas office on the corner of Hay Street and William Street.

'Can you give me your flight details please sir?' she asked with a smile.

'The flight number is QA 133, Perth to Harare, leaving on the third of December. I'd like to change to the next available flight after the third.'

'Yes, I have your reservation here along with a Mister Andrew Brown and a Miss Suzanne Taplin. Will they be accompanying you?'

'No, I'm travelling alone.'

Africa

"To travel hopefully
is a better thing than to arrive
and the true sucess is to labour"

Robert Loius Stevenson 1850-1894 El Dorado

6 Beside the Jade Sea – Andy

Blood had not reached my feet for half an hour. The slightest twitch on my part set off a wave of movement across the line of bodies beside me. One buttock held a precarious, aching contact with the seat. I tried to read, '... *I had seen a herd of elephant travelling through the dense native forest, where the sunlight is strewn down between the thick creepers in small spots and patches, pacing along as if they had an appointment at the end of the world ...*' With some difficulty I turned the page of *Out of Africa* with one finger of my left hand, my right hand was behind my head. The bus stopped in a village. Women and children stuck baskets of mangoes, bananas and bread through the window. I smiled and said 'No, thanks.'

They smiled back and said, 'OK'. I thought people were supposed to hassle you in Africa.

The bus was a washed-out blue; gushing black soot as it idled. Windows were cracked or missing, so a fine film of dust decorated each passenger.

More people wanted to join the bus. The conductor, a sweaty lump of fury, supervised the stacking and tying of sacks and bags to the roof. His two boys, who had climbed out of a window to reach the roof, obeyed silently, but once back inside they mimicked their boss and laughed behind his back.

The wave of new passengers piled on. The conductor pushed his way to the back seats and shouted to my neighbours, 'You have too much room, move, move, move!' They averted their eyes from the conductor and kept silent.

'Move up, move up,' he ranted.

I had to protest, 'This seat is made for five people!' Suzanne and Tim, sitting in comparative comfort two rows in front, turned and laughed. 'No, seven people, seven!' the conductor shouted back. 'Where can you put seven? Look at us!' My neighbours were no help. They stared, pathetically, at their knees. Were they typical of Africans, trusting in authority without question? 'You all take too much room, seven, seven, seven!' He had wild eyes and had been doing this job too long.

The long back seat of the bus was definitely made for five small people. The conductor, carrying a pile of white tickets in one hand and neat bundles of banknotes in the other, levered a newcomer onto the laps of two self-effacing young men next to me, squashing me further out of the window. He turned, walked half way down the bus and roared, 'Seven!!' God, I love cycling; you don't have to deal with this nonsense.

I was desperate to save the team for its own sake. At the eleventh hour, I had bought some time by getting Tim to agree to fly with us from Perth. He would at least come up to Turkana, to visit the Intermediate Technology projects which would be supported by the money being raised through the expedition. Once the visit to Turkana was over, we would split up for a two week break to think things over. We could just about afford it on the time schedule.

We had flown from Perth to Harare, in Zimbabwe, and up to Nairobi the following day. The bikes were now having a sleep down south in Nairobi, the capital of Kenya, while we were off, together, to see how the I.T. money would be spent.

Suzanne was keen to continue but, I knew, did not feel confident about cycling alone across Africa. I was not too keen myself. I had been mentally prepared for a team effort. Perhaps it was wishful thinking, but I sensed a shift in the relationship between Suzanne and me in the past week. 'Like brother and sister,' she had said.

Perhaps we had made a breakthrough and could get along. The danger was that we would set off across Africa and find the arguments flaring up again. That would be hell on earth!

We had already crossed the equator and were heading north along the Great Rift Valley to the town of Lodwar, in the Turkana desert. To the east lay the immense Jade Sea; Lake Turkana, home to Nile Perch, weighing up to fifty kilos, and twenty thousand crocodiles. Nearby, in 1959, Louis Leakey had found some of the oldest human remains in the world, perhaps two million years old. Close to the west was Uganda, to the north Sudan and to the north east, at the head of the lake, was Ethiopia.

After about fifteen hours, just before gangrene set in and my bum fell off, I decided enough was enough. I would stand for the remainder of the journey. I slid through the scrum of sweaty bodies to the front and tried not to watch the driver's high speed cornering as I rode the rocking bus like a surfer.

Much later, well into the evening, a man and his chickens got off in the middle of nowhere and walked away into the bush. This fortuitous event freed a spacious seat. It was too tempting. Here I could sit like a human being and, what's more, I would be in the perfect position to kick the conductor out of the door if the opportunity arose. I grabbed the seat and after a while chatted in the dark to the guy sitting next to me.

'I am lucky', he said, 'they feed me nicely and pay me to run up Mount Kenya. Me and the other boys run up every day.' He was stationed at the barracks of the 78th Tank Battalion at Tsiolo, but had never fired a gun.

In 1849 a missionary, called Krapf, claimed he had found a mountain with glaciers and permanent snow sitting right on the equator. Geographic experts dismissed these claims and the phrase, 'a load of Krapf' was born. In 1883, however, the experts were forced to eat their words when a Scottish traveller confirmed the existence of Mount Kenya. It was 1929 before the twin peaks were successfully scaled.

'They took me to South Korea', said my new friend, 'and I won a gold medal, in the steeplechase.'

'What, the Olympics!?' I asked in awe. I spoke loudly above the roar of the diesel engine and was unaware that the whole bus had stopped talking to listen to our conversation.

'I liked it in Korea. They gave us a lovely place to sleep, near the running track, and so much food! A man from Adidas even gave me a red tracksuit, with white stripes down the arms and a man from Nike gave me a pair of trainers. Oh, I won a silver medal in the 5,000 metres too.'

His name was George Simiyu Wanyonyi, a Turkana tribesman. He was going to see his family in Lodwar before flying off to a race meeting in Japan.

George went on, 'When we got back from Seoul, President Moi threw a big party for all the boys who had won a medal. He gave me so much money that if I wanted to I could buy a four-wheel-drive car.' He reflected for a moment. 'But petrol is so expensive that I take the bus.'

He looked indecently fit, tall, lean and muscular, and oozed charisma. People do not get that fit just for fun. I believed his story.

'Do you think we could be friends?' he asked as we pulled into Lodwar. 'We could write to each other and you could send me some training shoes from England one day. I have one pair, but they get wet every day and it would be nice to be able to wear dry shoes.'

John Munyes met us at Lodwar, a dusty wide street of a town. Although only in his mid-twenties, John was coordinator of the projects in Turkana, run jointly by Intermediate Technology and Oxfam. He was a Turkana tribesman, confident and good-looking, and would one day become an elder in the community. As an exceptionally bright young man he had been selected by I.T. to be trained in England and Nairobi to lead the projects. Exposure to another world was evident. His bright yellow *Channel* T-shirt and black Levis were souvenirs from England. 'I had many other English clothes', he told us, 'but someone stole them from me on a bus in London.'

We rattled around in the back of John's Landrover for several hours, bumping over dusty tracks, through a moonscape desert of red sand, hard packed pebbles and low scrub. John did not drive so bounced with us, while Samuel, at the wheel, skilfully rode the potholes. Alto-cumulus hung over sharp, black peaks under a washed-out sky. We arrived at John's base on the edge of a village called Kakuma and were free to walk around while he organised lunch. We had brought our own supplies but John insisted on providing our meals.

There was still considerable tension between Suzanne, Tim and myself, so we split up and wandered through the village alone. The huts were dome shaped, about four metres across, woven from saplings and roughly thatched with long grasses and goat skins. Groups of ten or twelve huts were enclosed in a compound formed by a circular windbreak, six feet high, which was no match for the strong northerly wind which blew great plumes of dust through the settlement. In each hut lived a family of mother, father and two or three children.

A small girl of about three years, stood staring at me, spellbound. She was on a mission to fetch water from an old oil drum and was holding a dull aluminium kettle. She wore a clean black and white dress in a lively patchwork pattern. I said, 'Hello,' but she kept on staring and did not react. I smiled and walked on.

A woman wanted to show me her hut. I had to stoop low to enter. Inside it was dark and surprisingly cool. Light peeked through small chinks in the grasses. The lower portion, close to the ground, was open to allow the howling, cooling wind to blow through onto a chubby baby which lay on the swept dirt, wrapped in a green and orange blanket. An older sister fiddled with the infant's hand. The hut contained no furniture and cooking was done over a wood fire, outside, behind the shelter of a further, smaller windbreak.

These huts, of prehistoric design, were not unlike our own dome tents: they were a similar shape, temporary and transportable, small and simple to erect. Although the huts did not, and never would, contain carpets, sofas, beds, pictures or televisions, they were certainly homes. They were places to love, to rest after work, raise children, welcome friends and neighbours and to spend hours talking and laughing. These were pure homes, where the lust for comfort was not the master. At this stage, these people had no expectations of owning satellite TV, fridges or carpets and were certainly better off for it. Should not a home be a place whose main function is to provide shelter, a place to rest, recuperate and be safe in preparation for the next challenge outside in the world? Homes should be places that you leave. A home should not be the reason for existence, as we are led to believe in the West, where for millions of people all daily toil is to provide comfort and luxury. If only we could slow down the development, production and sale of the things we do not need, we might free up the time to be happier, share out the limited resources a bit more evenly and make those resources last longer. If we all lived like these Turkana people, with almost zero consumption, the earth can sustain human, animal and plant life indefinately. If we all live like Americans we'll soon need another ten earths to support the consumption.

The Turkana women wore simple clothing, yards of striped or polka-dot cotton were wrapped around them and tied at the shoulder leaving one breast exposed; these shawls hung to their ankles. Around ankles and wrists they wore heavy metal bracelets, whilst ears held a line of twenty or more fine metal rings, each two inches in diameter. Their heads were shaven and smooth, save for a small cap of plaited hair on top. They chattered and giggled shyly amongst themselves, enjoying my attention.

They were fine looking people; their skins dark and shining with health. Around their necks hung hundreds of coloured bead necklaces, large ones on their shoulders, gradually decreasing in size as the pile climbed to nestle under the chin. The greater the number of beads the greater the family's wealth. Just below the mouth the more senior women wore a curved, beard-like, metal decoration, fixed through the flesh with a stud. The whole collection must have weighed a ton. Eventually rich women must die of strangulation!

Sheltering from the intense midday heat, we drank hot tea, served from a vacuum flask, and ate a stew of potatoes and chewy goat meat, accompanied by *ugali,* a stodgy mash of cereal, like dried porridge.

Ugali, milk and blood are the Turkana's staple diet. The goat, though, was a special treat, killed for us. We all wished they had not made such a special effort. We did not want to be eating their food; we wanted to keep as low a profile as possible. The Turkana are also keen on cakes made from crushed wild berries and cow's blood. Thankfully we were spared that treat.

'How many children do people generally have here?' I asked John.

'I think people like to have three children; some have more, some less. When times were bad in the eighties, people had more children.'

'Why?' asked Suzanne. 'Surely they had trouble feeding them.'

'Because the people did not feel that all the children would survive to become adults, nor that they, themselves, would be healthy enough to work throughout their lives. In bad times, having eight or ten children provides a good labour force and is a safeguard for the future of the whole tribe.'

'So you think', said Tim, 'that when parents are sure that all their children will survive they will not have so many?'

'Of course, that is only logical. Have you not heard of the law of supply and demand? You English have been practising the same technique in your families for centuries.'

In the afternoon, we were shown another village nearby. The drought of the early eighties had decimated the cattle population, and, since the Turkana had no food reserves, they had starved. Here, as in Kakuma, over the past five years, I.T. had helped the people to develop a successful system which had brought food security, while at the same time, allowed the villagers to maintain their culture and self esteem. There is a crucial difference between this approach and that of *'answers'* thrust upon tribes people by well-meaning outsiders which are, not surprisingly, quickly dropped.

'We did not cause the drought,' said John. 'Perhaps you did with your petrol fumes and your factory emissions. These people have never seen a factory, or many items which are produced in factories, but their friends and families have died from the environmental effects of factory output.'

Wealth here is measured in quantity of animals owned. These are skilled cattle people, nomads who spend most of the year following rain clouds to fresh pastures. By staying in one place for the rainy season, the Turkana are able to grow sorghum; a cereal crop, which is pummelled down to make *ugali*.

Through John Munyes and his team of mobile trainers, Intermediate Technology and Oxfam had trained the people in how to maximise crop production. The sorghum was a special strain, which could survive desert conditions and grow to maturity in just three months. John told us it cost about £5,000 to keep one trainer housed, fed and mobile for one year. Each spread their skills amongst hundreds of tribesmen as they zip about the desert on motorbikes, following carefully planned programmes. We did not know how the fund raising was going but hoped we could raise enough to enable the work to continue.

The sorghum field was about one hundred metres square.

'You see how this land has been carefully levelled,' John told us. 'Those mounds surrounding the field trap the rain water. We give the field a slight slope which allows excess water to flow through that gap, down into the next field and the next and so on.'

A boy of thirteen or so stood guard over the expanse of golden, two metre stalks, now bending in the hot wind. Perched on a raised wooden platform, he was well positioned to throw pebbles at any birds that dared to venture into the field. This living scarecrow threw with impressive accuracy, nailing a crow from thrity meters.

We were shown examples of wooden ploughs, made there in the village. They were a clever design, which agitated the soil but did not turn it over, an action which would have released vital water.

'Excess grain and flour are taken to the community store', John told us. 'Here it is carefully weighed on scales and recorded by the store-keeper, Rachel. The women of the village withdraw it daily, in small quantities.'

The store was piled high with sacks of grain, safe from weather and theft.

'If a family falls on hard times through illness or the crops fail there is always a reserve,' said John.

In good years there was so much sorghum that some could be sold outside the community or exchanged for goats. The goats provided skins and dairy products, particularly dairy products which can be sold outside for a profit. With these growing profits more and more goats and cattle can be bought. I found myself impressed, but surely people the world over had been engaged in trade for thousands of years. How had it by-passed the Turkana people? They clearly had not needed to trade formally until now. This local economy was simple and sustainable, they were able to provide for themselves and were not exploited or threatened by the fluctuations of the world markets. Also, the soil and the lake were not being poisoned by fertilizers and pesticides as in the developed world.

John continued 'We also teach the men how to treat their animals for sickness. They have to buy the drugs though, we do not give anything for free. They must even pay three goats to join the scheme.'

Only in this way will these people be able to sustain the projects, their lifestyle and their pride long after the white men and John Munyes have gone.

A meeting of elders, all male, held council under a shady, flat-topped acacia tree. The headman opened the proceedings with a ritual chant. In the sing-song tones of the Turkana language he called for attention:

'May God come down in peace to this tree, to the gathering of the committee.' The men replied in deep staccato unison, 'Yes, Yes'

'May he stay here forever.'

'Yes, Yes'

'Are there bad spirits here?'

'No. No. No'

'Has the devil gone forever?'

'Yes, Yes, Yes.'

Each man stood while he said his piece to the council. John, although not an elder, was very much involved in the debate. They were, John whispered, discussing how certain poorer members of the tribe would pay for veterinary medicines.

The men in the village wore little else but soft, high quality blankets, of yellow and red stripes; these were tied at the right collarbone and, like the women's, draped to the ankle. They carried thin staffs, two metres long, and small mushrooms of carved wood, which doubled as both seat and pillow. They also wore metal studs above goatee beards, heavy bracelets and long, finely fashioned ear-rings. The back rim of the ears had been sliced through to form a decorative loop. Their heads were partially shaved and from a small square of red clay on top, sprang white ostrich feathers.

Late arrivals walked slowly across the dust from the village beyond. They carried long staffs horizontally across their shoulders, drooping their bony arms over them like crucifixes.

When the meeting finished, a group of elders welcomed us, we sat in a circle; they on wooden pedestals; we on rush mats. They were proud men and pleased to see us. I felt that they showed too much respect, just because we were white.

It was confusing, we were in awe of them and they of us. We had not come as ignorant white people, 'here to save you', but as humble guests, hoping to find out how they lived. One or two men stared me full in the face and it was I who looked away first.

I was heartened by their spirit.

The head man joined us and we stood to shake his hand. He was ancient but very fit. His face was deeply lined and very dark, with high cheekbones, piercing clear eyes and a strong chin. A nobleman indeed. John translated while Tim explained that we were raising money in England to support further work in Turkana. The idea that riding bicycles could earn money was totally baffling to them all, and, come to think of it, it is rather odd. They were immensely impressed with Suzanne; a woman who could ride a bicycle across a whole continent! Tim and I were pretty impressed ourselves, but when we told her she accused us of being patronising.

Below us the valley was teeming with goats, long-horned cattle with humped backs and drooping jowls, donkeys and the greatest of all possessions, camels.

'A female camel,' John told us, 'can provide more than five litres of milk each day. When we mix it with blood it will easily feed a large family. Camels are now beyond price. They are only passed between members of a family, never sold.'

We had seen successful, well established projects with happy prosperous people and singing children, able to survive and preserve their culture. The money that was being donated to the 'Cycle for I.T.' fund would support the expansion of these projects to other villages in the region which were currently struggling.

Tim recalls: 'Here was the reminder we all needed. Here was a purpose to the expedition. In the heat and hardship of Australia it had been forgotten. I felt the three of us gelling again. The challenge of the journey ahead and the opportunity to do a little to help the spread of this good work were far bigger than our petty differences.'

As we prepared to return to Kakuma two figures appeared, running towards us across the windswept desert. When they reached the Landrover they talked earnestly to John. They were serious looking guys, tall, bare chested warriors from a village to the north, and were in pursuit of two men who had stolen a cow from their herd. They had been on the trail for eight days; if we could give them a lift on to Kakuma they might be able to overtake and apprehend the thieves before the cow could be sold.

'What will happen to the thieves if they are caught?' Tim asked.

'They will be put in prison for ten years,' John told us. 'We are cattle people, there are few greater crimes.'

The two warriors were fantastically fit. So tall and muscular, they seemed to fill the back of the vehicle. Before we could leave the village, though, a man approached in the fading light and spoke animatedly to me. I could not understand and directed him to John. It seemed there was a medical emergency; an old man in the village had a bladder problem and needed to go to the hospital in Kakuma. He was carried from his hut and laid on the floor of the Landrover. Two young men from the village accompanied him, one carrying a goat with which to pay the Irish doctor at the Mission Hospital. It was becoming a hell of a squeeze in the back so I saw my opportunity and sneaked into the front with John and Samuel.

'He will probably die', said John. 'They say he has not passed his water for many days and the witchcraft has not worked. Only now, when it is too late, do they seek real help.'

After a few days we returned to Nairobi, enriched by the experience of Turkana and happier than we had been for a long time.

Suzanne's boyfriend, Richard and Tim's girlfriend, Phyl, were flying out. We had arranged this break long ago knowing that, whatever happened, we would need to have some days when we did not have to look at each other's faces. The crunch decision – Do we go on together?, could be delayed still further.

Having started this thing, left my job, left Cassie, and sold the house, I had to make it work. Failure would be too much to handle; I would lose all self confidence. And what would I do in the future, now that everything was gone?

I was looking forward to having time to myself; Perhaps I might have to start getting used it, though I felt that if I was to go on across Africa alone I would either go off my head or die.

7 Rikki-Tikki-Tonga and the Bongo Bongo Man – Andy

It was Christmas Day. Charity handed me a small, white envelope. Charity was a wheeling, dealing, 'best price safari,' businesswoman in back street Nairobi. 'Miss Taplin asked me to give it to you,' she said, looking worried.

Inside was a scruffy piece of paper, torn out of a shorthand pad, its scribbled note read:

Dear Andy,
I hope this reaches you. I'm sure you'll be shocked, I'm not even totally sure myself, but I've decided to withdraw from the expedition. It has been the hardest decision I have ever had to make. I've looked at all sides. I can't expect Richard to wait for me for another seven months. I have had to choose which is more important to me and have decided to fly home with him when our holiday is finished. I wish you and Tim luck and know you will make it.
Love Suzanne.

Charity studied my face for a reaction. She could tell it was bad news. I phoned Cassie, at home in England, that afternoon.

'Cassie,' I forced through a nervous, cracking voice, 'Merry Christmas.'

'Merry Christmas AB. How are things?'

'Fine. Well actually not so good, Suzanne's leaving the expedition, but don't worry about that, I have something much more important to say.'

'Yes?'

'This is really hard for me to say ...' She was silent, which just added to the pressure '... I've thought about you every day across

Australia and it's all very clear to me now, I know we should be together.' I hesitated, she was still silent, I could imagine her folks preparing Christmas lunch in the background, wondering what was going on. For some reason I was close to tears. 'I want you to know that when I get back I'd like us to be together again; to have babies and everything. You don't have to say anything right now, I just wanted you to know, in case you were feeling the same and,' I tried to put a little laugh in my voice, 'in case you were thinking of getting married to someone else or anything.'

I could tell she was shocked. 'AB, isn't it usual for two people to be actually going out with each other when one proposes?'

'Yeah, but this is different. We've been together for a long time; circumstances pushed us apart and when I get back those circumstances will have changed. I'll have got this thing out of my system, and we can find a cheaper way to live than before.'

'I don't think it's very fair of you to drop this on me after all this time. You said I don't have to say anything now so I won't.'

'I wanted you to know. I don't want to get to my old age and discover that you felt the same. It would be a tragedy.'

'AB it's very sweet of you to phone me on Christmas Day but just leave it, you're lonely.' Her voice was harsh. 'Tim and Suzanne have their partners out there and you're feeling down, that's all.'

'No, Cassie I mean it.'

'AB please! Don't spoil my Christmas.'

I was speechless; in shock. This was not what I wanted to hear.

Finishing the call with a quick exchange of pleasantries, I was gripped by the need to escape this place. I was numb and oblivious to everything around me. I paid for the call and fled from the hotel in a blur of blind silence. That afternoon I wrote Cassie a long letter and got horrendously drunk.

After going on safari in Tanzania and climbing Kilimanjaro I came back to Nairobi and received Suzanne's note. By coincidence, Tim and Phyl were in town that night too and so I invited everyone along to the Norfolk Hotel to talk through Suzanne's decision. She held hands with Richard under the table as we talked. He looked like a decent bloke, and Suzanne was a different person when she was with him; happy and in love. I wondered why they felt their love would not survive another seven months apart, but they were adamant that they must go home together.

There was another week before we needed to hit the road. I felt that both Tim and I would continue individually if needs be, but that neither of us particularly relished the prospect.

I pulled Tim aside for a quiet word during the evening. 'I think it would be wise,' I said, 'if we both took the next few days to mull things over, let's speak on Saturday.' He agreed.

For some reason Richard chose to insult me and the evening nearly ended comically in a drunken fist fight. Suzanne's destiny was not to cycle around the world.

I still had a week or so left of our scheduled break and decided to make my way up to Watamu, on the coast north of Mombasa. The bus rattled north in breathless humidity, which lay like a blanket. Hot wind rushing through broken windows did little to ease the discomfort. I drifted in and out of sleep for a while before I spotted the girl of my dreams, an unmistakable flash of perfection. She was sitting four or five seats in front of me, looking out of the window at the blur of palm groves and sun bleached villages. Twisted boabab trees stood alone, marooned in golden sisal fields, but she did not notice them, her mind was far away. I could hardly take my eyes off her; the skin was deeply tanned, the nose small and the eyes bright. She turned away from the window so I could not see her face. Shining blonde hair was intricately braided, delicate fingers played with beads of coloured glass decorating the strands.

After an hour we stopped at Kilifi. Outside in the market place old women with naked, drooping breasts, like empty purses, sat chatting on sacks of grain. Young girls were covered and wore bustles underneath colourful, wrap-around cotton dresses, to accentuate hips and buttocks.

A space appeared next to the blonde girl. The temptation to punish Cassie was irresistible. *'GO ON!'* I told myself and jumped forward into the vacant seat, brushing her bare arm unintentionally against mine as I sat down.

Hello,' I said and she smiled. Straight scrubbed teeth, thin lips, no make-up.

'Where are you going?' I asked, pretending to be uninterested but friendly. Ten other passengers were listening, sod them.

'Oh, up the coast, I don't know.' She had long lashes and gigantic blue eyes, I dared not look too long. What was that accent?

'Me too,' I said, 'Watamu is meant to be *the* place. Have you been there?' She was confident. The T-shirt was brilliant white, probably new.

'No, I haven't been to the coast at all.' She wore a family of bead necklaces but no rings and cut down jeans with frayed ends. Long lines of bushy cashew nut trees slid by outside. 'Where are you from?' she asked.

'England.'

'You don't seem like the usual English traveller.'

'Oh? I keep meeting public school boys who think they are superior to everyone else in the world,' she said. 'They are so foolish. When I'm around them I feel that I only exist as part of their adventure; they think I should feel privileged to be with them and to be recorded in their diaries. They collect people for their diaries like other people collect stamps.' 'You speak excellent English, where are you from?'

'I am Dutch.'

The man in front could not resist it, he turned to look. Her name was Ellie, she was twenty-five and hopelessly vulnerable.

'My boyfriend dropped me; we were meant to be getting married' she stared dreamily out of the window again. 'I've lost it really. I don't know what I'm doing here.' I nodded, I wasn't exactly 'found' myself.

'I'm just drifting now,' she went on, 'looking for something that isn't anywhere.'

'Well you look pretty together to me,' I said, hoping I did not sound a prat.

'Ah,' she smiled, 'some people do seem to think I'm great, nice shape, happy, you know, but I'm not like that inside. Inside I'm useless. I'm usually too much in awe of people to talk to them, but they think I'm being cool.'

'Everyone has hang-ups and insecurities, even real top people. Presidents, stars, everyone you look up to, they all have to put on a show to make the fear go away.' A number of people were watching us now and straining to listen through the engine noise.

'Yeah, other people look so together to me, you're trying to tell me they're not?' She studied my face with mild interest.

'Absolutely. They're the same as you.' Ellie rubbed her forehead nervously and went on. 'Yeah the same as me, not cool, just scared.' This was getting depressing.

'Come on, it's too easy to reject yourself. If people say they like you and that you are a good person accept it and live with it. If you accept yourself you can do anything and be anything.'

'I know, I know, it's not that easy though.'

'Ellie, of all the 60 billion people who have ever lived on this planet, there is not one exactly like you. You are unique. Enjoy it. Besides', I gave what I hoped was a cheeky, winning smile, 'I think you're great.'

She had an idea to go up to Lamu in a few days, but thought, for now, she would go to Watamu, for New Year. Yeeeee Haaaaa!!!

As we got off the bus together I could not believe my luck. The other passengers gave us knowing smiles and nods.

After a slow, dignified start, chatting over cold beers and swimming in the warm water of the shallow bay, we jumped into a wild week of passion and partying. The week merged into one long day; making passionate, unrestrained, love in the thatched bungalow, or sleeping on the beach lying side by side, thighs and arms touching, laughing and talking endlessly. At night we danced and drank with the locals in the crazy, dark bars until three or four in the morning. It was fabulous. The perfect escape from the road, from Suzanne's departure and Cassie's rejection.

Meanwhile Tim said goodbye to Phyl and had a few days alone in Nairobi. The present day high-spots of Nairobi are the *New Modern Green Bar* and *Carnivores Restaurant*. The *New Modern Green Bar* opened its doors in 1968 and has only been shut for one hour since; for a census.

Tim recalls: 'I've been in some rough bars in my time, but this was the roughest of the lot. I was hardly through the doors when a hooker made a grab for my marriage tackle. I pushed her off and looked around, ready to make a run for it at any moment. I had a local guy with me who I hoped would give me some protection, so stuck it out. Coming off the bright street, my eyes adjusted slowly to the dark. A sweet cloud of dope hung in the air. People were lying about all over the place, drunk or stoned. Those that were still conscious were totally out of it. 'Let's buy beers,' shouted my companion over the blare of raucous reggae music crashing from the juke-box. At the far side of the room was a black cage, unlit. We walked over and my friend put forty shillings into a hole at waist level, on the counter. I couldn't see anyone in the cage, but two bottles of Tusker appeared in the hole. People were taking no notice of me as we drank so I started to relax a bit.

One guy finished his beer and threw the empty bottle at the wall where it smashed; no one reacted in any way. A fight broke out between two women in a dingy corner; there was a lot of screeching and punching. My companion pointed out a Japanese guy sitting on the floor with a 'tart' clinging to each arm. He told me the guy had been in Nairobi for at least five years. He couldn't drag himself away. What pathetic lingering death awaited him?'

At seven o'clock on Saturday night Tim was sitting on a stool in the Delamere Bar of the Norfolk Hotel, sipping a bottle of Tusker and chewing the fat with the barman. A little man walked through the bar, wearing a red waistcoat over a white shirt, a black bow-tie, black trousers and white gloves. He carried a wooden pole with a long rectangular blackboard fixed to the top. From the black board hung a little bell which tinkled as he walked. A message was chalked on the board, 'TELEPHONE MR. TIMUPY'.

'That'll be for me,' Tim told the little man. 'Where do I go?' In the plush foyer a coach-load of overweight Americans were nervously checking-in, while the doorman, in top hat and tails, supervised the movement of five coach-loads of suitcases. In a booth Tim picked up the phone and spoke, 'Hello?'

'Hello mate, how have you been?' I said.

'Fantastic.'

'Great.' I let a second pass. 'What do you reckon then?'

'Well, I'm game to go on together. How about you?'

'Yeah, me too, we'll be fine. I'll meet you at Mombasa Station on Monday morning.'

Relief! I might survive!

Vasco da Gama took a fancy to Mombasa in 1497, but his Portuguese sailors were fought off by the Arabs and it was another thirty years before the Portuguese finally took possession of the island. The Portuguese built Fort Jesus at the end of the sixteenth century to defend the prized port. The Arabs eventually won Mombasa back in 1698 with the help of a ship load of Welshmen. Arabs and Welsh slaughtered every living thing they found within the walls. I guess that's why the Portuguese have always had a strong aversion to rugby football.

The reason for all the interest in the port was simple: gold, ivory and slaves. Mombasa was the gateway to the riches of East Africa.

Rapid industrial expansion in western Europe at the end of the nineteenth century brought about increased prosperity and a rocketing birth rate. It also made large sums of cash available for investment. With too little space, too many mouths to feed and too much money about, the answer was simple: grab the land claimed by explorers, settle it with enterprising folk, have them grow food to send home, extract valuable minerals and create new markets for export from Europe.

Armies of British, German, French and Belgian civil servants zipped about Africa carrying armfuls of treaty papers, conning chiefs into signing away land and mineral rights for a few beads and the odd case of whisky.

The settlers were usually from the privileged, unimaginative, upper-middle classes. They completely ignored the traditional way of life of the indigenous people; their understanding of the land and the animals, the strong family bonds and the deep spirituality. The notion that the tribes-people were anything but worthless lay-abouts, and that they themselves were anything but all-knowing, superior beings, did not even enter the settlers heads. Trouble was in store.

Only one hundred years ago the British built the 'Lunatic Express', a railway from Mombasa eastward across Kenya and into Uganda, to exploit the fertile interior and to control the southern Nile. They called it the Lunatic Express because it did not appear to be going anywhere. I can imagine groups of local tribesmen sitting watching the furious activity from shade trees, saying to one another, 'If only they asked us, we could tell them there ain't nothin' out there but swamp and jungle and a whole lot of grass.'

With most of the gold already gone, slavery abolished and most of the elephants hiding, it was a bit of a gamble for the British to spend five million pounds on building the railway. 'Don't worry', said the engineers, 'we're bound to find something worth stealing.'

The Brits brought in the reliable resources of Indian labour to do the heavy work. The Indians keep the country afloat to this day. After three years of building they were half way to Lake Victoria. There at MILE 327, in the most inappropriate location, hot, humid swamp, a supply post was established. The shanty town which grew up around it was the embryo of, what is now, the great modern city of Nairobi, with skyscrapers, shopping malls, University and traffic jams. The Norfolk Hotel, where we said goodbye to Suzanne, was the first permanent structure in the colony.

Meryl Streep's Karen Blixen first laid eyes on Redford's Denys Finch-Hatton as she rode the Lunatic Express from Mombasa to Nairobi, in Hollywood's version of *Out of Africa*. Redford stopped the train in the middle of the bush and his men piled his ivory on Streep's crates.

'Shoo, shoo,' she called to them. 'My limoges!'

'Sorry', he said coolly, 'they didn't know it was limoges.' Redford followed up with the inspired line, 'I'm going on,' as he strolled off into the emptiness towards Kilimanjaro.

Most people we met claimed to have been involved in *Out of Africa*.

'I was Miss Streep's personal chauffeur,' said a taxi driver;

'I did the catering on *Out of Africa*,' said a cafe owner';

'I was the accountant on *Out of Africa*,' said a man hustling safaris on the street. Sure.

The narrow, cobbled streets surrounding Fort Jesus in Mombasa, still cling to those bygone days of war; you are still guaranteed a brawl if you wander about after midnight. We left Fort Jesus with a fine send off from the men of the Rotary Club at 10 am on 10th January. At 10.05, after our hosts had jumped into their cars and zipped back to their air conditioned offices. I lent my bike against a cannon and fixed a puncture. A truly magnificent start.

We took the ferry off the island and headed due south towards the Tanzanian border. Muslim women, veil robed, scurried to hide themselves as we approached a village. We stopped and sat outside a chai hut drinking sweet tea, being inspected by a couple of silent old men. Next to the chai hut, across the sand courtyard, was the *Ninja Video Bar*. The blackboard read, 'Tonit 7 – Al Pacino – Scar Face – 10 shillingi.'

The following day we reached the Tanzanian border. We were a little wary of Tanzania, and on good authority: we had been there a couple of weeks before. So many hoodlums. Whilst immoral and illegal, utilising the black market in Tanzania, as throughout the developing world, is part of the fun, and everyone does it. The objective of the game of *'Blackmarket'* is to declare a few dollars which can be exchanged officially in banks, while hiding a big wad which can be exchanged with shady businessmen for a much higher rate. The businessmen use the dollars to travel and to buy foreign goods for resale, which, in a way, does some good. In this game, anything the border guard finds he wins.

Tim stuffed five hundred American dollars down his smelly jock strap, while I went for style, placing seven hundred dollars under my bush hat.

'Be careful in Tanzania,' said the stern official. 'People are not always honest.'

'We will. Thanks,' I smiled.

I longed to scratch my dripping, itching scalp for the hour that we spent in the hut, filling in forms and answering questions. Fortunately for all concerned we were not searched, as both wads of money were soaked and somewhat unpleasant.

Once over the border the lovable, smooth road became an appallingly hot, tyre-sucking, sand track. Tarmac seemed to be an extravagant thing of the past only to be dreamt of. The extra effort required to shift the bike through the sand took us to boiling point.

All along the track we were greeted with warm astonishment. The villages popped up out of lush palm forest every three or four kilometres. The huts, with mud walls and rough thatch, were set twenty metres back from the road, women and children lovingly swept the smooth dirt area in front. They waved and shouted as we passed. Despite our exhaustion we waved back to everyone. When we stopped to rest and buy cold Pepsi, we were surrounded by happy, inquiring faces and endless numbers of hands demanding to be shaken.

In Australia we had met only a handful of cyclists; here we met twenty or thirty every hour. They were gently meandering around potholes, carrying loads of maize, urns of milk, chickens or mangoes, precariously perched on the racks of black, sit-up-and-beg. Chinese bicycles. One man carried buns for lunch, wrapped in newspaper and tied into a neat parcel. We were 'dinged' by these cyclists, waved at, shouted at, stared at, cheered, raced, befriended or sometimes just ignored. They came and went, their journeys far more sensible than ours. We were heading for Swakopmund, Namibia, on the other side of the continent, four and a half thousand kilometres away. They were going a couple of kilometres down the road.

Young lads sped up from behind and dinged as they shot past wearing cheeky grins. Tim exercised self control and stuck to his energy conserving, yet kilometre-eating pace. Sauna or not, I could not be beaten and gave chase every time. The lads soon faded or got off to push up hills. Being British, I could not contemplate such an act and always passed them. Some nutters went hell for leather to catch up again only to run out of steam once more. Tim and I marvelled at one man weaving up a long hill, sweat gushing over taught, ebony black muscles. On his rack he carried a one hundred kilogram sack of cement. He even had the balls to smile as we passed.

Kilometa ngapi Moa' (How far to Moa?) I asked in a chai (tea) hut. There was much discussion among the assembled group of dubious looking teenagers in filthy T-shirts and shorts. Eventually we were told, 'Moa isi eight bus stopis.' We did not pursue this, but did change a few dollars into Tanzanian shillings with the lads, to keep us going to the first town, Tanga. Being near the border the exchange rate was not very exciting, but we had no choice. We plodded on through the jungle. At the next village we stopped a chap, probably in his late thirties. In clean cotton shirt and slacks and surrounded by a huddle of ragged children, he was probably a teacher and would surely give us a good answer. 'Jambo, can you tell us how far it is to Moa and if there is a guest house or a lodge there?' asked Tim. 'Moa is very close, very imminent indeed, but alas, my dear friends, I greatly regret that you will find no suitable place to rest in the fine village of Moa,' replied the teacher.

'Wow, your English is extremely good,' I said.

He was flattered and replied, 'No, no, you are too kind. I believe I am terribly bombastic.'

A good answer indeed.

As dusk approached, Moa did not. A cyclist eased along-side and invited us to stay at his mother's house 'There are bad men on this road at night, you must not continue,' he warned. Ali was coming home from school. He was a bright sixteen year old with slightly buck teeth.

There are over one hundred and twenty different tribal languages in Tanzania, but fortunately for us there are just two official languages, English and Swahili. The young people diligently learn English at school. It is their passport to a job in the towns, from where they can send money to support the family.

Mother was not home, but Ali's numerous grown-up sisters, and crowds of their children, were. Big sister said we must ask the village headman for permission to stay. One of the children was sent off to find him and soon he came ambling along. The headman did not look like any head-man who might grace the pages of *King Solomon's Mines* or pop out of Wilbur Smith's pen. He looked like a normal overworked, stressed-up geezer, who had spent the day puzzling over a set of figures and worrying about the price of maize. We were just another inconvenient interruption. He wore white trousers and a white, over-sized, shirt which hung to his knees; both needed a good scrub. The eyes were piercing and quick as he looked us up and down. Ali told him our story and translated his reply. He was not going to waste time on us, *'Hapana,'* (No) he said, we could not stay here if the mother was not home, we should go off the road to the next village which was bigger. With that he turned and was gone. We did not feel we knew the country well enough to camp just yet, (especially with *'bad men'* about). So off we went with Ali, at right angles to the road, along an even softer sand track. After five kilometres we came to the bigger village which turned out to be Moa. At the far end of the thatched main street lay the Indian Ocean. Tall palm trees sprouted between the huts and men hung about doing a lot of nothing. The place was alive with snot-nosed children messing about and laughing. Some played with hoops, running barefoot beside them, others pushed home-made wire models of cars, complete with suspension and steering wheel.

Ali rounded up four elders who gathered round us in a huddle of hot debate. A crowd of fifty or sixty people quickly formed, staring at us, but keeping their distance. More elders were summoned. How best could they help these guests? They were enjoying spinning this simple situation out into a drama, taking it much too seriously. While they waffled, Tim played with the cheeky kids, squirting them with his water bottle, making them shriek with laughter and run away. They quickly came back for more and were squirted again. Eventually, Ali left the huddle and said, 'They can give the floor of the headman's office, but there is no water in the building.'

'OK', I said. 'We don't want to be any trouble to anyone.'

'No,' said Ali, 'This is not good. You must come back to my house even though my mother is away. I will not tell our head man.' We accepted.

Before we left Moa, we sought supplies from the stalls laid out on shady verandahs. Accompanied by Ali and a large gang of children we walked from one stall to the next, eventually securing a pineapple, giant tomatoes, ginger root, a pile of small onions, some strange dried figs and rice, all wrapped in pieces of old newspaper. Tim turned and went 'Boo!!' The children scattered noisily and quickly formed up behind us again. 'Boo!!' he went again. They were lovely kids, inquisitive and funny. These veggies would go well with the dried soya mince we had brought from Perth. The bill came to three hundred Tanzanian shillings; about forty-five English pence.

Slipping and sliding in the sand, we left the village. Fifty cheering children ran all around us, some clinging to the panniers, all giggling and shouting.

Ali rode next to us, proud of his position as host. 'They think you are wonderful. Never before have they seen such a thing as *wzungus*, (white men), on bicycles.'

It was dark when we got back to Ali's. He showed us through to the back yard, which was perfectly swept and enclosed by a high fence of woven saplings. In the centre was a concrete base on which we laid our mats and silk sleeping bag liners. We cooked up a curry sauce and rice over a burning palm frond. The frond had dropped off the palm tree which towered over us, growing from the corner of the yard. I cut up the pineapple and passed a saucepan full around Ali's three sisters and the dozen children. The men folk, like the mother, were nowhere to be seen and their absence was not explained. I gave the girls a bowl of curry, spiced up with home-made curry powder, given us by friends in Mombasa. These people usually ate *ugali* and rice; curry was a novel treat.

'You come outside and relax,' said Ali after dinner. We followed him through the dark house to the front yard. The kids of the family and others from the village were assembled, waiting for us in the moonlight. We were invited to sit on wooden boxes. 'The children will perform,' said Ali. One boy banged a drum, fashioned from an old oil can, another played a deeper toned drum; goat skin pulled over a wooden bowl. They quickly fell into an intricate rhythm. A dozen other children, some just toddlers, danced around the drummers in a circle, with a jerky, crab-like movement, singing sweetly. The rhythm was constant, the dance movements controlled. It went on and on, round and round, becoming hypnotic.

'What does the song mean?' I asked Ali, cupping my hand to his ear, to be heard above the singing and banging.

'They are singing a traditional Tanzanian song, they say 'If you want to seduce an African girl you must touch her left breast."

All across Australia we had been making recordings for BBC Radio, with a view to eventually editing them down into a series of programmes. To my mind the tapes had not, so far, been very successful, but here was a change in fortune. The sounds of Africa were far more promising. I ran off to fetch the machine.

We clapped loudly when the children had finished. Now it was our turn. Tim and I stood while the children sat around our feet. All we could think of was *'Wild Rover'*, which we sang with gusto.

The children replied with a song about Tanzania's game reserves and their wild animals. We gave them the *National Anthem, Old Macdonald's Farm* and *Twist and Shout*. Tim's speciality at Telford Rugby Club, had been Gary Glitter's *Leader of the Pack;* which he performed now. They joined in with the macho, hip swinging, air punching actions, screeching with laughter. The grand finale was Tim's rousing version of a Maori rugby chant. He sang the staccato lead while the kids echoed him, 'Ooh alay la' – *'Ooh alay la'*

'Rikki tikki tonga' – *'Rikki tikki tonga'*

'Ooh alay-ay alay-I alay-oh' – *'Ooh alay-ay ala y I alay-oh,'* and round again to 'Ooh alay la' – *'Ooh alay la,'* 'Rikki tikki tonga ...'

The chant started soft and slow, gradually increasing in speed and volume with each repetition, rising to a wild crescendo amid frantic dancing; all jumping around like mad things.

Later we lay on the concrete slab in the back yard, staring up at the stars through the leaves of the palm. For an hour, from the far corners of the village, came little, irrepressible calls of *'Rikki tikki tonga'* and *'Ohh alay la'*.

We woke before dawn leaving Ali and the clan waving and singing; they seemed to have got the words mixed up over night, *(Ikky pikky ponga)*. When the heat of the day hit, we had already covered twenty-five kilometres in the sand.

As we passed the villages, children waved and called *'Wzungu, wzungu'*. They ran across the swept front yards and onto the road, straining to keep up, big grinning mouths and bright eyes.

We bought delicious fresh coconuts in one village and ate them, out of sight, in the shade of a mango tree. Local cyclists continued to ding and chat to us as we headed on south towards Tanga. We called *'Jambo,'* (Hello) to everyone we met.

They replied with *'Habari gani?'* (How's things), to which we answered *'Nzuri sana,'* (Very Good), and on we went.

Everyone was happy, smiling and welcoming. Some called

'Habari Safari?' (How's the journey?), *'Nzuri Baridi!'* (Very cold) and they laughed.

There was no doubt that being on bicycles made us acceptable to the villagers; they were used to aid workers zipping by in fancy cars, often without even taking their eyes off the road.

A long line of children, more than one hundred of them, ran towards us along the track. They wore colourful Sunday best, bright white shirts and shorts, or white dresses with flowery trims of orange, red and blue. The children went on past, towards Sunday school, in single file, singing as they ran.

Baboons and monkeys sat in the track, scampering off when they saw us coming. As we pedalled by we could see their little faces peering out from dense undergrowth. We talked about Suzanne's departure as we rode along. I was angry with her for putting a love affair before the project. Tim was not surprised that she had left. We were both relieved, though. There would be no more of the bad feeling and misunderstanding which had blighted much of the Australia crossing. It was not Suzanne who was wrong; it was the chemistry and the circumstances. We both hoped we could avoid interpersonal problems; crossing Africa was going to be hard enough without that rubbish.

Forty-eight kilometres south of Moa, we reached the town of Tanga, an old port which lent its name to the German colony, Tanganyika. Britain had stripped Germany of its colonies after the First World War and changed the name.

It was only noon when we arrived, but we were absolutely exhausted. The sand track, scorching heat and humidity had drained away the last drop of leg power. We found the rambling old *Bandarini Colonial Hotel*, owned by an eccentric English woman, and called it a day. For the equivalent of $2 each we had an airy room with a balcony and a harbour view. With a whooshing fan, mosquito nets, comfy beds, clean sheets and cold water baths, this was pure luxury. Within five minutes of entering the room we were both sound asleep!

Later we made another exciting find, an Indian Restaurant. Maybe Tanzania was not going to be so bad after all. A high ceiling, white walls and open frontage gave the restaurant a southern

European feel. The vegetable curry in the display cabinet looked safe; the samosas did not, but we ordered both.

'Can we pay in dollars?' Tim asked the middle aged Indian owner with a nudge and a wink.

'How much you want to change?' whispered the Indian.

'A hundred, one note.'

'OK.'

We agreed a good rate of exchange. He told us to sit down and eat our meal while he collected the money from a friend.

After the meal we approached the counter again. The Indian was chatting with a customer who stood drinking a Pepsi. Tim put his hundred dollars on the white formica. The owner's eyes opened in horror at the sight of the note in front of him. He was flustered. 'You cannot use dollars here, do you not have Tanzanian shillings?' We were confused and struck dumb. The Indian retreated a few steps to his left and into the kitchen, out of sight of the man drinking Pepsi at the counter. He pointed wildly to the man for our benefit, and pulled his finger dramatically across his throat. The penny dropped and Tim called, 'I am sorry, I shall go to the bank and come back in half an hour with shillingis.'

We did not go to the bank, but came back, as promised, half an hour later. The Pepsi man was gone.

'You boys will put me in much trouble, much trouble, you must not be so open in Tanzania. That man was a plain clothes policeman.'

It was a good lesson, we had not been thinking. 'I am so sorry', said Tim. 'Did he suspect you?'

'I think we shall be all right, but he scares me,' he replied. Furtively this time, Tim handed over the note and received a brown paper bag containing a big pile of paper shillings.

The next morning we split up to do some jobs. Tim scoured the market for tomatoes, mangoes and bananas, and filled the fuel bottle with kerosene at the BP station, whilst I went on a mission to find a short wave radio which could pick up the BBC World Service. I managed to barter the Indian shopkeeper down to $17 US, a bargain. The purchase of the radio was very important to us. Now we had access to the daily shifts in African politics and would be able to avoid trouble-spots. We could also experience the joy of afternoon plays and live footie on Saturday evenings magically beamed in from London. Ironically, it was Tim's brother, Simon, who had installed the BBC transmitter on the Seychelles, a thousand kilometres off the coast of Tanzania, from which the signal was bounced.

I posted home a box of goodies and some letters, insisting that the clerk postmark the stamps in front of me. It was not unknown for Post Office staff to peel off the valuable stamps for resale and throw the letters in the bin. Home went thermal undies, track suit bottoms, film, the second stove and tapes for the BBC. Outside the Post Office I was confronted by a man in his early twenties, sitting on a tree stump, picking flaky scabs off his left foot. The foot and lower leg looked as if they belonged to an elephant; four times the normal size. His right leg was going the same way.

'*Jambo*', I said, squatting down in front of him, 'What's happened to your legs?'

'They are gone, legs no good. You have dollars?' He was calm and pleasant, resigned to his fate.

It was as though he had two plaster casts on the left leg, one on top of the other, but it was flesh. I guessed he was suffering from some form of lymph cancer. It was horrendous. I couldn't feel his pain and despair. I know the cold ache of loneliness and the desolate self pity of lost love like every-one else, but not this. This was real despair. 'Here,' I gave him some money.

'I don't think it is good to pick at the scabs, you will make more infection.'

'I know it. But he hurts.'

I am too lucky. This boy made me more determined than ever to complete the expedition, no matter what. I had the opportunity and was physically able to. It would be a crime to mess it up.

Suzanne had been carrying the team medical kit in Australia; this, the new radio and the water filter now had to be added to our already crammed panniers. Weight and space were vital considerations. In the hotel room Tim suggested we use '*Spoof*', a simple game of chance and bluff using coins, to decide who carried what. Being a novice, I lost the vital deciding round and was saddled with carrying the bulky medical kit and the radio. I swore I would get my spoofing revenge in the future.

If any piece of kit was indispensable it was the Katadyn water filter. We had sent this ahead from Sydney and collected it in Perth. If its advertised claims were met, it would prevent us catching amoebic dysentery, giardia, cholera and typhoid. I would not be surprised if it also prevented in-growing toe nails, premature hair loss and nagging mothers-in-law.

In Perth, I had serviced and refitted my Saracen with a new bottom bracket, chain, rear gear cluster and knobbly tyres. It did not really need these, but I wanted to play it safe. Tim, laid back as always, chose to put on new tyres, but to carry on with the other original components. This put us at risk of unfixable breakdown, quite unnecessarily. I could have shot him when I found out, here in Tanga where we could do nothing about it.

Thankfully, Tanga was the starting point for the new tarmac road. Built with European money, it ran inland from the coast before heading due south to Chalinze. There it would join the main road heading west from Dar es Salam across Tanzania, to the Malawi border. Somewhere along that westerly road we would climb out of the humid coastal region onto a cooler plateau, and the sooner we were on it the better. That would be more than five hundred kilometres away.

We left late after all the messing about, and cycled seventy kilometres from Tanga in tortuous heat. The palm forest gave way to open grassland. Villages continued to line the road and we stopped several times to rest and cool down. Not everyone spoke English, of course. Arriving in villages we chatted in simple Swahili, or mimed our need for water or food to the onlookers. Showing them the maps on the backs of our T-shirts helped to explain our presence. In each village an English speaker came forward and befriended us, whether we needed it or not.

That first evening out of Tanga, in a small, one street town called Hale, Elvis appeared out of the crowd to offer his assistance, (so that's what happened to him). The street was, like most others, swept and litter free.

Elvis had worked for the Tanzanian Government for twenty years.

They had sent him to study personnel management at Manchester University, in England, which was a great honour and gave him immense status. He was a fit fifty year old, organizing the workforce in the building of a major Hydro Electric Power plant nearby.

'Did you like Manchester?' I asked as we stood in the street, surrounded by the crowd. We were getting used to being stared at and carried on as if there were no one watching.

'No, I hated it', he said, 'I was there for three years and was very unhappy. The ordinary people wouldn't speak to me. They thought that because I was a black African I was stupid, an animal. I went to pubs a few times and tried to engage people in friendly conversation; they seemed offended that I had even spoken to them.'

Everything about Tanzania still felt alien and new. There was still no way we were going to camp until we settled down, so we decided to look for somewhere to stay. Elvis found us rooms in the *hoteli* (guest house) for one hundred shillings each, (fifteen English pence). His smart, professional appearance and manner seemed out of place in this grotty guest house, where he stayed for months on end while his wife lived and worked in Dar es Salam.

Elvis led us to a crowded cafe down the road, which sold warm fried chicken and cardboard chips which we forced down. Later, we wandered over to the ambitiously named *Sheraton Hotel,* a lodge with red carpet on the floor and a broken fan on the ceiling. Here we drank cold beers in comfortable armchairs, while the music of *Bongo Bongo Man* filled the air. Across the room the District Police Chief chatted up two prostitutes. Elvis asked, 'What did you both study?'

'I am a teacher', said Tim, 'of Physical Education and English.'

'I used to be a businessman. Now I am unclassified.'

He gave me a queer look, 'Now you are a cyclist!'

'I cycle a hundred kilometres each day,' I said, 'but I am not a cyclist.' Elvis was surprisingly ungrateful to us for treating him to a meal and drinks. Perhaps he thought we were rich Americans, or perhaps he saw it as payment in lieu of his disgraceful, racist treatment at the hands of our ignorant countrymen.

'What will you do if you meet people from a hostile tribe?' asked Elvis.

'We will smile and shake their hands,' answered Tim with our usual blind optimism.

'Do you not have a gun?'

'No, we think a gun would bring us more trouble.'

'But what will you do if you meet a lion?' he asked.

'We will ... er, I don't really know', said Tim, '... cycle faster I suppose.'

'*Salama,*' (Peace) I said to the astonished chai shop keeper, soon after dawn. *Jambo, Habari gani? Tunaomba chai mbili, na andazi mbili tafadhali,*' I asked in the chai shop, feeling pretty smug, (Hi, how's it going? I beg two teas and two doughnuts please).

We had left Hale at daybreak and cycled a couple of kilometres to the junction where our road forked south.

'ΛΛΛΛΗΗΙΙΕΕ,' said the man *Wzungus,* at dawn, on bicycles, speaking Kiswahili?? He could hardly pull himself away to make the tea.

We loved it. Swahili is a very melodic language; we found the basic phrases rolled off the tongue and were easy to pick up.

The hut was made of branches lashed together and coated with mud, now cracking and crumbling. The roof was grass thatch. On the wall hung a photo of the President. Beside him hung a photo of the ex-President Julius Nyerere, 'The Father of Tanzania', while beside him, the menu had been painted onto the mud wall in gloss paint; white on a red background. Tim and I sat opposite each other on narrow benches and leant on the wobbly wooden table.

Looking through the door we watched, outside in the dust, a man nonchalantly slit the throat of a protesting goat. He used a very sharp knife. The goat looked a bit surprised. The cut went all the way through the neck to the vertebrae. The goat lay on its side, kicking with its rear legs. This action turned it round in a circle while the head stayed still, opening the gap in the neck further. Children watched quietly as pints of blood flowed into a metal bowl which the man had placed under the neck. The goat's eyes were staring, the mouth open. '*Shit,*' it thought, '*Shit*'! The blood kept flowing. It was a full five minutes before the goat stopped moving.

The man came into the chai house carrying the corpse. He put it on the table, sat next to me and started to chop it up. The knife was drawn the length of its belly, purple guts spewed out under my nose making me retch. The man and the others at the tables laughed. A couple of powerful hacks with a chopper removed the head, which was thrown into a bucket by my feet. I turned my head away, creasing my face in disgust.

'How do you fancy a couple of runny fried eggs and some black puddin'? asked Tim.

Greasy tea came in plastic mugs. The chai man placed two andazi on the table in front of us. Perhaps he had been on a Macdonalds selling course, for seeing us eyeing the carnage, asked in Swahili, 'You liki goati for breakfasti?'

Truck drivers came in and were given yellow plastic plates piled with chunks of yesterdays half-cooked, gristly, grey, goat meat, which they ripped apart with ferocious teeth. One truckie shovelled at least eight spoonfuls of sugar into his mug of tea and gulped it down.

Outside the chai shop we gently stretched taught muscles, bringing whistles from the young girls waiting for a ride on a truck. They stood beside bundles of unknown goodies, wrapped tightly in white linen.

Workers, dressed in heavy denims, walked along the side of the road carrying hoes and picks, on their way to work in the fields. Other men sat in the back of a battered blue truck, their tools piled at the rear of the cab.

Clouds of black diesel fumes covered everybody in a film of grime, as the driver revved the vehicle like a new toy. I remembered an aid worker I had met in Nairobi jokig, 'Give an African a machine and he'll find a hundred ways to fuck it up.' We left him to it. The workers were being driven miles along the road to be dropped off. They waved as they passed. The truck stopped after a kilometre to unload a small group, allowing Tim and I to catch up and overtake. The young lads in the back found this hilarious and made fun of the driver, 'You are beaten by *Wzungus* on *beezcaillies*.' The truck pulled away and quickly overtook, the lads giving us the thumbs up. It stopped again, more lads got out and we overtook again. Now we climbed a long gentle hill, good for bikes but bad for trucks. Tim distanced himself from my childish behaviour and stayed back; I raced up the hill opening the gap between myself and the truck. I heard it change down, noisily grinding the gears. Its engine note became louder and louder behind me and I could hear the shouts of encouragement from the boys. Before the truck could catch me I reached the top of the rise, changed into top, shot down the slope and started climbing again.

My mind drifted away to when my brother Gordon and I used to wheel bikes out of the shed and call, 'Just off to the park Mum.' He was nine and I was eight, and we were expert liars. We would cycle straight by the park and onward, ten or twenty miles out into the Surrey hills, south of London. Here we would zoom up and down mud tracks terrorising dog-walkers, climbing trees and exploring the woods pretending we were commandos. It was great adventure. Then later, having tea with the family, we would smile mischievously to each other over sardines on toast and *Dr. Who*, so that everyone knew we had been up to something.

I was out of the saddle, straining near the top of the next hill, when the truck pulled alongside me. I turned, smiling at the boys in the back. They were leaning over swinging their arms, cheering and shouting encouragement. As they eased past it became obvious they were going to win, they took off their pork-pie hats and clapped. I waved and called

'*Kwaheri, kwaheri*' (Goodbye, goodbye).

'*Kwaheri mi rafiki,*' (Goodbye my friend), they replied.

The Masai Steppe lay to the west; a great plain the colour of lions. We passed bored looking Danish engineers who were supervising local labour in building a new, deliciously smooth road southward.

Being English we were a bit slow; it took us three days to figure out that the only people in Tanzania moving a muscle between the hours of twelve noon and four were we two. Everyone else was either asleep or sniggering at us from the shade of their huts.

We decided we would continue with the early starts, break the back of the kilometres before noon, have long lunches, siesta through the worst heat of the afternoons, then bang out thirty or forty kilometres before dark.

We were losing weight and physical power very rapidly. In this heat, over these hills, we were burning well over seven thousand calories each day and only putting in about four thousand. We also needed to drink eight to ten litres of water per day, which took ages to find and filter. Nothing in Africa was simple. Perhaps Suzanne was the wise one after all.

The distribution network for Pepsi was phenomenal. It could be bought in every village and had clear advantages for the people. Which was worse? Drinking cheap, highly sugared, fizzy drinks or river water contaminated with deadly diseases?

At one lunchtime stop we sat in the shade of a hut, dripping onto the wooden trestle. Blinding, white sun contrasted sharply with deep shadow. My arms were stinging with sunburn, despite the factor fifteen sun block. The mud walls were only three feet high. Above the wall was a similar sized gap before the low roof came sloping down. This gap allowed a wisp of breeze to cool the heavy air. A young woman in a red and white wrap-around dress cooked up rice and black beans for us and two other men crammed onto the bench. A baby was strapped to her back by the wrapped cloth and slept, quite happily, as its mother sang and chattered over the smoky fire.

This closeness of baby and mother, which we had seen everywhere since arriving in Africa, is a corner stone of strong families and produces well balanced children. The men often go off siring children all over the place, but the mothers hold everything together. Babies are never put down or left alone. If the mother needs to be free, she hands the baby to another child who takes over. The kids do not have dolls to play with, they have the real thing.

It was good to be out of the sun. In an hour we would find a shady mango tree to doze away the rest of the afternoon, hidden from inquisitive eyes. The woman offered cold *ugali*, cold rice, cold kidney beans, cold sweet tea and hot Pepsi. There was no electricity. She also sold goat meat, but after the head in the bucket incident, our goat gobbling days were over. Well that is not quite true because we found that every cup of tea and every plate of rice and beans came with a free coating of smelly goat grease.

As we sat waiting patiently, filtering and drinking water, four little heads popped up from behind the low wall. Their doll-like eyes, level with the top of the wall, were crawling with flies which were not shooed away. One little girl was on tip toes and kept sinking down and straining up again. We pretended not to notice the staring faces at first, but after a minute I raised my head and gave them a big wink. The heads instantly disappeared amid a wave of giggles. The softest, sweetest, whispers came from the far side of the wall. Six little eyes peered over again. We waited. This time Tim stuck his tongue out and they disappeared. When the heads popped up again, one little girl asked, 'Are you married?'

'No,' I said, 'Are you?' This knocked them into a another wriggling, giggling pile. When I pulled out my camera this happy gang of girls quickly dispersed, genuinely terrified.

The lady with the baby on her back waved her arms shouting *'Hapana, hapana, hapana!!'* (NO, no, no!!). The villagers believed their soul to be taken if they were photographed.

Witchcraft was still the principle means of getting your own back on your enemies. A visit to the witchdoctor could, the people believed, bring down a rival. A poor crop, a still-born child, an illness, were all believed to be caused by an enemy putting a spell on them. We respected their beliefs and committed not to take any more pictures of people in rural areas.

Wriggling giggling girls.

8 Crossing the Masai Steppe – Andy

Another exhausting hill. Tim pulled away and left me for dead. My right knee was starting to give me trouble on the steeper climbs, each turn of the pedal brought a sharp pain. Too much truck racing.

I slowed to a crawl where every metre had to be fought for. If I stopped pedalling I would not start again. I stopped pedalling. 'Damn!' My arms dropped forward onto the handlebars and my head sunk between them. 'Come on.' Blood rushed about, feeding muscles and calming everything down. I slurped some water from the bottle. My knee throbbed like hell so I leaned the bike against a tree and lay in the short grass beside the road looking into the empty sky. *'I've just discovered the wonder and richness of the real world,'* I thought, *'and yet I would willingly give it up, to return to that old world, for Cassie.'* Instinct was telling me to jack this in, forget my dreams, fly home and do whatever I had to, to win her back. *'But I know I can't, I'd be letting myself, and too many other people, down if I stopped now to sort out my own life.'* Pointing the bike across the road, to make it flat for the first metres, I wobbled and weaved slowly on.

At the top of the hill was a village. Tim's bike leant against a dirt bank on the left, beneath a chai house. The usual crowd had gathered to look. I was so hot and bothered I could not talk to them; I had to get into the shade and be alone. I found Tim in the cool of the chai house, guzzling his third *baridi* (cold) Pepsi and pulling at a piece of *Kuku* (chicken). The crowd pressed around the door watching the show. *'Leave me alone,'* I thought. Two donkeys came to our rescue.

They were being led down the road through the dusty village by two boys. The male donkey was very much in love and badly wanted to show his devotion. As they walked by the chai house the male made a lunge to mount the female, but she was having none of it and cracked him on the shins with an almighty kick of the back legs. The crowd turned away from us. In the confusion, the boys lost their grip on the ropes and the donkeys were off.

The male, in close pursuit of his beloved, was braying at the top of his voice. Round the village they chased, through the higgledy-piggledy mass of grass huts, women and children jumping out of the way, everyone laughing and shouting encouragement; the men cheered for the male donkey, the women for the female. We squeezed outside to watch. Dust flew as the animals crashed about. The two boys were highly embarrassed as they tried to keep up, commanding the donkeys to behave. At last the female was cornered and the male mounted once again. All looked lost but the boys arrived at the critical moment. One lad hit the amorous male on the rear with a stick, while the other pulled at his long ears. He quickly lost interest and gave up. Well, imagine how you would feel! The donkeys received a warm round of applause as they were led off, and the lovely villagers nodded happily at us, glad that we had shared their fun. I suddenly felt a little better.

Tim recalls: 'Tanzania was so different from anything we had experienced before. It was so wild, difficult and alien. We found we relied upon each other enormously for confidence and support.'

More than anything the water filter was guaranteed to draw a jaw dropping crowd. Several times each day we dangled the rubber pipe into a jug of contaminated mud, pumped it through the ceramic cylinder and 'hey presto' out would shoot pure, clear H2O. Most people were fascinated that we could do this; one or two were fascinated that we thought we needed to.

Evidence of severe, widespread dysentery was not hard to spot, and some village people were dying of cholera. A Tanzanian aid worker named Marcus, working for the Catholic Church, collared us in one village and poured out his heart. He was a Kikuyu in his sixties who had owned a grain marketing business in Iringa, in the south. When he retired he had started working with the villagers.

'I find it very hard to cope sometimes,' he said. 'We tell them and tell them, 'Boil drinking water for twenty minutes to make it safe.' We put posters in every village and teach everybody, but of course they don't do it.'

They take it off the fire as soon as it boils. It takes a child in their own family to die of cholera before they believe us.' He was surprised to hear that similar water filters to ours were available in Dar es Salam, the capital, but of course, the cost and the capacity would be unrealistic in trying to clean water for entire villages.

The messages on the television programme that started this whole venture came flooding back to me: '... five million children die each year from diarrhoea, ... fifteen billion dollars, the cost of five nuclear aircraft carriers, could put clean water into every rural community in the world within ten years ...' Now Tim and I were not watching it on the telly, we were in the middle of it and we still felt helpless. Money is only theoretical anyway, I mean it isn't grown or mined or built, it's just numbers on paper. The controllers of those theoretical numbers, Governments and Industries, choose not to pay up to clean the water. The bottom line isn't theoretical or profitable for the villagers though.

No villages had running water; the lucky ones had a hand pump or a well at their centre. In most, the water had to be carried from a river or stream in clay pots. The women and children spent hours each day fetching water, risking crocodile attacks as they stooped at the river bank, and using up precious time that could be better employed tending to young children, cooking or making things to sell. If it had been carried we did not take the water, we went to the streams ourselves. The Tanzanians were meticulous about washing their hands before eating, clearly the result of successful education and advertising. Pity they washed in contaminated water, eh?

We sweated on southwards, along the side of the Masai Steppe, happily calling *'Jambo'*, *'Habari Gani'* and *'Nzuri sana'*, about fifty times each day.

One big mama, hoeing in a field near the road, called, *'Jambo, Mambo!'* which had a good ring to it. Tim used it later, calling *'Jambo, Mambo!'* to a couple of girls carrying clay pots of water up the hill from a river. They laughed so much that they staggered and swayed along the road nearly dropping their loads. We found out later that it meant, *'Hey, Big Boy!'*

My idle mind became concentrated on dodging dead snakes and live caterpillars of all shapes and sizes. My favourite caterpillars were the fast moving, four inch, orange monsters, with extravagant red hair more than an inch long, which was swept back like smoke from a steam engine. Then there were the statuesque chameleons, who defied death by standing in the middle of the road pretending to be white lines.

We stopped to watch one curious lizard who walked with terminal indecision. He was eight inches of bright green leather with oversized legs. The front left and the back right legs were lifted together, held aloft, and rocked back and forward six times before he placed them forward onto the hot tarmac. It was then the turn of the front right and the rear left legs, with a cautious, exaggerated rocking movement. He had a reptile version of Parkinson's Disease. As a truck approached, rather than scamper across, he stood absolutely still until it was right on him then panicked and ran about uncontrolled, somehow missing the wheels. Once the truck was gone, rather than race to the safety of the grass verge, he returned to his slow rocking and rolling walk in the middle of the road.

'He is never going to make it across,' said Tim.

'No way,' I agreed, 'not unless he walks normally, he's too slow.'

We could not help him. One, two, three trucks somehow missed him as he scampered about between the wheels. He was almost on the other side when his journey ended with a sickening 'Splat!'.

Further along the road at Makata, we were befriended by the guest house owner; a tall gangling man with a shifty look about him and profound halitosis. He led us up a side street to what he said was the, 'Best hoteli in town'. Power lines and pylons dominated the skyline but the town had no electricity supply.

For thirty English pence we secured a small room each. The previous occupant of my room must have been a rhino. The bed had a one inch coating of mattress and a two inch coating of dirt; bed bugs were thrown in free of charge. The rhino had broken most of the cross slats in the bed, so I would have to balance on the four that remained. We squeezed the bikes into the rooms and made tea. The floor was concrete and filthy. The walls peeling brown gloss. A broken mosquito screen covered a hole in the wall which looked out over fields of maize. At the end of my bed were two metal barrels, I lifted a lid, dried maize. Tim shared his room with a pile of cement. *Bongo Bongo Man* music belted through from a group of lads sitting in the hall. I swear we had been hearing the same bootlegged tape in every village and it was beginning to wear a little thin.

It had only been a hundred degrees in the shade, every day since Tanga and no spare water, so I decided to treat myself to an all-over wash. Tim did not see the point. He said he would only get smelly again.

I found the washing facilities in the back yard, an oil drum full of muddy water. Hiding behind the drum, I stripped off and got down to it whilst keeping a lookout for peeping toms, snakes and rabid dogs. Beside me was a concrete base, on which large ceramic tiles surrounded a deep, black hole; the long-drop toilet. While I dried myself with my mini towel, a small boy came along and used the long-drop. He watched me silently as he went about his business and I about mine.

After dark, by the light of our head torches, we removed the frail padlocks from the doors to our rooms, replaced them with our unbreakable bike locks and went in search of food. The only way my door could be opened now was if the rhino came back to collect something he had forgotten, his shower gel maybe.

The stinking, gangling owner took us down to the market place. It was magically lit by a hundred or more oil lamps; like stumbling across a firefly's birthday party. The women of the town, and one or two of the men, waited behind rows of trestle tables which were arranged in a large square. In front of the women were steel cauldrons of rice, *ugali* or chicken. Beside these pots were piles of newspapers, and the oil lamps which illuminated the scene with weak, orange flames. In the centre of the square were more tables; behind these, men stood serving chai. Villagers and bus travellers, none white, sat opposite the sellers eating and drinking.

We did not need any help but our foul-mouthed friend took over, picking six uncooked chicken legs from a pile and handing them to the cook. The man behind the stall threw them into a pan of hot oil for a minute or two, pulled them out, then hacked them violently with a chopper, mauling each piece with dirty hands. He then wrapped them in newspaper and handed them back. Yummy! We paid and went to another stall for cold rice. When we sat down to eat this dubious fare the hotel owner reached over Tim's shoulder, snatched a handful of chicken and walked off into the crowd.

A deaf and dumb boy took a shine to us. Like many handicapped people we had seen, he was dressed only in a potato sack. Despite the socialist ideology, there was no governmental support for these people. We gave him some chicken. As we ate he stood miming to us; an aeroplane taking off, a bicycle and finally, playing a guitar. He wanted us to take him on our bicycles, then on an aeroplane back to England where he could be a pop star.

We continued on south, battling the sun until, at last, a sign proclaimed, *CHALINZE IS A PEPESI TOWN*. Here we would start heading west. Although we were trying to cross Africa from east to west, we had to miss out troubled Zaire and Angola, to do this we would have to cycle alternately south then west in giant steps. The westerly kilometres felt much more satisfying.

John Hanning Speke, the English explorer, passed this way twice on his journeys into the interior. The exact location of the source of the Nile had mystified men for thousands of years. In the mid-nineteenth century Speke and his companion, Sir Richard Burton, made it their business to find the source. They were the Neil Armstrong and Buzz Aldrin of their day; little over a hundred years separated the achievements.

Burton and Speke had been fellow officers in the Indian Army. Burton led the expedition; at thirty-seven he was a veteran explorer and a great scholar. He was a stern, studious man, with a long bushy beard, who feared nothing and demanded the highest standards in everything. Speke was seven years his junior, fair and dashing, relatively inexperienced and perhaps less scholar than adventurer.

In August 1857, wearing sturdy tweeds, they set out with a long line of porters from Zanzibar and walked west across the burning of the Masai Steppe, which now spread out endlessly to the north and west of us. We were conscious of following in Burton and Speke's footsteps. After six months, nine hundred miles and many adventures they reached Lake Tanganyika; Richard Burton wrote, *'Sometimes we lived in a dream, home seemed far away'*. Right on man. Burton was convinced that Lake Tanganyika was the source of the Nile, but Speke disagreed. (Tim and I had our own disagreements over the source of some of the smells that choked the air of the guest houses). Shortage of supplies and illness prevented both men from investigating further.

On the return march to the coast, Speke was inspired and, despite being partially blind, left Burton and cut north. He quickly discovered a great lake which he named Lake Victoria. However, he made the serious mistake of failing to circumnavigate the lake in order to prove that it was indeed the only source.

When Speke rejoined Burton six weeks later, Burton wrote in his journal:

'... We had scarcely, however, breakfasted before he announced to me the startling fact that he had discovered the source of the White Nile ... The fortunate discoverer's conviction was strong, his reasons weak ...'

The pair parted company on bad terms. Speke reached England weeks ahead of Burton and, with ungentlemanly haste, made his claim public. By the time Burton returned to London, Speke had already secured funding for a further expedition to confirm his theory and had recruited Captain James Grant as his number two, leaving Burton very much out in the cold and not at all chuffed.

Grant was a botanist, artist and sportsman and had a spirit that matched Speke's. They planned to prove the discovery once and for all, by walking to Lake Victoria then travelling the length of the Nile to Cairo.

They left Zanzibar in October 1860 with nine Hottentot privates, twenty-five British privates, seventy-five freed slaves, one hundred porters, twelve mules, three donkeys, twenty-two goats and a partridge in a pear tree. The porters carried beads, cloth and brass wire to trade with the natives. Believing Speke meant to take them into the bush to eat them, many porters took their pay in advance, swore an oath of loyalty and promptly deserted. Of Chalinze, where we spent the night, Speke wrote:

'there are no hills ... uniformly covered with trees and large grasses ... the villages are not large or numerous, but widely spread, consisting generally of conical grass huts – a collection often of twenty comprising one village. Over these villages certain headmen, titled Phanze, hold jurisdiction, they take blackmail from travellers with high presumption, they are low stature, thick set and their nature is to be boisterous. Expert slave hunters, they mostly clothe themselves by sale of their victims on the coast ... they always keep their bows and arrows in good order, the latter well poisoned ... Not infrequently we would pass on the track side, small heaps of white ashes, with a calcined bone or two among them. These, we were told, were the relics of burnt witches.'

These days Chalinze is a long line of fruit stalls and billowing diesel buses. The stall owners charge cyclists double the normal price, but make a wicked chip and tomato omelette. Slavery has gone, unless you count the young girls offering themselves for prostitution, and witchcraft, as in most towns, is alive and bubbling. The surrounding villages still consist of groups of conical grass huts.

The party reached Lake Victoria in July 1862 having walked a rather indirect route, and having spent six months in veiled captivity at the hands of a murderous king. Speke and Grant proceeded sometimes to sail, sometimes to walk up the Nile, eventually reaching Cairo in February 1863, two and a half years after setting out. Speke, incredibly, had once again failed completely to circumnavigate Lake Victoria, still leaving a doubt that some great river might flow into the lake from another source.

I'll bet his missus was cheesed off, *'You what! You forgot again! Oh, come off it John! Tell me the truth, you've got a floozie out there haven't you.'*

In London, in 1864, Sir Richard Burton again contested the scientific validity of Speke's claim.

On the eve of a public debate between the two men, to be held at The Royal Geographic Society, Speke died in a shooting accident. Some said it was suicide.

Young lads tried to sell us great tubs of marajuana as we prepared to leave Chalinze the next morning. While Speke had walked north-west from here we were heading due west to Malawi.

'Have you got the Hottentots?' I asked Tim.

'Yes', he said, 'but I should be all right to cycle!'

Two white cyclists appeared out of the parched landscape one morning. They were rolling down a hill as we were powering up. I could not believe my eyes. They really looked gaunt, dirty and dejected. We stopped to talk and exchange stories. Both sides were keen to know what was ahead. Tim and Helen were cycling home to England. They had both been teaching in Zimbabwe and were raising money in England for the school. Tim, like us, was an unshaven wreck. Helen's blue and white baseball cap and Tim's yellow, flowery cloth hat, were much less Burton and Speke than our own khaki bush hats.

Tim recalls: 'It was like seeing myself coming the other way; Tim and I looked the same, had the same name, were the same age and he was a teacher of English and PE just like me. He was riding almost the same bike, made by Saracen; he even played rugby. It was an incredible coincidence. I should have traded Andy in and gone off with Helen. No one would have known.'

Things were not going too well for them. 'The malaria situation is really bad in Malawi', said Helen. 'I've been taking the pills but I still caught it. I was knocked out for about two weeks.' They had taken a few lifts on trucks, pushed the bikes up hills, and had even flown across Zambia. It was our belief, that if you set out to do something, you had to do it properly. They were not so purist in their approach as ourselves, but then, we had not been sick.

'People say Zambia is boring and dangerous,' said the new Tim. The two descriptions seemed incongruous but I did not pursue it.

Helen looked pretty weak. I've also had dysentery for weeks', she said. 'We're going to give it a couple more weeks, but if I don't get better we're going to have to give up and fly home.' I felt for Helen. I knew from my time in Nepal it is no joke engaging in a strenuous lifestyle, in remote areas, when very ill. It had taken me a year to recover fully from that experience.

We felt if anything could defeat us it would be ill health. It was not a case of *if* we got sick but *when*. The water filter and malaria pills gave only partial protection. We were forced to eat dodgy food, and the water in the tea we drank everyday was probably not boiled for twenty minutes. Then there was the danger of accident; we carried pain killers, first aid, syringes and needles and periodically discussed how each one would transport the other to safe blood, in Harare or Johannesburg. This was a serious place.

What's Malawi like?' I asked, 'I hope there's more decent food there than here.'

'Malawi is brilliant, God, I envy you going that way,' said Helen.

Tim, though, warned us to expect trouble at the border.

'Have you found that everyone has been really amazed to see you?' I asked.

'Yes, we're getting tired of being stared at all the time,' said Helen.

'We've warmed them up for you, and you've warmed them up for us! Perhaps from now on we'll all be old hat.'

We took a day off in Morogoro. The objective was to sleep as much and eat as much as our bodies could take. After our primitive abodes of the past days we gladly splashed out $10 for a room with electricity, hot water, flush toilet, electric fan and mozzie nets.

We had arrived feeling totally drained. After a few cups of sweet tea, a shower, a nap and a couple of cold beers we felt half alive, but still needed loads of rest. Before going off in search of the famous *New Green Restaurant,* which claimed to make the best vegetable curry in Africa, we sat in the warm garden at dusk, slapping mosquitoes and listening to live coverage of a thrilling game between Spurs and Liverpool. The Liverpool keeper made a horrendous error in the final minutes to allow a Spurs goal, but Liverpool hung on to a 2-1 victory.

I was woken at nine next morning by a ringing phone (Yes, even a phone in the room!). I picked it up and said, 'Hello.'

A deep, husky woman's voice said, 'I want dollars,' and hung up. I replaced the receiver and, still half asleep, put my head back on the pillow with a faint wonder drifting through my brain.

The phone rang again, 'Yes?'

'I want dollars!'

'Wait, don't go. What do you mean. We paid last night.' I protested.

'No, I want dollars.' I gave up and went back to sleep, the mystery filled my dreams. We scraped in for the last breakfast at eleven o'clock, and waited until twelve for the omelettes to come. While we were gulping down the third pot of tea, a man walked up and sat down at our table. He introduced himself.

'I am the Government Auditor for Morogoro and I want dollars.' He had an insolent look in his eye.

'You too!' I said, 'Listen, we paid last night! I have a receipt!'

'No, no, dollars. You know, black market. I want dollars.' The penny dropped.

Acting innocent Tim asked, 'Isn't that illegal?'

The man was wearing a white shirt and black tie. He even had smart black trousers and polished shoes. He was in his early twenties and, definitely, was not the Government Auditor; anyway we were not likely to start selling black market dollars to a government official. It was totally weird.

'Yes, it is very illegal. You must be careful, but you can trust me, as I say, I am the Government Auditor.'

We politely refused his services and wished he would go away but he continued talking. 'Tell me my friends are you married?' he asked.

'No,' we replied together.

'Hmm, when do you suspect marriage?' he asked.

'Always,' I said. He smiled but was lost.

As we passed the reception desk the husky, deep voice of the morning called in a secretive tone, 'Hey you two, I want dollars.'

In the afternoon Morogoro United were playing Railway United, so we wandered through the ramshackle mud huts and crossed the stream on stepping stones to reach the stadium. It was a big concrete structure with a running track around the perimeter of a pitch which had long forgotten the colour of grass. A covered grandstand ran down one side. The whole crowd, perhaps five thousand people, was crammed in here; it was far too hot to sit in the sun.

A solid mass of very dark faces watched us walk along the front of the grandstand looking for a seat. A few men called *'Wzungu,'* which sent a ripple of laughter through the thousands. We smiled back foolishly.

Both teams were skilful, fast and had impressive close control. For the first half hour there was much goal mouth action and a few near misses. We kept a low profile and from the crowd's reaction figured that the home team were the blues.

Just before half time the nimble blue winger passed two men and slammed the ball into the roof of the net from the edge of the box. We instinctively threw up our arms shouting, *'YEAH!'* which was a bit of a whoops. Morogoro were in red.

The sea of dark, curious, faces turned towards us. Tim and I were the only people standing and the only whites in the place. Feeling just a little conspicuous, we sat down at the speed of light. Men near us nodded and laughed, nudging each other, the laughter spread outwards.

'Wzungu! Wzungu!' they called. There were more shouts in Swahili, which we could not understand and these had people guffawing and nodding to us. They took our error in good spirit but it was all too much for one old man at the front. He stood seething, shouting abuse at us and waved his walking stick. When another man told him to sit down, he hit him on the head with the stick and started to climb the concrete terracing towards us, waving and shouting. It took four spectators and a policeman to restrain the old hooligan. He was eventually led away, still waving his stick, and ejected from the ground. The crowd loved it. They clapped laughed, nodded and from all corners of the stand called, *'Wzungu, Wzungu,'* like a new football chant. Happily Morogoro found their scoring touch and the game finished 4 -1.

After the football, Tim found he was suffering from a *Famous New Green Stomach Upset* and retired to bed, while I serviced the bikes in the cooler hours of late afternoon. I adjusted the brakes and gears, checked tyre pressures, took a buckle out of Tim's rear wheel, cleaned the chains and finally gave them both a hot soapy wash and a good talking to. The chain cleaner was a handy

Italian job, which worked kerosene into the links and flushed out abrasive sand, which would have worn out the components in no time. This was the second service they had enjoyed in a week.

We preferred cool early morning starts but, as had often happened on the mornings after a day off in Australia, we were slow to get it together and did not hit the road until nine. For the first time since leaving Mombasa, though, we had total cloud cover, so the usual searing heat held off. We chugged along happily, greeting and waving to women working in the maize fields, making good ground. We were starting to find our feet in Africa!

Spectacular dark mountains stood north and south. Even when the cloud did break in the late morning it was not as hot as on previous days. This must mean we had, at last, passed out of the humid coastal region. The map showed that in the next few days we would be climbing into the mountains.

Gradually, the villages became fewer and farther between. The hand-worked fields were replaced with wild scrub. We surprised a middle aged woman as she defecated in a ditch beside the road, passing the time while waiting for a lift on a matatu (Toyota pick-up). Small, pale trees and thorny mopani bushes dotted the great plain of the Masai Steppe to the north. Roadside grass rustled with startled, unseen snakes or rodents.

A triangular warning sign, with red border and white background, carried the picture of an elephant. Our muscles were strong and solid but we had to work hard, heads down, teeth gritted, concentrating and fighting the pain to hold a fast pulsing of the pedals, hour after hour, mile upon mile. At noon, we took advantage of the rare isolation, to pull off the road and into the bush to brew tea. We were now well used to having crowds staring at us, though it was good to be alone for a while.

A little later we came to a large road sign, about five metres square which read:

MIKUMI NATIONAL PARK

DANGER WILD ANIMALS

NEXT 50 KMS

This did not come as a surprise as the map showed the road running through the reserve. The surprise, though, was that there was no gate and no officials to stop us cycling on. As the idea was to *cycle* across the three southern continents, we would have felt we were cheating if we took a lift through the reserve, even if it was on the orders of a game warden. We pedalled on past the sign. Suddenly we were in a world of wild animals.

I had experienced a similar feeling of vulnerability a few years before, when snorkelling with Cassie, whilst on holiday on the Great Barrier Reef. We had jumped off the boat, knowing that sharks were in the water, put on face masks and looked below to indeed see two small sharks circling six metres beneath our feet. The captain had assured us they were only reef sharks, about six feet long, 'They don't usually attack people,' he had said, totally unconcerned. We had swum about for half an hour as the sharks continued to glide around watching us. I had had a strong feeling that I was not meant to be there; the same feeling I had now, cycling through this game reserve.

Tim and I stuck close together, not speeding but rolling gently along, constantly scanning the bush on both sides of the road, adrenaline pumping. We felt wild animals were quite shy and did not really expect to see anything so close to the road. After only ten kilometres we saw a shape on the tarmac ahead. As we approached, Tim slightly ahead, the shape remained still. Tim called back excitedly, 'Look at this!!'

It was a lioness. She was dead. From the look of her she had been hit by a car within the last hour or two. Although there was no great mutilation we could see her skull was cracked. She would have died instantly. The tongue drooped from the open mouth; the teeth coated in a film of blood, her palate was split and out of line with the rest of her skull, and there was also a deep gouge in her left flank. At a metre long, we guessed that the lioness was about a year old; fading spots of cub-hood clung to muscular legs.

'We better skedaddle', I said to Tim, 'the rest of the pride might be nearby.'

'Christ, yeah! They might think we did this with our bikes,' he replied. We had to laugh, despite the circumstances. Senses were heightened now as we cautiously continued, studying the dense greenery. 'How fast do you think lions can run?' I asked.

'I don't know', said Tim, 'and I don't want to find out.'

We cycled on, going deeper into the Reserve, looking nervously for any movement in the bushes. Patches of shade under impenetrable tangle hid everything. We were making a poor job of disguising our fear.

'What time is it?' Tim asked.

'Three o'clock, why?'

'We're safe then, it's past their lunch time.'

A warthog broke cover and crashed away from the road to the left into the bush. The perpendicular tail gave away its zig-zag course. A mixed herd of wildebeest and zebra stopped munching grass to watch as we passed; one moved and they all took flight. They ran for a hundred yards and, as though forgetting there was danger, stopped and started to eat again. Five giraffe were spooked, running surprisingly gracefully, they were moving at thirty or forty kilometres per hour, but the gait was slow motion. A herd of elephant grazed a few hundred metres to the north. Dangerous buffalo and angry baboons gave us the willies. Further along the road, under a shady acacia tree only thirty metres from us, a mother elephant and her calf pulled leaves from a bush with differing degrees of success.

We had seen wild animals in the game parks of Kenya and northern Tanzania from the safety of a Landrover, but this was very different. We were now actually out there amongst them. The Park and its administrative Headquarters were not open to tourists, so our arrival on bicycles caused some surprise. People were expected to drive through without stopping. We did eventually persuade the wardens to sell us a bed for the night. For a couple of hours, though, they insisted they were closed and asked us to continue our journey through the reserve in the dark. Hmmm.

We left the makeshift jumble of the Park Headquarters buildings soon after dawn, sneaking past grazing elephants and a curious giraffe. *'Thought cyclists were banned,'* he mused.

After fifteen kilometres we were out of the game reserve. We stopped to change dollars into Tanzanian shillings at the bank in the small town of Mikumi. We filled in three forms and waited forty-five minutes to change $70; quick for Africa. It was an important move in the game of *'Blackmarket'*.

We needed an official stamp, or two, on our declaration forms. A late breakfast of coffee, andazis and samosas in a truckers' café was slowed by an Elton John tape playing in the background. We could not drag ourselves away, 'Just a couple more songs,' I begged. I was so tired; not that Tim was raring to go. The waiter brought more coffee and andazis and warned us not to cycle through the game reserve.

'We have just come through it,' Tim chuckled, 'we are heading west.'

'But the *simbas* and *tembos?* Do you not see them?'

'What?'

'Many lions and great elephants!'

With exaggerated nonchalance I said, 'Oh, Yes, we saw a few.'

'Are you not scared!!?' asked the waiter.

'Oh, no, not really,' I said, lying through my teeth.

Boy, it felt good to see the look of amazement on that waiter's face.

In eight cycling days from Mombasa we had covered nearly seven hundred kilometres, an average of eighty-four kilometres per day. Despite the extreme heat and humidity, shortage of water and adequate cycling food we were moving much quicker than we had in Australia.

Tim recalls: 'I felt we were being physically and mentally challenged as never before. Months of cycling had built up a reserve of stamina which allowed us to move faster for more hours, thus we also had more time available to stop and talk to the locals or rest tired muscles under some shady tree. The planned siesta did not always happen. It was a compromise; if it was so hot that the going was slow, we could not afford the time to stop. We had to make our target distances. We were very happy with our progress and surprised that, so far, we had stayed healthy.'

It was nearly noon by the time we had pumped up our tyres and bought kerosene at the Mikumi petrol station, next door to the truckers' café. We bought a supply of peanuts and dizzies (small, sweet bananas) from two small boys on the forecourt and headed on.

The sun climbed higher, the cloud burned away and our brains boiled. We climbed and fell through emerald terraces, the surface alternating dangerously between rough, broken tarmac and sandy gravel. We shot down hillsides jinking to avoid pot holes only to find the wheels suddenly skidding and twisting in soft sand.

We estimated our planned destination, Mboyoni, to be sixty-five kilometres from the town of Mikumi. A short day, but we were tired after one hundred and eleven kilometres from Morogoro the previous day. Sixty-five kilometres came and went, seventy kilometres, eighty, no Mboyoni, no villages at all. Our water ran out, our peanuts and dizzies ran out. The hills kept coming and the sun kept beating. We doggedly heaved on along the side of a deep valley, a wide, dirty river murmured far below us in the ravine. At four o'clock we hit the *'bonk'*, runners call it the *'wall'*. Legs were rubbery and numb. A cloud of weariness floated around me. My hands were tingling. We were dangerously dehydrated; neither of us had peed all day. All reserves were used up.

'I'm feeling a bit weak and silly,' called Tim, 'I need to drink.'

We stopped in the shade at the road's lowest point. The river, though, was still a hundred metres below, down a steep rocky slope, thick with vegetation. We decided to spoof for who would climb down to fetch water; spoofing being the only fair way to decide who does the dirty jobs. It is a very simple game, you have three coins each, you place one, two or three of them in your right hand, which you then hold out in front of you. The object is to guess how many coins are held, in total, in both right hands. Although I was carrying both the medical kit and the radio across Africa through losing in Tanga, this was somehow a much more important one to win.

'Four,' I said on the second round.

'Hmm, good call,' said Tim, 'three.'

He opened his hand, two coins, I opened mine, two coins.

'Don't be long, mate', I said, ecstatically, 'I'm a bit thirsty.'

'Sod it,' he said with not a glimmer of a smile. In fact, Tim's face was a picture of unhappiness as he inched down the steep slope, into the snake infested thicket, towards the crocodile infested river.

'Have a nice time,' I called and he managed to break into a laugh.

'You bastard!' he said, 'We should have brought some Hotentotts to do this.'

I put my hat over my face and lay in the shade, my entire body awash with sweat. Ants crawled over me, biting just once before being splattered. I chuckled at the thought of Tim fighting off a crocodile for a cup of tea.

We reached Mboyuni at the one hundred and four kilometre mark, very, very tired. I bought eight Marindas (fizzy orange), sickly sweet, warm and bloating. We sat on wooden crates in the market, grey faced, staring blankly, gushing sweat, unable to speak. The more Marinda I drank the worse I felt.

After twenty minutes we roused ourselves to go in search of lodgings. As we pushed the bikes through the crowd, a group of incredible looking young men greeted us. Their fine radiant features, and plaited hair, tinged with ochre was, to our western eyes, a little effeminate. Spotless purple robes looked brilliant against rich skins. Two men wore robes of a large tartan pattern. Earrings dangled from long holes in the lobes, and each man wore a single string of coloured glass beads around his neck. These were Masai, fearless men from a long line of warriors.

The Masai tribes who occupy the great plain of the Masai Steppe are pastoral herders, lovers of land, family and cattle. Their cattle carry large bells around their necks and roam immense distances throughout the year. It is a similar lifestyle to the Turkana's, except that the fertile grasslands offer far greater food security. They are renowned as fierce and untamable and will kill anything which threatens their cattle.

These young guys did not carry the long, razor-sharp, stabbing spears of old, but thin wooden staffs and certainly meant us no harm. Soon a school teacher, George, came forward from the crowd to help. 'These men are Masai, they love you very much. They have never seen white men on bicycles and want to look at you and ask you many questions.' We were desperately tired and needed to be alone, but could not refuse them. When we had told our story we asked a few questions of our own.

'Is it true that each of these men must kill a lion before he can take a wife?' I asked.

'Ah, it was this way, but they like to have many wives and there are not enough lions left,' laughed George.

'How do they manage to look so healthy?' I asked.

'They live on milk and blood. Sometimes they eat meat.'

'Do they not eat vegetables?' asked Tim.

He talked to the men and they laughed. 'They say that vegetables are for women.'

They were the most healthy looking people I had ever seen; very strong and supple, with gleaming teeth and clear eyes.

'Why do these two wear tartan robes?' asked Tim. The two young men were proud to be picked out from their friends and simpered like girls.

'Your Doctor Livingstone gave them tartan,' said George.

Incongruously, one was wearing headphones and a Walkman. 'What is he listening to,' I asked George.

The young Masai pulled one ear-piece away from his ear and summoned me over. I put my ear close to his, 'Ah, Bob Marley'. It made a change from the Zaire music.

During the Mau Mau uprising in Kenya, the British recruited the local Masai to form special units. It is said that a Masai patrol was ordered to bring back any Kikuyu arms they could find. The following day the British Commanding Officer was shocked to be presented with a pile of severed limbs.

President Nyerere had left his mark on Mbuyoni. He had been the main force behind the bloodless revolution which ended Britain's colonial rule. Nyerere was a staunch socialist and on assuming power had immediately organised his people into communes, *Ujamaas*. Ten million people were resettled against their will and put to work in twelve hundred newly established villages. Some *Ujamaas* grew only cotton, some coffee, sisal, or tobacco, some raised cattle, some mined gold. All colonial plantations, processing plants and banks were nationalised. Soon the country was prospering, there was ample food and education was available to almost all. But this communism had in-built problems. European investors were unhappy about supporting an extreme leftist regime and the people objected to being moved. When the finances dried up the people wandered back to their homelands.

Here in Mbuyoni, we stumbled on the legacy of the *Ujaama* communes. Rows of trestle tables lined both sides of the road. The first table in line held five or six small pyramids of onions. The next table held the same and the next, all twenty tables held pyramids of onions. Truck drivers bought large numbers of the vegetables and sold them in Dar es Salam. The people of Mboyoni did not eat onions.

I had spent the two hours since arriving in Mbuyoni sat in my shabby concrete cell making tea and filtering water to rehydrate. The mosquito net was more holes than net. The water for washing smelled of urine. The room was filthy. My candle went out. My knee ached; my head throbbed and I was absolutely fed up. I was infuriated with Tim who slept soundly in the next room. When, at last, I put my head on the grimy pillow I found a packet of condoms in my ear, compliments of the management. After two minutes Tim pushed open the door of my cell and shouted, 'Wakey, wakey, time for some onions!!' Fortunately we found eggs and, with great difficulty and amusement for all, taught the chai shop man to make onion omelettes. I dozed off during my third helping.

The sun had soaked its way deep into the mud walls of the rooms and its heat seeped out all night. As I lay unsleeping and cursing, cramp seized my left leg in a tight vice, making me cry out. I eased it with intense concentration. The stench of my body was unbearable. Mosquitoes or not, I could not stay inside this oven any longer. At 2 am I dragged my mattress out into the relative cool of the court yard and laid it on the swept dirt. Within two minutes, by coincidence or perhaps my inspiration, Tim ghosted out of his room with the same idea. He had been tossing and turning for hours in a pool of sweat and thought he had malaria. 'This is a horrible bloody place', he murmured, 'we must start camping again.'

Tim recalls: 'I can usually sleep anywhere: trains, bouncing buses, rocking boats, I don't care, but this place was squalid. We were both miserable and worn out and desperately wanted some sleep, the claustrophobia and the heat were overpowering and made it impossible.'

Mildly amused by our discomfort Tim said, as we lay in the yard, 'Someone once said, if you're unhappy it's because you're not trying hard enough'.

'Bollocks!' I said, 'I can't try any harder.'

By 7.30, after another onion omelette, (what else), we cranked onward, weary and quiet. Tim had thought to pick up a load of hard boiled eggs from the chai house. These would keep us going. We had also picked up a small box of toilet paper, which could be coming in handy at any moment.

The first thirty-five kilometres were flat. We were quiet, eyes red-rimmed and gritty from lack of sleep. I spent an hour unwinding taught muscles and freeing heavy gunk from my lungs. Happy villagers cheered us as they walked down the side of the road, on their way to the fields.

We pretended to be happy, but we knew that, on top of everything else, we had the biggest, nastiest hill to climb. By the time we reached its base we were athletically warm, the depth of stamina was there, but it was going to be bad. We do not get off and push bikes up hills, I reminded myself, *not ever*. Nature was saying *'Take that!'* and threw in a ten kilometre, one-in-four climb, in one hundred and fifteen degree heat. I took this personally.

'OK, well take this!,' I said and attacked it full on, put my head down, and just kept going. Tim's approach was more sensible. He kept a slow, steady pace and saved his energy. Nasty hills were a test of mental as well as physical stamina. A white aid worker, coming down the hill in a $40,000, four wheel drive, Landcruiser, opened his electric window and called smugly,

'You've only just started! This hill goes on for miles.'

Tim recalls: I thought, 'You bastard! I'd like to see you get out and have a go.'

Muscles protested, my knee stung, sweat rolled in rivulets down my cheeks, my chest heaved and my mouth hung open in a crooked '0' gasping for air. I tried to remember what it felt like to kiss Cassie. It had been a long time.

At a false summit I thought a group of lads might be bandits, but they were just *dizzy* sellers, who jogged alongside stuffing them under my nose. I was not going to stop for anything. At the top I gulped two litres of water and waited for Tim. The ultimate irony occurred as he reached me: a giant, articulated Pepsi lorry crawled tantalisingly past. We could even hear the bottles clinking. I could, quite happily, have crawled into the long grass and slept; snakes or no snakes.

A couple of kilometres further on we collapsed into a crowded chai shop, and drank cup after cup of foul, lukewarm chai. The woman had poured half a field of sugar into the pot despite our protests.

'Why are you doing this to yourselves?' a man asked.

'Doing what?' I thought, *'Cycling across the southern continents or drinking this foul tea?'*

He was sitting in the shade of the thatch, his bare feet up on the table.

We could only shake our heads. 'Perhaps you are doing this to make history?'

We said no, that was not it, we were doing it because it was our challenge and because we thought we could. 'We want to prove to ourselves', I said, 'that it's okay to live however you want, as long as you don't harm anyone.'

The man was thoughtful, 'This is a much extreme way of proving a point, no?'

'Yes', said Tim, 'but Andy and I are very dim. If we were doing something less extreme we might forget the point sometime in future.'

An old, green truck stopped in the road below us; the driver was hoping to sell bags of maize. Our friend stood and exchanged words with the driver in Swahili. He sat down laughing, 'I told him you are cycling across Africa and he thinks you are mad.' Tim said, 'Tell him, thank you very much, we love him'. This he did, bringing a great laugh from the driver and the others.

As we left, an hour later, the man said, 'We wish you success. We are proud to be your friends.'

'Thank you,' I said, 'We are proud to be yours.'

We were exhausted as we waved goodbye, even after the long rest. The city of Iringa was still fifty kilometres away. It might as well have been five hundred.

Iringa was the centre of this tobacco growing region. It held a surprise for us; it sat on top of another great hill. On this one I surprised myself, and the twenty passengers piled in the back, by somehow overtaking a lorry and beating it to the top. Once in the comfortable *Isimila Hotel* we knocked back six litres of water each in half an hour.

In 1959, the year of my birth, the writer Evelyn Waugh visited Iringa. In *'A Tourist in Africa,'* he wrote:

> *'Iringa is a cool pleasant town with a railway station but no railway and an excellent Greek restaurant. The natives of the place are called, if I heard it aright, 'Hehe', a warlike people who defeated a German column and hold themselves superior to the Masai ... They mostly go to work in the copper mines and return dressed as cinema cowboys. There are many of them swaggering about the streets with spurs, ornamental leather-work, brilliant shirts and huge hats, but most of the inhabitants of the town are Greek or Indian.'*

Now the Greek restaurant has gone, the railway has come and, sadly, no one was outwardly impersonating Alan Ladd or Cary Grant. The only cowboys in town are the guys actually running the cinema. Seven billboards outside displayed seven different films, one for each day of the week. Today was Wednesday, an American Kung-Fu film. This was a disappointment, if it had been Tuesday we could have seen Warren Beatty in *Shampoo,* (I don't know though). By the dilapidated look of the posters I guessed that these seven films had been showing for many years. We arrived at seven twenty-five. A funny little man with buck teeth greeted us at the pay desk and took our thirty shillings. He gave us tickets then opened his door and led us into the gloomy, vaulted auditorium to our seats. There were no other customers, not one. Tim and I sat and chatted for a while. The lights dimmed and Pathe News came onto the screen. Pictures of a very youthful Queen of England came up, followed by Prime Minister Harold Wilson greeting President Anwar Sadat of Egypt. I was disappointed, had it been slightly more out of date we could have watched the same newsreel as had Evelyn

Waugh. The loud speakers had suffered a hard and unhappy life, played at top volume for so many years, or perhaps they were just fed up with playing the same old stuff all the time. They were so worn out that only a low, unintelligible mumble was audible. Pathe News finished and the main film jumped in immediately, well into the story. We had been deprived of at least the first ten minutes. Kung-Fu films were designed for places like this; you do not need to be able to see the beginning or hear the dialogue to follow the plot. It was not exactly challenging. We were watching this, thinking there must be something more meaningful we could be doing with our time, when the funny little man popped up in front of us and said, 'You want Pepsi, bwana?'

'Oh, err, yes please,' I said cheerily. 'That's very kind of you. Two each please.'

'Give money now', he said with a smile, 'and I get.'

We gave him a few coins and he walked away. A moment later the film stopped and we sat in the darkness, wallowing in surrealism. After five minutes the man came back with the cold Pepsis.

'Sorry, shopi across road closed,' he puffed, 'so I walk a longi way.'

He handed over the drinks and we gave him a big tip. The man stood over us while we drank. As soon as they were finished he stepped forward and took the empty bottles. 'I take back shopi,' he smiled, and was off again.

After a further five minutes he must have returned, for the Kung-Fu started again. Half an hour later the projector broke down and the film burned in a giant cauliflower on the screen. We slipped out unnoticed and embarrassed. The poor man had really, really tried. He would have looked out of the little window of his projection room and seen us gone and his evening would have been totally ruined. I could hear the sigh of disappointment as we slunk down the dark street. Some of these people can break your heart.

We walked back to the *Isimila Hotel*, where Dowdy, the friendly waiter, served up cold beers and watched, spell bound, as we made and played a game of *'Owzat'*. Tim's team, *The Richie Benaud President's Eleven*, featuring WG Grace, Len Hutton and Sir Godfrey Evans attacked the spin bowling of William the Conqueror early on and amassed a huge total before tea. Despite a valiant fifth wicket stand between Frankie Howard and Michelle Pfeifer, my *Barry Manilow All Stars Eleven* went down by three wickets.

Since leaving Mombasa, we had shaken twenty-nine thousand, two hundred and seven hands (roughly), a world record, even more than the Queen. *'What's more'*, I thought, *'Her Majesty only shakes pleasant, manicured, Daimler hands. We, sadly, shake dysentery, cholera and HIV+ hands.'*

The ridge of the Great Rift Valley takes an odd twist here, at the junction of southern Tanzania, Malawi and northern Zambia. We found ourselves climbing up the side of the valley twice in a couple of days.

At the town of Yulole the road went on west to Mbeya and into Zambia, while a fork headed south to Malawi. This was where we were heading. Yulole had grown as a result of the fork in the road.

Rows of pale mud-built shops lay twenty metres back from the road on each side; the area in front was rough, sandy waste-ground. Some of the buildings were garages, lorries and cars were scattered about waiting or being worked on. Men peered under bonnets, while others hung about smoking. One guy was fixing a dented wing with flattened tin cans, another was making sandals from old car tyres. Some shops sold mangoes and bananas, others colourful cloth, others were chai stalls or cafés.

As we rode through town, my eye caught a sudden movement to the right, on the waste-ground. A rat had broken the cover of its hole and was in the open, running scared, trying to make for the safety of the buildings. A boy threw a rock and missed, other boys followed suit. With every rock the rat changed direction. Just as safety was in sight a nimble boy caught it a glancing blow with his foot. The rat rolled and, for a moment, was stunned. Its hesitation was fatal. The boy, athletic and swift, had regained his balance and, before the rat could sprint on, a boot caught it with full force. The creature flew five metres through the air, limp and spinning, landing dead in the dust. The boys congratulated themselves and threw the corpse at each other.

Tim changed money in the bank. A friendly armed-guard was on duty outside. 'We were robbed last month,' he informed me proudly, in some way revelling in the inherent danger of his job. I waited with him in the shade of the porch, reading *Out of Africa* and watching the town ... *'The Masai have reported to the District Commissioner at Ngong, that many times, at sunrise and sunset, they have seen lions on Finch-Hatton's grave in the Hills. A lion and a lioness have come there and stood, or lain, on the grave for a long time ...'* Lions like that would not eat us, much too cool.

An enterprising Indian had set up a café in town. The bank manager escorted us to the door and told Ali to look after us. The vegetable curry and mint raita were a welcome change from rice, beans and onion omelettes. On the wall hung a team photo of Manchester United with Bobby Charlton, Dennis Law and Nobby Stiles.

The road south was the worst yet, neither soft nor hard; neither tarmac, rock nor sand. A change of surface every five metres, made the climb all the more exhausting. We struggled up and up for ten or fifteen kilometres, again my right knee protested. The top lay three thousand metres above sea level, we collapsed on the verge. Oh, it was bliss. After a few minutes rest I felt greatly refreshed and managed to eat a couple of *dizzies*.

A truck passed, crowded with people. On the back, standing on the tail board, hanging on to the frame for dear life, was a white man. I waved, he nodded. He was in no position to wave back, as the truck was bouncing all over the place. 'There's no way that guy is going to stay on there,' I said to Tim. 'I bet you a banana we see him down the road with his head caved in.'

A little way down the road we stopped in the market place of Tukuyu to look for somewhere to sleep. A youth appeared in front of us carrying a big tray of samosas for sale. A gigantic growth, the size of a tennis ball grew from his forehead, covered his right eye and rested on his cheek. We were horror struck, mainly because it was so sudden an appearance. Later we were embarrassed that we had reacted with such obvious shock and had refused his samosas. The poor guy, it was not his fault he was so hideously ugly. In the morning I made a point of buying a supply of samosas from the lad, but was still horrified. I would never have the guts to be a nurse.

In fifteen cycling days, three rest days and two sick days we had cycled one thousand two hundred and fifty, hard, hot, kilometres. We were knackered and knew if things continued to be so hard, our physical and mental reserves were likely to be used up very quickly. We would be in trouble. We were only a quarter of the way across Africa, Swakopmund seemed too far away. And what of South America? My mask of optimism was starting to crack.

9 Ladies who are not gentlemen – Tim

In the Chichewa language Malawi means *'The land of reflected light'*. Entering the country from the north, it was easy to grasp the relevance of the name. The whole of eastern Malawi is dominated by the calm blue waters of Lake Malawi. It is a long, thin sliver running almost the entire length of the country, north to south; a distance of four hundred kilometres. The lake is never more than one hundred kilometres wide and accounts for approximately one third of the total surface area.

To the north and north east lies Tanzania. To the south and east is troubled, war-torn Mozambique. In north Malawi, the western ridge of the Great Rift Valley plunges into the waters of Lake Malawi, creating a formidable escarpment. At the top of this escarpment lies a high plateau running parallel with the lake, stretching west to the bush lands of Zambia.

The River Shire flows south out of the lake through the Shire Plateau, an area of temperate, fertile country which extends to the mountain mass of the Southern Highlands. The river continues its path south before merging with the great Zambezi on its inexorable journey to the Indian Ocean.

As Andy and I wheeled our bikes towards the border post at the end of January, I remembered the words of Tim, the English cyclist.

'Watch out for the Tanzania Malawi border, it's the heaviest in Africa,' he had warned us a couple of weeks before. 'If you have anything at all to hide, they'll find it. They'll pull your bikes to pieces and leave you to pick up the bits.'

'We don't have anything to hide', I thought, *'apart from a thousand dollar wad of blackmarket cash.'*

The gamble now facing us was a simple one – we either declared our stash and everything would be twice as expensive in Malawi, or we smuggled our wad through the border and everything would be half the price. Of course, there was always the chance of being caught by an over-zealous border official, in which case we were looking at a stretch in Lilongwe nick or, at the very least, confiscation of our precious *'green backs'*. Both Andy and I like a little flutter now and again, so there was really only one possible decision – put it all on black and spin the wheel.

In the Tanzanian bush Andy had set his devious mind to the challenge of getting our cash past the border guards. After a couple of days' plotting whilst cycling, he came up with the answer.

'We'll put it inside our tyres,' he declared.

'What?' I asked.

'There should be enough room for the notes and the tubes will mould around them.'

And so it was that we arrived at the official looking, white-washed border post with a thousand dollars stashed in Andy's front tyre. We leaned the bikes against the wall, watched carefully by two smartly uniformed officers. They took an immediate interest in our machines, pointing at them and starting an earnest discussion. Perhaps they were bicycle buffs wanting to discuss the merits of gear ratios and tyre pressures.

I stepped into the cool darkness of the hut and was immediately relieved to be out of the glaring sun and away from the constant attention of bush flies.

'Good afternoon, gentlemen,' said the dapper official seated behind a well ordered desk. 'Please may I be having your documents?'

We duly handed over our passports. He gave them the most cursory of inspections, stamped them and handed them back.

'Everything in much good order,' he said politely and waved at his two mates outside who were still examining the bikes. 'Okay gentlemen, you may be going on your ways. I am wish you fine travel.'

With that we got onto our bikes and rode off. As soon as we were out of earshot of the guards Andy started ranting furiously, 'I don't bloody well believe it! I spent two days dreaming up that plan and that bloke hasn't even got the decency to go through my bags!'

We churned out the last fifty kilometres to Karonga through flat wetlands, past neatly tended fields of maize. People working in the fields straightened from their toils as we approached and greeted us with vigorous waves and friendly smiles. Along the sides of the road were an assortment of locals; small groups of barefooted children skipping and wrestling, old women bent double under heavy baskets and the occasional cyclist on a battered old bike wobbling his way from one village to the next. We stopped at a bottle shop on the outskirts of town to change $50 with the lady owner.

Whilst I watched a group of adolescent boys taking the tops off Coke bottles with their teeth, Andy managed to get four kwacha to the dollar. This was about twice the official bank rate. We had placed our bets, the wheel had stopped spinning and black was today's lucky colour.

The heavens opened as we entered the town. Great floods of water cascaded down the road transforming everything instantly to thick, reddish-brown mud. We rode slowly past a well stocked grocery shop, a clothing store, a smart looking bank and a book shop. The centre of town was choked with traffic. We had to dodge big trucks as they belched foul black diesel fumes and sent up great sheets of muddy water to drench us even further. Huge raindrops were hammering against our water proofs as we finally pulled off the road by the *Government Rest House*. It had been one hundred and twenty kilometres and ten hours since we had bought samosas from the lad with the tennis ball growing out of his head back in Tukuyu. It had seemed like a week.

The *Government Rest House* was situated by the beach on the edge of Lake Malawi near to the intriguingly named *'Welding and Disco shop'*. The Rest House was basic but clean and tidy and run by a friendly manager who knocked on our door shortly after we had checked in.

'Do you have laundry you would like washed?' he asked.

I thought of the stinking bag of soiled cycling kit that lay humming in my pannier. We had not had the chance to wash anything since Iringa, more than a week before.

'Yes, we do have some laundry but it's pretty disgusting. Do you have a washing machine?' I asked.

'Oh no, we have the man who will do washing by hand for small cost,' he said.

We met the laundry man who was thin and cheerful. I judged him to be in his mid-forties. His name was Job. We gave him our filthy washing feeling a little guilty. I noticed a pair of my underpants in the putrid pile. I bent down to retrieve them as I would not have wished him to wash these by hand. Job snatched the underpants out of my hand.

'No, no, give them to me,' he said enthusiastically. 'I love underpants!'

The waiter looked smart in his red blazer. His snow white felt gloves contrasted sharply with the very black skin of his face and his appearance would have been immaculate but for the old blue yachting pumps he wore without socks.

We were sitting in the dining room of the pleasant *Club Marina* in Karonga. The Club was an up-market hotel, restaurant and bar, catering for travelling business-men and wealthy locals. The hotel prices were over our $10 per day budget but the restaurant was reasonably priced.

Andy and I had been dreaming about this meal for two weeks now and it promised to be a gastronomic delight. The restaurant was clean, bright and airy with half a dozen tables covered by crisp, white table cloths. Through the window I could see a small, neat garden full of the reds, yellows and purples of a dozen exotic blooms.

'What do you have to eat?' I asked the waiter.

'For eating sir,' Moses told me with the solemnity of a depressed undertaker, 'I have one sausage and one bacon but he is highly frozen.'

'Okay that sounds good to me,' I said, 'we'll have whatever you've got.'

'And for puddings you are having?' he asked mournfully.

'Well what have you got?' I asked again.

'We are having fruits salad and one time we are having ice creams.'

'Ice cream for me please,' I told him eagerly.

'And for me!' said Andy.

After taking our order the waiter turned and moved at a very dignified pace towards the kitchens. He emerged a couple of minutes later to inform us sombrely, 'Much apology mister, but ice cream is all fucked up.'

We returned to Moses and his little restaurant several times over the next couple of days. Our bodies soaked up the calories – fried breakfasts, steak and chips, liver and onions and freshly caught fish, all disappearing at an alarming rate. We were often so hungry we ordered everything twice, each with extra bread and butter. The restaurant was a communal meeting place for travellers staying in Karonga on their way south through Malawi or north into Tanzania. On one occasion, as we were about to tuck into another huge plateful of grub, the door opened and in walked a young sandy-haired guy followed by two attractive young women. He spotted us in the corner and walked directly to our table.

'You made it then?' he said in a London accent.

I looked at him quizzically. 'Have we met before?'

'Not exactly,' he said. 'I was hanging onto the back of a truck that passed you back in Tanzania, a couple of days ago.'

'Oh, that was you was it?' I said, remembering him passing us on the hill out of Yulole.

I looked across at Andy. 'In that case you owe me a banana!'

'That was me all right', said the guy, 'thought I was going to die on that trip. I'm Alistair by the way.' He turned to the two girls standing behind him. 'Meet Annie and Macy.'

We invited Alistair and the girls to join our table. Annie and Macy were Canadians, about twenty years old with masses of long, dark hair, both wearing cut-off jeans. Annie was sporting a pirate-style red bandanna.

'Annie, Alistair and I just met yesterday,' explained Macy. 'We've all been hitching individually through Tanzania.'

'What! Hitching in Africa on your own?' Andy asked incredulously.

'Don't be such a boring old fart,' said Annie, obviously annoyed. Macy joined the attack, 'We're big girls. We can look after ourselves.'

'That's right', said Annie, 'I punched a guy on the nose the other day for trying to grope me as I walked down the street. It was great, you should have seen his face. Was he shocked or what!'

Karonga nestled on the fertile shores of Lake Malawi. In the evenings we sat on the sunny terrace of the *Club Marina* drinking ice cold Carlsberg lager, universally known as *'Green'*. In Malawi there was a simple choice between *'Greens'* and *'Browns'*. The bottles which had green labels contained lighter beer than those with brown.

We met Wisdom Kaumphaw in the bar of the *Club Marina*. He was a local business man, a large gentleman with smoky yellow eyeballs and a generous, rubbery face. His belly was colossal and strained against the buttons of a long suffering pinstripe waistcoat. He reminded me of Idi Amin, the infamous former Ugandan dictator. Oddly, his feet were small and dainty, in a pair of black leather brogues.

'Are you Scottish?' he asked me.

'No, I'm English,' I replied.

'I'm half Scottish,' Andy told him.

'Ah, Doctor Livingstone was Scottish,' he told us. 'He built many missions here. We like Scottish people.'

'Are you a religious man Wisdom?' Andy asked.

'Alas, no,' he sighed, 'but I used to be Scottish when I was younger then I lost interest and gave it up.'

After leaving Wisdom we took a stroll down by the lake and watched the antics of a group of young boys, frolicking naked and unabashed in the lake, bobbing and diving like sleek ebony eels. I sat on a gnarled piece of drift wood to watch a saffron sun sink beneath the mirrored surface of the lake. I chuckled when a bizarre image formed in my mind of Wisdom Kaumphaw, dressed in full highland garb, complete with tartan kilt and sporran marching up and down the beach playing a wailing set of bagpipes. I pondered the oddity of Malawians with Scottish ancestry.

In 1858, to the north of where I sat, Burton and Speke were walking across the great expanse of the Masai Steppe towards Lake Tanganyika in search of the source of the Nile. They were unaware that a thousand miles to the south, Doctor Livingstone was embarking upon his own expedition in search of another great lake.

Livingstone followed the great Zambezi River into the African interior. At Sena (now in central Mozambique) he decided to go north, up the Shire River. The small steamer, *'Ma-Robert'*, chugged through a wide and fertile valley watched by hostile Manganja tribesmen. Standing alone on the foredeck the big, formidable Scotsman was an imposing figure with bushy greying beard, blue sailing cap with faded gold band, red-sleeved waist coat and old grey tweed trousers. Occasionally he ventured ashore to shout to native audiences who were hidden in the bush watching his every move.

'I am one of the English', he boomed, *'I am your friend. I have come to save you.'*

Not surprisingly, the natives chose not to show themselves.

A Manganja chief heard about this strange white man in the *'burning canoe'* and a meeting was arranged. The chief stood on the shore, whilst his warriors hid in the reeds ready to fire off a shower of arrows. Doctor Livingstone stepped ashore alone, walked up the beach, swept off his cap, held out his hand and smiled.

For the rest of his life the chief dined out on the story of how he had met the famous explorer.

'How could I give the sign to kill a man who smiled like that?' he was to recount a thousand times over the years. Livingstone was delighted by the brimming river and rich land he found, and recognised this as a great opportunity to bring the Christian gospel to an immense population.

'When will this fertile valley resound with the church-going bell?' he wrote in his journal.

After several days travel he found the Shire River blocked by cataracts just to the north of Chikwawa. Livingstone learned of a well-used path that skirted the cataracts and of a large lake a few days march to the north. He headed back down-river determined to return to find the lake on a future expedition.

Livingstone wrote in a letter to his friend Murchison: *'I think twenty or thirty good Christian Scotch families with their minister and elders would produce an impression in ten years that would rejoice the hearts of all lovers of our race.'*

In February, 1859, Livingstone made preparations to explore the land to the north of the cataracts. He loaded his steam launch with provisions and fifteen Makololo tribesmen and steamed back up river.

The party left the launch and continued past the cataracts on foot. After a week long trek, they emerged onto the great Shire Plateau which extended northwards to the mountain mass of

Zomba (now the Southern Highlands of Malawi). There was still no sign of the lake but they found a cool, healthy and well-watered country which Livingstone considered to be the most beautiful he had seen in the whole of Africa. In the midst of all this beauty, the group heard stories of the warlike Yao clan, who had been incited by the Portuguese to attack neighbouring tribes and carry off captives to be sold into slavery. This did little to improve Livingstone's opinion of slave traders.

Livingstone had to return south for provisions before making his third and final journey up the Shire River in search of the great lake. He was suffering from dysentery and chronic haemorrhoids, and strongly suspected the camp cook of poisoning the mulligatawny soup. As ever, he continued undeterred. On 17th September, 1859, he did at last reach Lake Nyasa (now Lake Malawi) and became the first white explorer to gaze upon its shimmering waters. In the early evening the group spread their blankets under the hanging roots of an enormous banyan tree, and slumped down exhausted as the sun dipped behind the great rampart of Dedza Mountain.

Livingstone continued his work in Africa, exploring the watersheds of the Nile, Congo and Zambezi rivers. No word of him filtered out of the interior for several years and it was rumoured that he had died. The New York Herald commissioned the journalist Henry Norton Stanley to find him.

It was some twelve years after the discovery of Lake Nyasa that the famous meeting took place between Livingstone and Stanley. They met at Ujiji on the shores of Lake Tanganyika on 10th November 1871. Stanley recalled:

'I pushed back the crowds, and, passing from the rear, walked down a living avenue of people, until I came in front of the semicircle of Arabs, in the front of which stood the white man with the grey beard ... I would have run to him, only I was coward in the presence of such a mob – would have embraced him, only, he being an Englishman, I did not know how he would receive me; so I did what cowardice and false pride suggested was the best thing – walked deliberately to him, took off my hat, and said: 'Dr. Livingstone I presume?'

'Yes', said he with a kind smile, lifting his cap slightly. I replaced my hat on my head, and he puts on his cap, and we both grasp

hands, and I said aloud: 'I thank God, Doctor, I have been permitted to see you.' He answered, 'I feel thankful that I am here to welcome you.'

After six months of telling people we were English cyclists riding mountain bikes around the southern hemisphere, we were getting a little bored with recounting our story. There in the bar we invented a game of ad lib. This was a bit of harmless fun, which involved one of us spinning a yarn with the idea of putting the other in as tricky a situation as possible, and then watching him try to talk his way out of it. Hopefully, it would entertain the locals and give us a break from our cycling story. Andy started the game.

'Well, actually we're travelling actors from Finland,' he told a mixed group of businessmen and prostitutes at the bar. 'We're on a six month tour of East Africa as members of the Finnish Company of Wandering Thespians.'

I listened to this with growing unease. I knew any moment now he was going to drop me in it.

'My friend Sven here does an excellent Macbeth soliloquy. Would you like to hear it?'

'Oh yes, Macbeth!' one of the drinkers exclaimed, 'Let us hear it.' The whole group turned to me in expectation.

'Oh yes, splendid', I stalled, 'Macbeth soliloquy, yes fine.'

'Thanks Brown', I thought, *'I'll have you for this.'*

'Okay, here we go. Macbeth: Is this a bottle I see before me? Out! Out! Damned spirit.' At this point I stabbed my chest with an empty bottle of *'Green'* and went down on one knee in the first throes of an epic death. 'And once more into the breach dear wildebeest!' I gasped and finally expired on the floor of the bar. This was as good as I could come up with under the circumstances.

Amazingly the Malawians loved it and started clapping and shouting, clearly not understanding a word I had said but enjoying the melodramatics all the same, as I shamelessly hammed it up.

'Beautifully, beautifully. Give us more!' one of them shouted.

'Okay, you want more, well my friend Olaf here', I said pointing to Andy, 'does a marvellous Hamlet. Don't you Olaf?'

'Hamlet! Good one,' Andy said raising both eyebrows. 'Of course, my favourite: Alas poor moose! I knew him Horatio. Untimely ripped from his mother's womb.' He really began to fly now, voice booming – Olivier at his best. 'When shall we three meet again? In thunder, lightning or rain? When the hurley-burly's done, when the beer's drunk and won.' With that 'Olaf' dramatically downed an entire bottle of *'Green'* to great cheers and slid down the bar.

The evening became even more bizarre as Andy, still in the guise of a travelling Finnish actor, began talking to a woman at the bar.

'Where are the other actors?' the woman asked.

'They are sleeping in a wooden caravan in the town square,' Andy told her. 'I have to buy food for my actor friends. What do you think I can buy for them?'

'I have a pig that I will sell to you,' she said.

'And how big is this pig?' Andy asked.

'This pig is this big,' she said, indicating an imaginary beast which came up to her knees.

'What is the name of this pig?'

'This pig has no name.'

'Then I shall call the pig, Ronald,' declared Andy . 'How much for Ronald?

'For this pig Ronald it will cost twenty kwacha.'

Andy shook his head, 'This pig Ronald is very expensive. I will give you no more than fifteen kwacha for him'

'Fifteen kwacha!' A large lady, in a flowery dress, bellowed in disgust from the other end of the bar. 'I will give you ten kwacha only for this pig!'

'What! This fine pig, ten kwacha!' shouted the first lady. 'You are cutting my throat!'

'Twelve kwatcha, no more,' retorted the second lady angrily.

I rubbed my eyes and looked around me for the pig which seemed to be very much alive and well. The argument about Ronald's value raged on in the bar, as Andy and I quietly slipped away.

From Karonga we pedalled south following the fertile shoreline of Lake Malawi, source of food to many native people. We were heading towards Cape Maclear at the southern end of the lake where we planned to have a few days rest before tackling Zambia.

Andy and I rode side by side through a land rich in crops – tea, coffee and mangoes. It seemed that we were waving and answering greetings every few minutes throughout the day. We stopped to buy mangoes and bananas and to chat to friendly Malawians. These people had little in the way of possessions but were rich in spirit and contentment, their lives untouched by the stress and greed of Western culture.

As I pedalled amongst these happy people a memory from long ago stirred my thoughts. A picture of a beautiful young girl I had once known formed clearly in my mind. She had long, silky chestnut hair, smooth skin and a cute slightly turned up nose. I remembered how we had been close for a couple of years before I had gone away to college and she had moved down to London. I did not see her for several years until she looked me up one weekend in Shropshire. We went out for a drink and she told me about her life in London. She had met a rich businessman, fallen in love and got married. Life had been great for a while. She no longer had to work, had her own Mercedes sports convertible, flights to New York by Concorde and holidays on a yacht in the Caribbean. Shopping was by Amex Goldcard in Harrods and cooking by French maid.

'Sounds like a great life,' I had told her. She had shaken her head.

'It's great for a while', she had said, 'but you quickly become bored with such an empty, aimless way of life.'

'Why don't you go out and get yourself a job then?' I had asked.

'Don't think I haven't longed to, but whenever I've discussed it with my husband he just goes up the wall. You know the old male ego bit, 'no wife of mine is going to go out to work' and all that bullshit.

Now he even refuses to discuss it. I often long for the days when I had no money and the two of us used to roam about the country having fun in my old red mini.'

In the months that followed she had grown more and more frustrated and became deeply unhappy. The conclusion had been a divorce within eighteen months.

Here was a girl who had lived a life most people dreamed of and yet the reality was, that despite all the trappings of wealth, she had come to detest it all. I knew she would have loved Malawi.

Leaving the sleepy little lakeside village of Chilumba, eighty kilometres south of Karonga, we found ourselves at the bottom of the great escarpment of the Rift Valley for the third time within a week.

Stopping at a small thatched chai shop we chatted to the owner.

'Is this hill very steep?' Andy asked him, suspecting it was the start of another huge climb.

'Oh no,' the man replied cheerfully, 'this is a somewhat moderate hill.'

I would have liked him to have joined us that afternoon as we struggled up this 'somewhat moderate hill'. We pedalled up and up for ten kilometres and gained eleven hundred metres in altitude in the hot sunshine. Personally, I would have said it was a somewhat murderous hill.

At one point I caught Andy talking to himself as we gasped and sweated our way up the hill inch by painful inch. As I drew closer I could just make out what he was saying:

'If you can keep your head when all
About you are losing theirs
And blaming it on you.
If you can trust yourself
When all men doubt you
But make allowance for
Their doubting too ...'

'It will not be long now' I thought to myself, *'until the men in white coats come to take him away. I hope when his time comes he will go quietly.'*

Andy found inspiration in Kipling's poetry and often used it when the going became really tough. I was a little less cultural in my approach and took to ranting, raving, and a form of basic Anglo Saxon poetry to keep myself going.

We stopped several times to rest on this long, long hill. As agreed all those months ago when planning in England we were determined not to push the bikes up any hills or take any lifts – that would just not be cricket old boy! At first there was a bit of a macho thing between the two of us – who could get up the hills the quickest, endure the most pain and prove something to the other. After seven thousand kilometres and two thousand three hundred and forty two hills, we had lost interest in the game.

Now we did our own thing and got to the top at whatever pace we liked but would we get off and push – *NEVER!*

As dusk fell we finally reached the top of the escarpment and lay panting and sodden with sweat by the side of the road, struggling to force air into tortured lungs. I looked up and spotted a sign on a simple brick building:

WELCOME TO C.MPONA GROCERY

FRIENDLY FOODS

Dragging my tired body across to the shop, I bought two warm Cokes from a crippled lad sitting in a wheelchair behind a rough wooden counter. Matchstick thin but seemingly oblivious to his frailty he gave me a big smile along with the drinks.

When I came out of the shop I found Andy surrounded by thirty or more children ranging from tiny tots to teenagers, all wanting him to take their photograph. Before we could get away, we had to take a dozen photos and promise to post them back to the kids.

Now began a long, slow descent to the plateau. We relished the chance to rest numb legs and cool overheated bodies. Darkness was fast approaching as we raced down a twisting ribbon of road, dark hills covered in thick vegetation rising high on either side. We found a camping site tucked away in lush grass beside a fast flowing river. This was the first time we had camped since Kilimanjaro. In Tanzania we had been adjusting to the weird and wonderful ways of the *'Dark Continent'* and had not had the confidence to pitch our tents for fear of cut-throat bandits, stampeding wildebeest and man-eating lions. As with most things, ignorance and superstition rather than reality were the source of our fears. Here in Malawi we felt quite comfortable pitching the tents by the side of the road in the middle of nowhere.

After a tasty meal of savoury mince, rice and mangoes we were treated to a magnificent natural phenomenon, as a powerful electric storm blew in and raged all around us. The clouds were a boiling cumulus. Every few seconds, great flashes of white light and forked prongs of lightning danced around the dark mountains turning black night into bright day. There was a strange absence of thunder; the whole show unfolding in eerie silence. We both lay outside on our sleeping mats deep into the night unable to tear ourselves away from this awesome display of pyrotechnics. In the back of our minds lay the fear that we could be swept away in a flash flood should a rainstorm break out but, like stubborn English fools, we stayed put regardless. In the morning the river level had risen by more than a metre and murky brown water lapped at tyres and toes.

We continued riding south for the next few days on our way to Mzuzu, passing many villages made up of twenty or thirty thatched huts, some with mud walls others fashioned from crude red bricks. As we entered each village hordes of bright-eyed, grubby kids would appear magically from every corner to skip alongside our bikes. They were always in rags but, beneath grimy clothes, the skins were glossy black and the smiles wide and white.

'*Wzungu, wzungu!* Give me ten *tambala!* (pennies),' came the chorus of shrill voices. Andy liked to stick out his hand and echo the words of the children, 'No – you give *me* ten *tambala!*'

This always confused the little beggars. 'Hey, hold on this isn't how it's supposed to happen. We get money from *wzungus*, they don't ask *us* for money!'

We usually sped past like the wind leaving them trailing and chuckling in our wake.

At the beginning of February we rode into the modern city of Mzuzu, the second largest in Malawi. We found the modest *Government Rest House* and made the acquaintance of Mister Ngoma, the night watchman. He wore the doleful expression of a mistreated bloodhound, with skin chiselled and grooved by the harshness of a lifetime of struggle. The whites of his eyes had been stained blood red adding to the hound dog effect.

'How long have you been night watchman here Mister Ngoma?' I asked him. After giving the matter considerable thought he replied, 'Er, twenty.'

'Twenty years?'

'Er ... yes.'

'So you must know this place very well by now?'

After more thought he answered, 'Er ... no.'

We stayed three nights in Mzuzu, during which time I had several chats with Mister Ngoma. Our bizarre and comical conversations delighted me simply because he was such an uncomplicated, wacky guy.

'What did you do before you were a night watchman Mister Ngoma?' I asked him on the second night.

'I am working in gold mine in South Africa.'

'That must have been hard work?'

Again deep thought, 'Er ... yes, no, no, yes. Hard work, no.'

The yes's were definite and bold, the no's regretful and hesitant.

'Why did you leave South Africa?' I asked.

He raised his right hand to display the stumps of thumb and forefinger.

'Much dangerous place,' he told me solemnly. His face was blank – the black mask of Africa behind which native people hide their emotions.

Once an African has retreated behind this mask it is almost impossible to guess what he is thinking or feeling.

'You had an accident in the mine?'

'Much accident, no more work mine.'

'Did the owners of the mine pay you any money because you could no longer work?'

'Er ... pay, money, no, yes, forty rand for finger.'

I converted this in my mind. Mister Ngoma had received about eight pounds sterling, at present rates, for the loss of his fingers. I was horrified yet fascinated.

'How much would they give you for an arm?' I asked.

'This', he pointed to his leg, 'eighty kwacha.'

'Eighty kwacha if you lose a leg?'

'This', lifting an arm, 'no this', raising the other leg, 'hundred kwacha.

Yes, no. Sixty kwacha.'

By this time we were both thoroughly confused. I decided to change the subject.

'What about family? Do you have any children?' I asked.

'Family? Children? Er ... no ... yes, five baby, no six baby, yes.'

The mask dropped and returned to the normal mournful look.

'It must be hard to feed them all?'

'Much difficult problem, much problem.'

'Is food expensive here in Mzuzu?'

'No. Much money, one bag maize, twenty kwacha.'

'Do you eat meat?'

'Yes, no, no meat. Chicken five kwacha, much money.'

'Does a night watchman get good pay?'

'Bad. Much bad pay – thirty kwacha.'

'Thirty kwacha a week?'

'Er ... yes, no, kwacha. Thirty, yes, for one month.'

Mister Ngoma worked from six in the evening until six the following morning, six days a week for the princely sum of £6 per month. Andy and I were ashamed. We had just spent the equivalent of his month's wages on dinner in the *Tropicana Restaurant* in town. We put twenty kwacha into an envelope and slipped it into his hand the following evening.

'Mister Ngoma, this is for your family. Maybe you can buy them a chicken,' I told him.

He stared blankly at the notes then at me, and a tear ran down his leathery cheek.

'Mister Ngoma please don't waste it on cigarettes and beer.'

'Cigarettes, yes ... no. Cigarettes ...'

The whole of Mzuzu had been without water or electricity for three days. Nobody could tell us why, things were just not working. We had heard a rumour that the *Mzuzu Club* had its own generator and therefore hot food and cold beer. We felt like having a night out so we headed to the club with the intention of letting off steam.

The *Mzuzu Club* was a plush colonial establishment catering for wealthy local businessmen and a variety of expatriates. I looked at Andy in the creased and faded cotton shirt he kept for 'special occasions.'

'Look at the state of us,' I laughed. 'I couldn't get into my local pub back home looking like this.'

Andy inspected my soiled, flowery shirt and grubby cotton trousers.

'What are you worried about? You've only had that shirt on for five days. The stink will clear us some space at the bar!'

Fortunately, the bar was poorly lit by candles and Mister Ngoma had, kindly, found us a bucket of cold water to wash in before we came out.

Nobody seemed to be worrying about our unusual attire.

True to expectation the beer was cold and before long I found myself talking to an attractive girl at the bar. She leaned forward and whispered softly into my ear, 'Gladys is my name, I'm from Sierra Leone. Do you want to change dollars?'

This was quite an opening to a conversation.

'My name's Tim, I'm from England. What rate will you give me?'

'England, a beautiful country. I once had a boyfriend from England. I'll give you three kwacha for one dollar.'

I was beginning to feel like some kind of double agent in a bad spy movie.

'A boyfriend in England, that's interesting. Give me four and you've got a deal.'

'I'll give you three and a half, no more.'

'Okay It's a deal.'

We went into a dark corner and I handed over a twenty dollar bill.

'Here is sixty kwacha' she said. 'We must go back to the bar and I will change a twenty kwacha note to give you the rest.'

We returned to the bar and drank another bottle of beer. I turned to talk to Andy and when I turned back to Gladys, she had melted away. So had my ten kwacha.

Andy was talking to a dumpy man in a business suit with sly darting eyes, wobbling jowls and nervous manner. His name was Sadiq.

'I am British as well,' he told Andy. His accent was Indian but the goatee beard and hooked nose were strongly Arabic.

'I was living in Croydon when I was offered a job over here. I've been here for four months and my family will join me later in the year.'

Sadiq was drinking expensive Scotch whisky by the tumbler full. He was a lonely guy.

'I can change your dollars if you want. I have good connections in this town. I know important people.'

I had had enough of money changing and was beginning to tire of Sadiq.

'Hey Tim, how do you fancy checking out the disco?' Andy had read my mind. It was strange, but having spent so much time in each other's company we were developing an almost telepathic understanding.

'Andrew,' I said, downing the dregs of my *'Green'*, 'that sounds like an excellent idea!'

The disco was in another part of the club and turned out to be good fun with local businessmen and their wives or mistresses strutting their stuff to energetic European rhythms.

I found myself standing at the bar next to a smart middle aged man in a pinstripe suit.

'Excuse me', I asked, 'could you pass my *'Green'* please?' He duly passed the bottle.

'Thank you,' I said. 'You are a gentleman.'

He seemed to be flattered by this comment, 'Oh, thank you very much and you, are you gentlemen also?' he asked.

'Yes, we certainly are gentlemen,' I told him.

'Well,' said Andy, 'we are gentlemen except when we are with the ladies.'

The man gave Andy a strange, quizzical look. 'And where did you meet these ladies who were not gentlemen?'

There really was no answer to that one.

The *Mzuzu club* closed up at midnight but we had met Douglas, the resident Disc Jockey, who was very keen that the evening should continue and insisted we go with him to another club in town. We were having fun so we agreed.

The *Apollo Club* in downtown Mzuzu may have been a little ambitious in its claim to the status of night club. Drinking and drugs den would have been a better description. It was a shack with flimsy tin walls, dirt floors, roaming prostitutes and raw blaring reggae music.

We walked into a room lit by harsh blue neon light, crates and bottles strewn everywhere. The air was thick with dope, booze and sweat. A lone dancer swayed in the middle of the dirt floor, moving sensuously to the primaeval rhythms of the night. Barefoot, clad in threadbare work trousers and yellow grime streaked singlet, the eyes glazed, fixed on some point way beyond the confines of this tinpot haven; lost in some private ecstasy. A body lay slumped in a corner and young men leaned against tin walls glaring with hostility. I was glad to be seen to be with Douglas. This was definitely not a place for whities to wander into alone unless they were willing to fight their way back out again.

'Seems like a nice place,' I said to Andy.

'Yeah, sort of place you'd bring a girl for a night out.'

'Oh well, it's all part of growing up and being British,' I told him. 'Come on let's have a beer.'

I sat on a wooden crate by the bar and ordered two *'Greens'* from the barman, who looked as if he had drunk more beer than he had sold.

'Hey man! You sittin' in ma place!' A deep voice boomed aggressively in my ear.

I turned to be confronted by a huge boulder of a man with a big, shaven cannon-ball head, shoulders like Tallboys and biceps that wouldn't have been out of place on Frank Bruno. He could have wrestled rhinos for fun.

'Oh no, I'm dead,' I thought. *'What a way to go. I can see the headlines – British cyclist has head ripped off in Malawian drink and drugs den! What will mother say?'*

I tried to reason with the boulder, 'Sorry about that mate, here it's all yours. How about a beer?' I ordered more *'Greens'* and kept on talking. It turned out that the boulder had a name, Dunstan Gansi, and was a communications engineer with the Malawian army based at Moyde Barracks here in Mzuzu. He was also a nice guy.

'Sorry 'bout that shit man,' he said after a couple more *'Greens'*. 'I do not care for white people. I was in your country a few years ago, in Oldham, on an army training course for radio communications. The people were not friendly, not friendly at all, just ignored me wherever I went. I did not like your country.'

'I'm sorry,' I told him, remembering our friend Elvis back in Tanzania, who had also had a similar experience in England. I felt embarrassed that my countrymen could be so inhospitable.

'It's okay man, I understand,' he said, 'they do not like the black skin over there.'

'It's not like that everywhere in England,' I told him. 'Where I come from people don't really worry what colour you are. Lots of my friends are black. I don't even think about it.'

'You have a good way of thinking my friend,' he said. 'You are welcome in my country. Let us take more *'Green'*.

'Yes, more *'Green'*. Sounds like a good idea.' It was certainly a much better idea than being kicked around the dance floor. I turned to see how Andy was getting on. He was nearby having a chat to a young guy with vacant looking, bloodshot eyes. I tuned into their conversation, listening to Andy jabbering on.

'Yes, but I told Margery when she put the serving hatch outside that you can't teach a dinosaur Swahili once it has visited Hawaii.'

What on earth was he drivelling on about? I listened to a little more of this gibberish.

'I have often wondered why German elves insist on cooking sandals without rabbit sauce!' he continued.

What really amazed me was the youth actually seemed to be following these strange ramblings and was joining in with his own comments.

'Germans ... yes. Sandals ... mmm. Rabbits ... there are too many, too many, aah.'

Andy and I staggered out of the *Apollo Club* at some ungodly hour, mission accomplished. We had succeeded in letting off steam after the hard pedalling of the last few weeks. It did seem that since entering Malawi there had been more steam-letting than cycling. In the morning we would suffer with bad heads as payment for our night of fun. It would be worth it.

The following morning we went in search of the money-changers of Mzuzu. Gladys's cash was not going to last long. There was a black market for American dollars in Malawi but it was not as widespread, or as easy to find, as it had been in Tanzania.

Our first port of call was our friend Sadiq in his chaotic little shop in the centre of town. He seemed to be selling a little bit of everything and a lot of nothing. The goods on sale ranged from cheap imported china tea sets to old computers and car tyres. The whole place was disorganised and badly presented. We found Sadiq sweating in the back of the shop amongst a jumble of typewriters and wheelbarrows. He looked as if he may have overdone it on the whisky the night before.

'Good morning Sadiq,' I greeted him.

'Hello my friends,' he answered warily.

'We thought we'd take you up on your offer of changing some dollars,' I told him.

'Ah, yes, well,' he stuttered. 'You have come at a bad time my friends.

I do not have much money here at the moment.'

'I see, so how about the important people you know' I asked, 'would they be interested in changing money?'

It turned out he knew one important person – the manager of the *Mzuzu Club* which he frequented every night of the week. We tried our luck with the manager and were not exactly surprised when he refused to have anything to do with us and had us escorted off the premises.

Next on our list was the central shopping area which was full of shops run by fat, prosperous Indians. The story was much the same in every shop:

'We are not changing dollars at this time. It is too dangerous, the police are arresting people and causing much trouble. Be careful with the police, they will surely put you in prison if they find you changing dollars.'

We spent another couple of fruitless hours searching before we found a small restaurant on the outskirts of town. The owner was reluctant at first but eventually agreed to change our dollars at twice the official bank rate. This made the last few hours seem much less of a waste of time. We ordered a pot of tea to celebrate the deal and sat down at a table next to a young lad.

He smiled.

'Hello, how are you?' he greeted Andy.

'Hello, I am fine thanks and you?' Andy replied.

'I too am fine.'

Most Malawians are taught English in school and the standard greeting they learn is: 'Hello, how are you,' to which the standard reply is:

'Fine thanks, how are you?'

The young lad looked to me, 'And you my friend, how are you?'

'Well actually', I told him, 'I'm tired and hungry if you really want to know.'

The lad looked perplexed and turned back to Andy, 'Your friend, he does not speak English?'

'No, he is Chinese,' joked Andy.

'Ah, Chinese,' he seemed to accept this answer. 'So my friend, you must teach him English as soon as possible.'

'Yes, I must,' said Andy. 'Perhaps you could help me.'

'Oh yes, I must help,' replied the boy sternly.

10 Half-Way around the world – Tim

The dawn rays of the sun touched the tent and the heating process began. I was already sweating softly inside my tiny cocoon. It was becoming an oppressive, stinking prison from which I had to escape. Throwing off my sleeping bag, damp with night sweat, I thrust my head out of the flysheet and gulped in a lung-full of sweet morning air.

For the past two days we had been pedalling south from Mzuzu. Progress had been slow at first as the road undulated through a series of thickly forested hills. We were aiming to cover ninety kilometres each day on our way south towards Lilongwe, the capital of Malawi.

There was no sign of movement from Andy's tent. He was obviously catching up on much needed beauty sleep. I made a start on the daily morning chores, mixing milk powder and oats and brewing sweet, green tea. I cut a loaf of bread into thick white doorstops and smothered them with strawberry jam and peanut butter.

Tuning to the World Service on our tiny short wave radio, I listened to *Focus on Africa*. It was a familiar catalogue of bad news – civil war raging in Somalia, attacks on government troops in Mozambique, suppression of democracy in Algeria and anti-government rallies in Nairobi. Never a day passed without reports of civil unrest, disease, famine and war from some part of this massive, troubled continent.

By now Andy had come out of his coma and set to work filtering water scooped from the nearby river. It never ceased to amaze me that muddy brown river water could be magically transformed into clean drinking water simply by pumping it through our filter. In under an hour we had eaten breakfast, packed up all the kit and pushed the bikes through long dry grass back onto the road

The first hour on the bikes was always tough: muscles cramped, tight and heavy. We rarely talked at this time as we struggled to loosen up our bodies and tune ourselves mentally into the day. I had become acutely aware of the need for harmony between mind and body. If the body was not fit and healthy then this type of relentless exercise would find it out. Mental preparation was crucial to keep our motivation week after week, travelling through strange landscapes and difficult conditions. We had three thousand kilometres in front of us before reaching the coast of Namibia, a distance I was finding difficult to cope with. We gave ourselves goals to keep up morale – thirty kilometres and stop for a brew, ninety kilometres and camp, five hundred kilometres and take a day's rest. We found it much healthier for the mind to think in terms of small, achievable targets that frequently arrived.

One morning on the road from Mzuzu to Lilongwe Andy came up with some important data.

'This morning', he said with an air of great authority, 'we will reach the halfway point around the world.'

'Is that right?' I said.

'Seven thousand, four hundred and fifty seven kilometres or approximately four thousand, five hundred miles of cycling from Sydney.'

'That's incredible, Andy', I told him, 'and I suppose now you're going to tell me how many pedals we've done.'

'Ahha! Funny you should say that,' he said with a big, smug grin.

'I've worked that out to be two million, five hundred and sixty three thousand revolutions, give or take a couple!'

Halfway around the world turned out to be the middle of nowhere. A lonely spot in the bush with little to recommend it. Just up the road a large black road sign read:

LILONGWE – 160 KM

This was all that marked this major milestone on our journey. We propped our bikes up against the sign and shook hands.

'So we've made it halfway then', I said. 'What do you think our chances are of going all the way?'

'It's very interesting you should ask that', he laughed, 'because by my calculations I reckon the chances are somewhere in the region of two hundred and twenty three to one, against.'

Back on the bike I tried to get my mind around the fact that we were approximately half way through our journey. I retraced the route across Australia visualising faces, restaurants, bars and mile upon mile of lonely, straight road. We had already pedalled an impossibly long way and yet here we were only half way. We had expended so much energy, courage and determination to get this far but knew the worst was yet to come over the coming weeks and months in Africa. Could we really make it? Surely something would go wrong soon; our luck had been just too good to last. I had a mental picture of myself swimming way out in the middle of a vast, black ocean. A sign stuck out of the top of a large, gently swaying buoy:

HALF WAY AROUND THE WORLD
MALT SHOVEL 7,500 KM WEST.

I swam on slowly in darkness around the huge buoy and started heading back the way I had come. On the horizon I could make out a tiny pin prick of light, almost invisible. I was on my way, on the long, long journey home. It's sink or swim time. Come on, you've always been a swimmer. The picture faded. I put my head down and started to push the pedals just a little harder.

The road was black asphalt, level and smooth, solidly built by Europeans, unlike many we had travelled in Tanzania which resembled war zones rather than highways with their ruts and pot holes. On this good road surface, with muscles beginning to loosen, the pace picked up. Sweat began to fill eyebrows, trickle into eyes and plaster T-shirts to backs.

We were trundling along now at twenty-five kilometres per hour across a flat plain past dense banana groves, fields of bright yellow maize and lush green pastures. Malawi is blessed with a more temperate climate than Tanzania due to the presence of the lake, which has great influence on the weather.

A distant figure waved at us from a maize field. It was a woman who had been toiling in the fields as we approached. She was standing waist deep in golden maize, dressed in a bright yellow cotton dress with a splash of red cotton wrapped around her head.

I thought of old friends, Wink, Honk, and Pasc. I tried to picture their faces and work out where they might be and what they could be doing at that particular moment. I thought of Phyl and whether our relationship could stand these months apart and how things would be when I finally returned home. I wondered how the lads at the rugby club were doing? What month were we in? February. Ah yes, the month of snow and rain, training and playing in six inches of mud. No thank you! *'You must be getting old Garratt'*, I thought, *'you used to love all that stuff.'*

'Another twenty k's and we can stop for a brew,' Andy's voice brought me back to reality and saved me from further mental ramblings.

We pedalled on into the warm afternoon sun, grunting and panting up the hills, freewheeling and gasping for air down the other side. After fifty kilometres we leant the bikes against a shady palm tree and had lunch. I pulled out the pots and pans. Andy produced the stove and kerosene bottle.

We settled down on our sleeping mats with a bowl of chicken soup and pasta and listened to a play on the radio. Christopher Columbus was having a hard time of it with the natives as well as an ear bashing from the Queen of Spain. Before long I had dozed off, contentedly, in the cool shade of a banana tree. Ah the simple things in life!

The last hour's riding was always the hardest: keeping tired muscles turning the pedals, finding the rhythm, and the flow, changing down the gears for the steep hills, keeping it all going – only a few more k's now. We passed the eighty kilometre mark, time to think about finding water and a camping spot.

My cyclometre now read ninety kilometres; the day's work was done, another small goal achieved. We pulled the bikes off the road and started searching for a suitable bush camp. This day we were lucky. We had reached the Beo River, and slumped down on the banks amongst the long, dry grass, out of sight of the road and oblivious to snakes. Andy found some classical music on the radio and we sat side by side watching a huge, dying orange sun sinking slowly into golden fields of maize. Sunlight danced across a slow river to the soothing accompaniment of a Chopin piano concerto.

We made tea, intending to wait for dark before putting up tents. It was not long before we were disturbed by three young men who magically appeared from the long grass. I stood up quickly and took the initiative.

'*Muli bwange,*' I greeted them, shaking their hands and putting on my friendliest smile.

'Hello,' said the leader of the group in English.

'We are from England and we are cycling through your beautiful country.' I could see Andy wince at this piece of sycophantic rubbish. Amazingly it had the desired effect.

'You are liking our country?' asked one of the men.

'Oh yes, we like Malawi very much. It is a fine country with friendly people,' I told him.

'That is good', said the leader, 'but why are you resting here? We are farmers and this is the land of our village.'

'Well, we have ridden our bicycles for fifty miles today. We are tired and we wish to sleep here tonight.'

'You must stay in Beo, in *Government Rest House,*' one of the farmers told me.

'It's okay, we have tents to sleep in so we don't need a rest house.'

'What is tents?' the leader asked.

'They are small houses made from material which we can build and sleep in for the night. In the morning when the sun comes up we will take them down and cycle towards Lilongwe.'

'White people always sleep in the town,' the leader persisted.

'We like to sleep outside,' I told him. 'Look, we have everything we need here.' I showed him our stove, food and cooking pans. 'We really don't want to have to pedal all the way back to Beo. We would be very happy if you would allow us to stay here. We shall respect your land and leave when the sun rises in the morning.'

The group of men moved away to the banks of the river to talk amongst themselves. They returned a few minutes later and the leader gave me a solemn look.

'Very well', he said, 'you may rest here tonight but be careful of the crocodiles.'

With this they turned and disappeared once more into the long grass. Andy looked at me in alarm. 'Crocodiles!' he exclaimed. 'What bloody crocodiles?'

Once the village delegation had gone, we got on with the evening chores. Time passed quickly as Andy and I worked in harmony putting up tents, filtering water and preparing the meal of soya mince and cassava, washed down with steaming mugs of sweet coffee.

As usual the camp conversation was of distances, routes, people and places. Some from the past; some yet to come. The sun had long since disappeared when we lay back in the long grass to stare up into a star-bright sky. A few bats flitted around our camp site and the rhythmic sound of drums drifted over us from the nearby village. I felt intoxicated with peace and contentment until the mosquitoes started to whine around my ears and the night began to chill. It was time for bed. It had been fourteen hours since starting out that morning. Now it was time to sleep and rest tired bodies in preparation for the process to begin again with tomorrow's sun.

It was another hundred kilometres from the campsite on the Beo River, south to Lilongwe, on a very good quality sealed road. As we approached the outskirts of the city, we came across a gang of forty or fifty men, all stripped down to dark brown cotton trousers, working on both sides of the road. Each man held a small, wicked looking scythe and was well muscled in both back and shoulders. Black skin glistened and shone in the bright sunshine as the gang toiled, waist deep, in long parched grass. I discovered later, these men were paid the miserly sum of three kwacha per week (£1). Labour in Africa is not in short supply and governments are not slow in exploiting this fact. A few kilometres after pedalling past this first group of labourers, we rode slowly past another band of about the same size and then another and another. An army of hundreds of workers was out tending the grass. Why bother with tractors and mowers when you can use a few hundred men to do the job for a fraction of the price?

Entering Lilongwe along *'Presidential Way'*, we rode under huge ornamental archways decked with green and white flags and colourful bunting. It really was so nice of these people. They really should not have gone to all this trouble just for two visiting British pedallers!

We stayed in a pleasant guest house on the outskirts of the city for a couple of days, before locking our bikes in a storeroom and hitching down to the southern end of Lake Malawi. This was a departure from our route, but many travellers went to this peaceful haven and we felt the need for some western company.

We arrived in Cape Maclear crammed into the back of a battered pick up truck along with a dozen Malawians, all of us sitting on bags of maize. It was a long and rough thirty minute ride.

'Good morning sir,' said a youth as I jumped down from the truck.

'Do you require nice room by beach?'

'No thanks,' I told him. 'We have a tent.' I was in the defensive mode I always adopted on arriving in a new place – trust nobody and accept nothing until you have had time to look around and see what the place was all about.

'Ah, you have tent!' The youth gave me a brilliant white smile and continued undeterred. 'Then I can show you best camping place in whole of Malawi.'

'Maybe,' I told him and looked at him properly for the first time. He was a fine looking boy, regular features and the muscular, V-shaped body of a middle weight boxer. I judged him to be about sixteen years old. 'What is your name?' I asked.

'My name is Amman,' he said. 'And this is my friend Arran.' He indicated another boy of similar age who had been hustling other people.

'We can find you room at Mister Stevens',' said Amman.

I remembered this was the place recommended by two English lads back in Karonga. We had been told of another quieter spot which would suit us better.

'Do you know the *Golden Sands* campsite?' Andy asked him.

'Yes *Golden Sands* is very good – less people than here and very pleasant beach. If you like we take you there.'

There was something about this lad I liked. He seemed to have achieved the happy balance between helping and hustling.

'Okay, let's go then,' I told him.

The lads took our panniers, balancing them on their heads as we set off through the village, thick, soft sand sucking at our boots. The blue waters of the lake stretched away to the right as we passed stoutly built thatched huts and the occasional rough brick building. Fat, naked little kids chased each other amongst the huts; their thick limbs and chubby black backsides radiating a healthy sheen. Scabby dogs skulked and roamed the village looking guilty and down trodden; much the same as scabby dogs everywhere. Groups of women sat in front of their huts, chattering happily, suckling infants from glossy breasts. In front of some huts lay old grey tarpaulins on which lines of small silver fish dried in the afternoon sunshine.

The village was built on the very edge of Lake Malawi and there was evidence everywhere of a fishing culture. Coarse fishing nets, fashioned from rope and nylon, hung between huts. Old men sat cross-legged in shady corners repairing damaged nets. On the beach lay heavy dugout canoes, the most valued possession of these people, vital for transport as well as for catching food. Each one was about twenty feet long and capable of seating six or seven people. Whilst we walked I chatted with Amman.

'Do you go to school Amman?' I asked.

'Ah, school. Yes sometimes,' he said. 'But it is expensive to buy books and uniform. Maybe I go next year and become doctor.'

'It will take many years of study to be a doctor,' I said.

'Then maybe I will be engineer,' he said cheerfully. 'School is necessary but I can make money here, working for travellers like you and mister Andrew.'

I asked him about the government and the politics of the country.

'It is not good to talk of such things,' he said, suddenly becoming serious. 'There are people who spy for the government and we have big troubles with the police if we talk with you.'

This was a common fear throughout Malawi. It was almost impossible to get a Malawian to talk about politics and, in particular, about the president, Doctor Hastings Banda.

Britain declared Nyasaland, as it was then known, a protectorate in 1891 and introduced tea and coffee plantations which grew quickly and prospered using native labour. The increasing use of forced African labour on white settler plantations lead to unrest amongst the Malawians.

Opposition to British colonial rule surfaced in the southern highlands and became a serious threat in the 1950s. More and more land was being expropriated by the British, a hut tax was introduced and traditional slash-and-burn methods of agriculture discouraged. As a result, increasing numbers of Africans were forced to seek work on the white settler plantations or became migrant workers in Rhodesia and South Africa. By the 1950s, one hundred and fifty thousand Africans were leaving the country every year.

It was at this time that the Nyasaland African Congress was formed to oppose colonial interference in traditional agricultural methods. Support for the Congress was limited until Doctor Hastings Banda was invited to return home and take over the leadership. By this time, Banda had spent forty years abroad in the USA and Britain studying and practising medicine.

On his return to Nyasaland, Banda was so successful in whipping up support that, a year after he took over, the British were forced to declare a state of emergency and threw Banda and other activists into jail, suppressing all opposition and killing more than fifty Africans in the process.

Opposition continued to gather pace to such an extent that in 1961 the colonial authorities had to release Banda and grant the country independence. Banda's Malawi Congress Party swept to victory in the elections that followed, and Malawi gained independence in July 1964.

Although he gained power through the democratic process, it was clear from the beginning that Banda had no intention of relinquishing that power. He demanded his ministers declare allegiance to him. Rather than do this many of them resigned and went into exile. Having now dealt with the opposition, Banda strengthened his dictatorial powers by having himself declared *'President for Life'*.

Thousands of political prisoners languished in Malawi's jails, and as Amman had told us spies and informers were still a reality. Criticism of the President was considered treasonable and dealt with savagely.

Whilst we were in Cape Maclear, a leader of an opposition party returned to Malawi after years of exile in Zambia. He was arrested before his feet had touched the runway and whisked away by security police in front of the cameras of the world's press. Banda's spokesman told waiting journalists, *'...Any person opposing the President can expect to be fed to the crocodiles.'*

We found the *'Golden Sands'* at the far end of the village. It was a quiet spot with a clean, beach of white shale. The campsite was spread out amongst shady trees, but we managed to get a good deal on a *rondaval* (circular beach hut) and booked in for a few days of rest and recuperation.

'What about tomorrow mister Tim?' Amman asked. 'Would you like canoe trip? If you wish Arran and I get canoe and take you fish and swim. We show you best beautiful island in Lake Malawi.' This boy was so willing I did not have the heart to put him off.

'Okay Amman. If you can get a canoe come for us in the morning and we will discuss a price.'

'Very cheap sir,' he said. 'Best price in village.'

'Yes, I'm sure it will be,' I said, having difficulty suppressing a smile.

Andy spotted a small, yellow tent and a touring bicycle propped up against a tree. We decided to investigate as we were always keen to meet fellow cyclists and swop stories. As we got closer to the tent I could see somebody inside.

'Hello, anyone home?' Andy called out. A girl's head appeared.

'Hi, we're cyclists,' I said. 'We saw your bike and came across to say hello.'

'Oh, hi!' she said in a soft American accent. 'How are you guys? I've got malaria.' Suzanne was from California. She was painfully thin, with long bony limbs, very fair skin and long platinum blonde hair tied back in a pony tail. She was deathly pale and had the deliberate, slow movements of a very sick person.

'I've been here for three weeks now,' she told us in her soft West Coast drawl. 'I'm trying to get my strength back so I can carry on cycling. I caught malaria in Tanzania six weeks ago and I've been very weak. I sleep a lot – sometimes eighteen hours a day and there are times when I don't know what planet I'm on. It's like being high on grass for days on end.'

Suzanne had suffered more than her fair share of bad luck through Africa. She had cycled all the way through Europe and planned to ride down to South Africa.

'Before I got sick I had a big crash in Tanzania,' she told us. 'I was going very fast downhill, my foot slipped off the pedal and the chain wheel cut into the back of my leg. I had to spend two weeks in a missionary hospital before I could carry on.'

'How do you find travelling alone as a woman in Africa?' Andy asked.

'Well, they think I'm crazy but I don't really mind. We're all crazy in California anyway. Lots of the women ask me what I've done with my husband and children.'

Suzanne had very nearly died from her bout of malaria. I was amazed at her determination to continue with her trip, even though she had been so desperately ill. So far we had been incredibly lucky with our own health. I silently prayed for our luck to hold.

Andy chatted to Suzanne during the afternoon when she was not dozing. In the early evening he came back to the *rondaval* with a proposition.

'I've been thinking,' he said.

'Oh yes,' I said, wondering what new scheme he had thought up now.

'What do you think about Suzanne riding along with us for a while?'

'Well, she's very weak Andy, and I don't think she's in any shape to ride for a long time yet.'

'We could wait a few days for her to recover. She wants to ride through Zambia, the same as us, and that's not a place for a girl on her own.'

'As far as I see it,' I told him, 'we are just about on schedule to reach Swakopmund in the middle of April, if we can keep up the pace we've been going. That means we will need to average ninety kilometres a day. I really can't see Suzanne riding five kilometres a day the way she looks at the moment.'

'I suppose you're right,' said Andy, 'but you know me – always a sucker for a pretty damsel in distress.'

As it turned out, Suzanne had her own plans anyway and, by the time we were ready to move, she had decided to pedal towards Lilongwe at her own pace, to regain some of her fitness.

The sun had not long been up when Amman came knocking on our door. He was wearing a freshly laundered white T-shirt and a pair of cool, mirrored sunglasses. The T-shirt read *'On On ... 650th Durban Hash Run.'*

He looked more like a successful young business executive on vacation than a poor village boy.

'Good morning mister Tim,' he greeted me. 'It is beautiful morning for canoe journey.'

'Hello Amman, isn't it a little early yet?' I said, screwing my eyes up against the early morning sunshine.

'No, no, it is best go very early. Fishes, they are hungry and wait for you to catch them.' he told me enthusiastically.

I had to hand it to him, he was a good salesman. I could see him doing well selling canoe trips down the River Severn back home in Shropshire.

'Okay, Amman. So you have managed to get hold of a canoe then?'

'Oh yes sir, best canoe in village. Also swimming masks for you and mister Andrew so you see fishes in water before you are eating them.'

'Thanks! That's very thoughtful of you,' I said. 'It will be nice to see what we are going to be eating for lunch. So how much is this canoe trip of yours going to cost us?'

'Very good price. We have paid a man ten kwacha for canoe and another man two kwacha for swimming masks. We have bought food to eat with fishes for five kwacha. This makes seventeen kwacha. Me and my friend Arran, we do not need much wages for very hard work of paddling canoe, catching fish and cooking dinner – let me say five kwacha each. This makes very moderate price of twenty seven kwacha or thirty kwacha if you think it is very good journey.'

'Oh you want a bonus as well?' I laughed.

'This is custom in Malawi, if men do good work.'

'I'm sure it is,' I laughed. 'I'll tell you what Amman, we'll give you twenty kwacha for the trip.'

'Twent- five kwacha and bonus if it is good trip.'

'Twenty kwacha and maybe a bonus,' I told him, enjoying the friendly haggling.

'Okay mister Tim, twenty two kwacha and a bonus – this is a deal?'

'All right, it's a deal.'

Arran and Amman sat at the front and back of the canoe which had been hollowed from a single large tree trunk. Andy and I squeezed our legs into the narrow opening that ran from one end of the canoe to the other and had to sit rather awkwardly on the side. The two Malawian lads paddled the vessel with great energy and skill and we were soon out in the deeper water of the lake. Amman stopped the canoe.

'Now is time to fish,' he said, handing us roughly made handlines.

After an hour's peaceful fishing, we had caught half a dozen small fish between us.

'Okay, this is enough fishes to cook,' Arran told us and we paddled on, this time with Andy manfully working one of the carved wooden paddles. Half an hour later we reached a small, uninhabited island two or three kilometres from the main shoreline.

'This is beautiful island where we cook fishes and you swim,' said Amman.

We tied the canoe to a tree and the two lads set about building a fire on the beach using drift wood. Andy and I swam in the lake using the masks that Amman had brought along. It was like swimming in a vast tropical fish tank amongst a million brilliantly coloured fish; a quite unique experience. I felt like Jacques Cousteau on his holidays.

We spent the afternoon chatting, eating tasty grilled Chomba fish with salad and basking in the sun in between dips in the lake. Dusk was gathering over the lake when we paddled back, stopping on the way to catch our dinner. After half an hour Andy, bored with fishing, handed me his specs and dived into the darkening waters, eight hundred metres off shore.

Andy recalls: 'As I swam towards the beach I remembered somebody telling me there were hippos in the lake and that they came out at night. It was now completely dark. I was fifty metres from shore when something made me look behind. I froze in horror as I saw a big, dark shape following me in the water. I began to panic and splash and let out an involuntary wail of fear as I frantically swam for shore. After twenty metres I turned to see if the thing was gaining on me, it was – SHIT! It was now only ten metres away and gaining fast. I swam on expecting at any moment to feel my legs being crushed between massive jaws. I was tiring quickly and it was almost upon me now.

'Hey mister Andrew,' came a voice from above me. 'You swim like a Ninja!'
'I turned and squinted into the darkness trying to focus on the ferocious beast before realising I couldn't see properly without my specs. This wasn't a deadly hippo – it was only Tim and the lads bringing in the canoe!
"How are you going mister Andrew?" asked Amman as the canoe pulled up alongside.
"Oh, fine, just fine thanks," I replied feeling ever so slightly foolish.'

We finally reached the shore and dragged the heavy wooden canoe up onto the beach.
'Here you go Amman, I said, handing him a ten kwacha note. 'I think you've earned your bonus.'
'Thank you mister Tim and tomorrow I will give you best barbecue in Malawi for only five kwacha.'
'Perhaps' I said. 'Come back and see us again tomorrow.'
Andy and I left them on the beach as they sorted out the canoe and fishing gear. We sauntered back through the village feeling very mellow after our day paddling on the lake. As we reached

the far end of the village I could make out two figures lurking in the shadows thirty metres ahead. They were silhouetted against the moonlight at the end of a dark tunnel of trees. I stopped on the path and turned to Andy.

'Hello, could be a bit of trouble here,' I whispered.

'Yeah looks like it,' he whispered back. 'Keep on your toes mate.'

We continued to walk slowly down the tunnel which pressed in on us. As we approached the end of the passageway two muscular youths stepped out, blocking the path.

'Good evening gentlemen.' Andy greeted them using his best BBC English accent. 'And what can we do for you?'

The larger of the youths stepped forward, within touching distance. I could now see his face, it would have been impossibly black but for the dull white gleam of the eyes.

A burst of adrenaline fizzed through my body. *'Okay, here we go',* I thought, *'Andy will have to deal with that one and I'll sort out his mate.'*

'Hey man,' the larger youth said in a soft, sinister voice. 'You got laundry needs doing?'

It was difficult to leave the tranquillity of Cape Maclear, with its friendly people and leisurely pace, but, once more our mission was calling strongly. It was time to get back on the road.

We braved the pick-up truck back to Monkey Bay and caught an old lake steamer, the *'MV Mtendere'*, which was heading north. We joined a number of other white travellers on the 2nd class sun deck and watched as the green shoreline of Lake Malawi drifted past in bright sunshine.

The steamer dropped us at Chapoka, where we had a piece of good fortune in the shape of a lift back to Lilongwe, travelling on the back of a huge, open trailer along with a dozen other hitch hikers. The journey lasted five hours and was one long, wild, bone shaking fairground ride. Andy and I held on for dear life and loved every minute.

It felt strange to be back in a large city again after our time amongst the thatched huts and wooden canoes of Cape Maclear.

Lilongwe is a busy, modern African city complete with multi-storey office blocks, golf course, burger bars and ice cream sundaes. Best of all, we discovered a modern supermarket.

It was all there – peanut butter, chocolate biscuits, marmalade, pasta, soya and soft toilet paper, just sitting on the shelves looking at us. We were like a couple of kids let loose in a sweet shop. I finally had to put my foot down when Andy started to look longingly at a bottle of scented bubble bath. After all, there *are* limits to a man's decadence!

The next couple of days were spent on our usual business in large cities. We persuaded a bank manager to let us buy cash with credit cards, set up an interview with the *Daily Times,* Malawi's national newspaper and collected our post.

Picking up post was our favourite job. We had set up a series of mail drops along our route using the poste restante system operated by most countries around the world. Communication by telephone was difficult, to say the least, and so precious letters and *'Red Cross'* parcels were our only link with family and friends back home. Andy went into the main post office to pick up letters from Phyl, Cassie, families and other friends.

'Are you one of the gentlemen travelling by bicycle for Africa?' asked the large post lady.

'Yes, that's right. How did you know?' Andy asked her.

'I saw a picture in the newspaper,' she told him.

'Oh, I see.'

She gave him a lovely smile and said, 'To ride bicycles around the world to help the people of Africa – that takes a little love I think.' She stepped forward and smothered him with an enormous hug that somehow made all the effort worthwhile.

There was one other pressing piece of business that needed attention – a visit to the dentist. I had lost a large filling, chewing on a particularly grisly piece of goat meat, back in Turkana. We had brought along an emergency dental kit as part of our medical equipment and I managed to give myself a couple of do-it-yourself fillings along the way. I did not relish the idea of visiting an African dentist but here in Lilongwe we had heard about a Seventh Day Adventists' dental surgery that would do emergency dental work at a reasonable price.

We found the surgery on the outskirts of the city. It was a slick, modern building. The practice was run by two dentists, one American, the other Swiss. The American, Bob, welcomed us.

'Good to meet you guys,' he said with a grin. 'Nice bikes. Used to do some mountain biking myself, back in the States. So how are you finding riding across Africa, pretty wild, eh?'

'Yes, it gets a bit hairy at times but so far we've been lucky,' I told him.

'Where are you headed next?' he asked.

'We plan to go into Zambia and ride west across to Victoria Falls,' I said.

'Wow!' said Bob. 'Better be careful over there. Zambia is a really wild place, not like Malawi. People get bumped off all the time over there.'

He seemed to be very cheerful about all this. I suppose he could afford to be – he was not coming with us.

'Well, the least we can do for you guys is fix your teeth up before you go,' said Bob, 'coz when you leave here there sure as hell ain't gonna be anything out there.'

I had my filling expertly replaced by Bob's very professional partner, Peter.

'How much do I owe you Bob?' I asked him in reception afterwards.

He looked at me as if I were mad.

'Absolutely nothing. Anybody crazy enough to ride through Zambia gets it for free!'

11 Too much close encounters – Andy

'Be very fast my friends', urged the customs official, in smart blue uniform and peaked cap, 'dark is coming. Soon bad men on road. You must hurry.' He took me by the arm and led me off. We had reached the border post one hour before dusk, having cycled a hundred and thirty kilometres from Lilongwe on fast, flat road. From here we still had to cycle another twenty kilometres to reach the safety of the border town, Chipata. The guard whisked us to the front of a long line of locals and a handful of white travellers who had come off a bus. One whitie complained at our special treatment, even though the bus would still be sitting there in half an hour.

Passports were quickly stamped, and we jumped back on the bikes to race the setting sun. Youths chatted in groups, hanging out beside the road. They lessened our fears by returning our greetings. The rest at Cape Maclear had been just what our bodies needed; we had eaten well, slept well and done very little else. A record day of one hundred and fifty kilometres was an encouraging return to the road.

At dusk, we found ourselves arguing with hordes of pushy money changers. They were young lads in smart jeans and baseball caps, and with an air of greed and desperation about them. They operated illegally on the forecourt of the BP petrol station in the middle of Chipata. We were tired and hungry but kept our wits about us. They were offering a ridiculous rate of exchange and we 'kicked them into touch'.

We treated ourselves to hotel beds, hot baths and lukewarm steak. This was likely to be our last opportunity for some days.

We had been led to expect hostility from the people and hundreds of kilometres of tedious bush. It is true that Zambia is not blessed with great lakes or snowy mountains, beautiful cities or famous game parks; most of the wild animals had been poached. It was also true this was one of the world's poorest countries, caught in the grip of severe drought. I felt, however, it might hold some surprises for us.

There was only one road running from southern Malawi across Zambia to the capital, Lusaka, in the west. To the south lay Mozambique.

One negative story after another had certainly given us the jitters. Adrian, an irrigation engineer I knew in Scotland, a South African car salesman in Lilongwe and Tim and Helen, the English cyclists we had met in Tanzania, had all warned strongly against crossing Zambia by bike. The car salesman had said, 'Not if someone paid me $10,000'. A journalist in Lilongwe had told me that a number of white residents had been murdered recently for no apparent reason. 'They are not like us,' he had said.

The morning after crossing the border was Tim's birthday. We each ate three breakfasts to celebrate. For once in his life Tim was overjoyed to receive a pair of socks; I had found them in a shop in Lilongwe. One of his three pairs had recently fallen in half after a severe bout of sweat poisoning.

Tim recalls: 'Family and friends had sent cards and packages to the Post Office in Lilongwe. People had gone to so much trouble. I knew they were thinking about me today, especially my mum. It brought back to me the tremendous support that was with us. I never knew a pair of underpants and a bar of chocolate could mean so much!'

Ahead of us lay eight hundred kilometres of scrub and dense bush before we would reach Lusaka. By all accounts Lusaka was not a very wise place to go anyway.

That morning in Chipata we procrastinated for as long as possible: we had more tea; wrote and posted a couple of cards; changed $100 in the bank for twelve thousand Zambian Kwatcha, a great wad of dirty notes; we checked and pumped up the tyres; adjusted breaks and gears; had a Coke; had a pee; had a chat to some locals; but then, at last, we ran out of ideas and just had to get on with it.

As usual, children happily waved and shouted 'Wzungu, Wzungu' in surprise and greeting as we passed through mud hut villages. Bare feet racing to keep up, teeth glistening in wide, chuckling smiles. Bums falling out of long dead shorts.

It is the mystery of Africa. People expect nothing more from life than hardship and struggle. They treat every blow and reminder of their impossible position with good humour. Here were two privileged white men, carrying unimaginable wealth, free as birds, able to come and go, whilst they, the village people, must stay to face poverty, sickness and drought. Yet so strong, so proud are they that, as in Tanzania and Malawi, they seemed to be welcoming us with open arms.

Balancing villagers waved as they sped past on trucks piled high with sacks of maize, imported to ease the food shortages. Every few kilometres we saw lone peasants, sitting beside the road on bundles wrapped in white linen. Their villages were far off in the bush, out of sight. As a pick-up or truck approached they would stand to flag it down. Not a big wave, or a thumb stuck out, but a subtle action; as though they were bouncing an invisible basketball.

One hundred degrees Fahrenheit reflected up off the road, (I know it was a hundred because I counted every one of them!) Beside us stood great fields of maize, each worked lovingly by hand. Now they looked sad and withered. Villagers continued to hoe forlornly. In the face of disaster they showed great courage and tenacity.

'What do you say we stop at the forty kilometre mark for some tea?' Tim suggested.

'Fine by me,' I said. A cuppa, shade and a chat with the locals would be welcome.

We pulled up outside a wooden hut on the edge of a village. I stretched my back and shoulders to relieve the strain of the morning. My shirt was soaked with sweat and hung off me like a sack. I hung the bush hat on the handlebars, removed my sun glasses and wiped the grime off my face with a dusty sleeve.

A man in his late thirties sat erect on a wooden, high-backed chair outside the hut, in the shade of the thatch. His sinewy fingers guided folds of cloth under the needle of a pedal-powered sewing machine. A drop of sweat rolled off his balding head and slid down his wide nose, falling onto the trousers he was creating. He pretended to work but kept a beady eye on us. He looked dignified in his clean white shirt and black waistcoat.

I smiled broadly, *'Moni'* (Hello) and shook his outstretched hand.

'Muli bwange?' (How are you?) he asked. A stream of fine golden dust, thrown up by the hot wind, pirouetted around the side of the hut.

'Chabwino,' (fine) I said, shielding my eyes from dust. 'Where from?' he asked in English.

'From Mombasa', I said. The tailor jerked back, the mask of disinterest broken.

'MOMBASA!! AAYYYIIIEEEEE!!' he exclaimed, almost painfully.

'NO!! NO!! NO!! It is too much far, too much far. He is not possible to bicycle to this place from Mombasa.' He was very sure of this and did not expect there to be further discussion. He could have been talking to small children.

Tim laughed and said, 'We have.'

'No you haven't.'

'We have.'

'No, you haven't,' he said chuckling and shaking his head.

'Yes.'

'Too much far, too much far' he persisted.

I could not resist this charming character, 'And you know what?' I said, 'Before Mombasa we cycled across Australia.'

'AAYYIIEE. You didn't,' he argued.

'We did.'

'No, no you didn't.'

'Yes we did.'

'It is not possible.'

Entertaining as it was, this was going nowhere.

'Can we buy some chai somewhere?' I asked.

The tailor ignored this, 'Where to?'

Reluctantly Tim said, 'Lusaka.'

'NO! AAYYIIE, no, no, no, too much far.'

'And after Lusaka we shall cycle to the coast, in Namibia,' Tim went on.

179

The tailor waggled his finger and shook his head sternly. 'NO!!' he ordered.

Tim went on, 'Then we will cycle across South America.'

He was smiling and shaking his head, 'AAYYIIE! You are too young, too young.'

We all laughed.

Tim and I went off in search of tea, leaving the tailor to his trousers. We found a little wooden chai house a short way off. In the dark hut we slowly revived with cup after cup of sweet, black tea. This was served in red plastic cups, embossed with flying ducks.

I checked the bikes. Outside the villagers were admiring the dusty black machines. The value of the bikes and kit would have set a large family up for life. They kept a respectful distance, though, not touching a thing. They counted the gears and studied the odd looking handlebars. One chap was very taken with the knobbly tyres. 'Is it a pikki-pikki?' he asked his friend.

'No a beezcaillie,' he was told with a smirk.

I turned to the young tea shop owner, 'What's a pikki-pikki?'

'It is a small motor bike. The engine goes pikki-pikki-pikki-pikki-pikki-pikki.' He paused and said flatly, 'That man is a jackass.'

Refreshed, we stepped out again into dazzling brightness, liberated the bikes and walked over to say goodbye to the tailor.

'May I buy your bicycle?' he asked.

I did not bother mentioning that it was worth over a thousand dollars. 'Well if I sold it to you, how would I cycle to Lusaka?'

He had thought of this. 'You can sit on your friend's crossbar, or run beside him.'

'Ahh, sorry, but Lusaka is too far to run, we must cycle,' I replied, swinging my leg over the saddle.

He stood and shook our hands, 'My friends I salute you. You are too brave.'

'Thank you. Why don't you come with us?' I joked, 'You sit on my crossbar.'

'AAYYYIIEEE no, no,' he shook his head in mock regret, 'I would come, but aaaah, there is a man who needs these trousers.'

A boy played his banjo. Off beat and out of tune, it was still a relief from the silence of the bush. The neck of the banjo was a long smoothed branch, kinked near the top. The strings were animal gut, tightened around rusty nails; the body an old oil can; its noise was mysterious. He sat with four friends in the patchy shade of a small thorn tree.

The village of Kampala had popped up out of thick scrub, stretching endlessly under the sapphire sky. Huts of golden thatch and parched mud walls were scattered, indiscriminately, over a wide area. Between the huts and away to the south lay fields of tall maize, lovingly tended by hand; mainly women's hands. The stalks, taller than a man, rustled in the scorching wind, bleached, colourless and dead. There would be no harvest this year. Perhaps one day these people would have access to the fancy sorghum seeds, so successful in Turkana.

The banjo boy's white, pork pie hat swayed with the rhythm of the tune. He was lanky, awkward and self conscious. We cooked our lunch of pasta and onion soup. The boys did not ask for anything. They sat and watched and listened to the music. With a whisper, one boy sent his friends into fits of laughter. We smiled to show we were not offended by being the butt of their jokes. The crowd swelled to twenty or more as women, youths and young children wandered over. We nodded a greeting at each new arrival; none spoke to us. Everybody crowded in under the tree, almost silent now.

We finished eating and started to clean the pans with sand. 'I'm going to get this pan so clean', said Tim, 'that you can eat your dinner off it.'

A woman spoke up; talking rapidly and pointing to the eastern sky. We mimed, helplessly, that we did not understand her language. This caused great hilarity. A thin lad of seventeen or so stepped forward and said in English, 'My grandmother asks if you have seen rain.' He held a big, black Chinese bicycle, his blue cotton shirt was too big and hung about him like a sack. The boy's name was Kings Steve Mbawo.

I thought for a moment and answered him slowly, 'Please tell your grandmother we thank her for the use of this land to eat and rest.' I paused while he passed this on, then continued, 'We did see rain in northern Malawi three weeks ago, but we have seen none since.' She looked solemn as Kings told her this. A low murmur ran through the crowd.

The grandmother had once been a fine looking woman. She was now hunched and loose flesh hung from her arms. Her skin was dark, wrinkled velvet. A blue cloth gathered her hair, washer-woman style. Her plain cotton blouse set off a colourful wrap-around skirt. Her name was Martha. She was well-groomed; probably a village elder. I guessed she was in her forties. Though she was less than half the age of my own grandmother, Granny Viewing, at home in Wiltshire, Martha would be considered old; to have 'reached a good age'.

Kings translated her words for us: 'We see clouds often, but they move away without breaking. Not one drop has fallen here in two months and soon the rainy season will end. Why does it not rain?' This was impossible for us to answer and I told him so. Kings Steve nodded and spoke for himself,

'Do you think it is the new Government?'

'No', said Tim, 'I don't think so. The Government cannot bring rain.

Have you heard of a thing called global warming?'

Kings nodded, 'Yes, we have heard about this. People in South Africa are poisoning the air.'

'Well, it's not only South Africa', I explained, 'it's all developed countries and many developing countries too.'

'Not Zambia,' said Kings. He was probably right. 'Why would Zambia poison the air to bring drought on its self?' He went on to blame the new Government again. 'Chiluba promised us wealth but has brought us disaster. We need Kaunda back or we will starve like in Ethiopia.'

'People must give the Government time,' I said, feeling like a marriage guidance councillor. 'They will change this country in time, but it can't happen so quickly; I am sure they will send you food.'

'Huh! If food or rain does not come to this village soon we shall all be dead.'

The drought was hitting all of southern Africa. Further south in Zimbabwe, the livestock had already started dying. Once the cattle stocks die it takes many years to restock, to raise new herds.

Millions of people could die and untold damage would be done to the economies. They might scrape through this year, but what if the unthinkable happened? What if it did not rain next year either?

'I would like to live in your country,' said Kings Steve, 'where everyone has money and food and there are many jobs.'

The dilemma, of course, is that the hopes and dreams of millions of western youths have been stolen by their own Governments. Poor housing, poor education, no jobs, no future, potential with no outlet; these afflict the whole world. Who is better off?

The new President of Zambia, Chiluba, had won the recent election, the first in 27 years. He had ousted President Kaunda with promises of economic and social reform, freedom for the people and improved education and health care. It was a landslide. *'Vote MMD and Set Yourself Free'* was his catchphrase. But the rains had failed him. Now he was fighting to feed his people, reforms took second place. Chiluba was travelling the world, searching for financial support and cheap maize. Thousands of tons of maize were to be imported from Brazil and North America, but it would take time and distribution would be difficult.

I felt helpless and embarrassed. Tim and I could do nothing for these people. The west seemed so far away, the remoteness of this place crept over me. I reached out and grasped a maize stork. The cob had not been far from ripe when it had died. Now it broke away and collapsed in my hand. We offered the grandmother some dried pasta. She studied it and laughed. Kings Steve said, 'Thank you, we only eat maize. You must keep this for your journey.' The bikes were quickly packed up and we all shook hands. As we pushed onto the road Kings Steve came after us.

'You will write to me please?' he asked and we exchanged addresses, as we had with ten or more Zambians already.

'Good luck,' we called feebly and left them. It was impossible not to be profoundly moved by these people and their plight.

Late one afternoon we stopped at a small, white post, looking like any other small, white post. A crowd of young men streamed out of a hut to see what these strange white men were doing.

Studying his bicycle computer Tim declared 'This post is half way across Africa.' None of the men had paid any attention to the post before, but now they saw it in a whole new light.

'This post!' somebody exclaimed, examining it. We were all photographed standing beside it, laughing and jostling. Distance markers on our map told us we had pedalled two thousand four hundred and twenty-one kilometres from Mombasa in a total of forty-six days.

We rode on west into the descending sun, the colour of cherries and custard. Bush hats pushed low over our eyes against the glare. We came upon a small boy walking along the road. Two tiny sisters trotted behind. He was about four years old, his clothes were in their mid-forties. The trio were off on some important mission in their babyland of the Zambian bush.

On seeing us the boy stopped; the girls stopped, so we stopped. He faced us, solid and brave as a lion; tight lips and gigantic dark eyes.

To prevent accidents, a round hole had been cut in the front of his filthy shorts. This allowed his little willy to hang free. On his right foot he wore a big, green wellington boot. The left foot was bare. On his head was a colourless baseball cap bearing the words *'The Hour Has Come'*, a relic of the recent election campaign; daddy was an MMD supporter.

I said, *'Moni,'* softly. The girls sank behind their brother.

He remembered his English lessons and proudly greeted us, 'Good morning teacher.'

Although it was nearly six in the evening we replied together, 'Good Morning'.

He was satisfied with his handling of the meeting and so continued on his journey, the girls followed in his wake giggling. We were transfixed.

A little way up the road he turned and called, 'Goodbye *Wzungu'* We laughed and waved back, cycling on slowly. They stood there, waving and giggling, until we had waved our last goodbye and pedalled out of sight. There is a phrase that flies about among the aid workers: 'In Africa the big trick is to live to be five years old.' What chance would these little ones have in the approaching famine?

Burned-out shells of buses and trucks lay pitifully abandoned beside the road; rolled there by the army after the Renamo massacre. A rotting monument to the murder of one hundred and twenty innocents. Now the bush was claiming them. Nature was trying to put the horror and the loss into the past. We cycled by silently.

Here the road ran close to the Mozambique border, a theoretical line in the bush only ten kilometres to the south. The previous night we had stayed at the village of Katchalola, in the only hotel on the route to Lusaka. A cold bath and a bed had been very welcome.

Heaving over a succession of short, steep hills, the sun beat down without remorse. We plodded on, hour after hour, not daring to stop to make tea. This was bandit country, an area to get through and look back on; not somewhere to actually be.

We started to climb yet another hill, dense greenery pushed in from both sides. One hundred metres ahead, figures filed out of the trees, six, no seven youths. They formed a cordon across the road and started to walk slowly down the hill towards us. Each held a *panga*, a long bush knife, nonchalantly pointing to the ground. The lads oozed menace. Dirty, cotton shirts hung out scruffily; a couple wore porkpie hats. We stopped together, Tim and I, wary.

'What do you think?' I asked. So was this to be it? The moment we had dreaded since the thing began? The headline hitting murder – or disappearance – bodies in shallow graves in the bush. I wonder how it feels to be hacked to death. Did I remember to write a will?

'We could turn back', Tim said thoughtfully, 'but it'll be a thousand kilometre detour.'

We would have to return to Lilongwe, then all the way back north through Malawi and cross Zambia on the northeast/ southwest road. It was unthinkable.

I added, 'Or we could go back to Katchalola and catch a bus through here.' We both knew that would be cheating, though, breaking our rules. The rest of the expedition would be for nothing. This too was unthinkable. Or we could plough on and take our chances.

Tim and I held each other's gaze and grinned mischievously.

'It might be nothing anyway,' I said. 'Shall we risk it?'

Tim raised a clenched fist in front of his face and shook it, 'This is what it's all about mate', he said. My pulse was beating faster.

This bunch were very odd. They did not actually look like guerrillas, perhaps they were just bandits.

People generally walk along the side of the road in tidy single files, never across it blocking the way; and unless they had all had a dentist appointment it was too late in the morning to be going off to work in the fields.

We tried to look immortal, brave and mean. We felt just the opposite. Adrenaline buzzed through me as we approached at a medium speed.

At fifty metres Tim gave a cheery, *'Moni. Muli bwange?'* and a wave of peace. People had always returned our greetings, not these guys though.

There was no answer. They stopped and just stood there watching – Sod it. The guys' faces were deadpan. They looked bloody mean now. They had definitely passed the audition.

I quietly urged Tim, 'Come on. Let's do something.' We seemed to give each other confidence.

We jumped on the pedals and squeezed out full power. Pulling on the bars, straining back and shoulders, legs pumping. We changed up a few gears and charged for a gap in the cordon, to the left of centre. Tim was just in front. We were really moving, maybe thirty kilometres per hour. If we collided we would do someone some serious damage. The nearest guy to Tim, on the right, jumped back to save himself, raising his panga as Tim piled past. I leaned my shoulder in towards the guy and he took another step, losing his balance for a second. With yelps of surprise from the lads and manic laughter from us we were through. It was so quick. *'Yaaa whoo!'* we exclaimed.

Two hundred metres up the hill, safely out of range, we stopped. I swivelled in my saddle. They stood there, still spread across the road arguing with each other. We did not hang about. For the next couple of hours we recounted the blow by blow details, congratulating ourselves.

'For God's sake don't tell your mother!' said Tim.

The Luangwa River runs north to south, bisecting the country. The Luangwa Bridge is in a strategic position, with the Mozambique border only a kilometre to the south. We knew it would be heavily guarded.

We had heard stories of foreigners, suspected of spying, being arrested, harassed and beaten here. Adrian, the friend in Scotland, had been arrested twice here while working in Zambia on an irrigation project. Zambia had served as a willing haven for freedom fighters from Zimbabwe and South-West Africa in the 1970s and 80s, and had become very wary of white outsiders wandering about.

Recent improvements in relations between Zambia and South Africa may have changed things, but we were not sure what to expect. In Kaunda's time any white person was seen as a potential South African spy or, at least, a supporter of colonialism and thus, an enemy of the black man. The soldiers did not necessarily know what a spy was, but to catch one was their greatest ambition.

After a long, exhausting climb in draining heat, we sped down, drinking in the cooling breeze as the bikes topped 50 kph.

The bridge appeared through thorn trees. At the base of the hill, close to the start of the bridge, a rusty sign lent against a Gerry-can in the middle of the road. It told us *'STOP'*, so we stopped.

With a criss-cross geometry of cables and girders the bridge spanned the wide, muddy river.

'Very impressive' I thought, *'must remember not to photograph it.'*

First we had to deal with the guards. A group of eight young soldiers slouched in the shade, on the wreck of a burned out car. Perched on the bonnet and roof they looked bored to tears and half asleep. A couple of older, more senior guys, sat high on the bank above them. In heavy green uniforms they sweltered. They had all read the *Guide to Looking Mean and Suspicious*, but their power stemmed only from their rifles.

One stern young man reluctantly stood to deal with us. We put on our happy, chatty, great-to-see-you faces and enthusiastically showed our passports. The guard searched for the Zambian stamps and studied them long and hard. He finally nodded and handed the passports back.

'Where do you cycle from?' he asked.

Tim talked them all through the maps on the back of my T-shirt.

'We've cycled here from Sydney,' he said, 'and it's taken us all morning!'

They tittered not.

He ploughed on, 'Yes, it is very hot for cycling; we are totally mad.

Ha, Ha.' They liked this and relaxed a bit.

Tim, though, was on a roll and overplayed his hand a touch. 'Are you here guarding this beautiful bridge to stop people like us blowing it up?' he grinned.

They all thought, *'WHAAATTTT!!!!!!'*

I thought, *'Oh goody, we're going to be arrested. Maize mush and dirty water for the next two years.'*

The officer pulled a revolver from a leather holster, he aimed it and, without hesitation, shot Tim dead.

He didn't really, just kidding.

Tim recalls: 'They looked so fed up, I thought I'd lighten it a bit. When I saw their reaction I knew I shouldn't have bothered.'

None of them replied. They tensed up and managed to look even meaner; eyes narrowed; chins jutted out. I could see little lights ping on in their heads: *These are SPIES!! SPIES AT LAST!! We can capture them, impress the General and get away from this boring, bloody bridge.'* The standing soldier held Tim's gaze. 'What do you mean? Who are you?'

Tim held up his open hands, looking worried. 'Only joking

guys, only joking'. They were not smiling.

'Why do you say you blow up our bridge?'

'I wa... It ... It was just a joke, OK,' Tim pleaded. We really didn't want to be arrested.

'You are not funny,' barked the officer on the bank.

'No, I agree. I'm not funny', shaking his head like a contrite schoolboy, 'not at all.'

'No', confirmed the officer, 'You say you are cyclists, how can we know who you are? Now you make trouble.'

'We *are* cyclists. He is only joking,' I said.

There was a long silence while they studied us. I wondered what we should do next. The guards were waiting to see what the officer would do.

'Go!' he said.

Deciding to continue the eccentric Englishmen act, I piped up,

'Anyway, we've enjoyed meeting you all, but we really must get moving.' I swung my leg over the saddle and scooted off.

Tim followed suit. 'Yup, thanks a lot. We really do like your bridge,' he called over his shoulder.

'You are not funny!' called the officer on the bank, but his men had already given way to a fit of sniggering. I suppose they thought, 'What the hell, who cares anyway,'

As we cycled out onto their beautiful bridge together, I muttered,

'Gosh, you are a wag.'

'Why, thank you,' Tim replied, feeling very pleased with himself.

Up around the bend a small community had grown up, servicing the garrison and the traffic using the bridge.

'Let's get a drink,' I suggested.

I sat on a log outside a kiosk gulping hot coke, not cheap at about fifteen English pence a go. The Coke man suggested I sit in the shade, but I could not spare the energy to move.

Every pore in my body gushed pure water, not the usual salty, sticky stuff., this was actually flowing. The villagers slept or sat motionless in the shade, watching the day and the mad cyclists slip by. Women sipped water from clay mugs and passed them around to their children.

The Coke man let us have a bagful of muddy river water from his oil drum, and soon we cycled up the hill out of sight of the village to make lunch. Finding a shady tree, overlooking the valley, we got to work on the pasta. A few cars and trucks passed in both directions as we cooked and ate.

A rifle shot rang out across the valley, the echo cracking off the far hillside. My mug of tea went flying as we both jumped with surprise. The shot had come from the bridge. Had they decided they needed a spy today after all?

12 Much further by bicycle – Andy

We were not quite sure where we were. There had been nothing but bush for hours. Evening was approaching and we were out of water; we had filled our bottles beyond the bridge but that had not lasted long. The map showed no villages, just a town which could have been anything from fifty to eighty kilometres ahead. We were starting to get concerned. Without water we could not have tea!!!! In reality, if we did not guzzle lots of the stuff tonight we might possibly die of dehydration. Working our bodies hard in temperatures over forty degrees we had, as in Tanzania, been filtering and drinking ten or twelve litres each, per day. Today we had drunk only five litres each, rehydration was vital. If we did not manage it, a dry, eighty kilometre ride to Rufunsa tomorrow could be very dodgy indeed.

I was confident something would turn up; it always had before. I pulled Tim's leg about drinking baboon's blood as we passed a troop of them on the road. Another ten kilometres rolled by. As dusk approached we came across a young man in a black hat, selling bananas from a rickety stall.

His customers would be passengers from the occasional truck or bus. A person, of course, meant there should be water nearby. *'Moni,* do you speak English?' I asked, disguising my tiredness. He nodded. I asked, 'Can you tell me where we can find some water?' He looked at the ground. 'You must go to Rufunsa.' Now, this meant either we were much closer to the town than we had thought, or he was on the old, *'White men only sleep in hotels'* track. 'How far is Rufunsa?' I queried.

Turning a bunch of bananas over and over in his hands he said, 'It is very close'.

This was a bit vague so I gently persisted, 'How many kilometres?'

He bowed his head again and rubbed his brow with thumb

and forefinger, thinking hard, shifting his feet uneasily. Eventually he decided. 'If you have transport it is seventy kilometres, but if you only have bicycles it is much further.' I let a few moments pass while we both considered this notion.

'Much further by bicycle?' I asked.

'Yes,' he nodded solemnly.

'I see.'

I decided to take another line. 'Can you tell me, please, is there a village, nearer than Rufunsa, where we can get some water?'

'My village is very close, but you must go to Rufunsa, it is also very close.' I thanked the lad and soon the village did emerge. A lady of spacious dimensions called from the doorway of her thatched hut, guiding us off the road and down a steep, dusty track.

'If you only have bicycles'

At the bottom was a miraculous scene. Clear water flowed from a rocky outcrop. Amongst a lush sprouting of ferns and grasses, five or six teenage women splashed and frolicked, half-naked, in the pool. Firm round breasts glistened and jiggled as the women worked, washing clothes. Slightly older women scrubbed pans using sand and water. We called greetings and held back while the women covered themselves with pale cotton tops, then beckoned us over.

Remains of a corrugated metal drum, a yellow plastic watering can and a pair of white plimsolls littered the bank, worn bare by a million to-ings and fro-ings of women at work.

We filtered slowly and drank quickly. I fancied I felt pure

water flowing through my veins; fingers and toes tingled with exhilaration. One woman, in a white cotton dress, spoke a little English, her name was Mathilda. She had a pretty smile and, unlike the others, was not at all intimidated by us. They were high up in the hills here and had been fortunate with the rain. The crops had survived and the people were happy.

On Mathilda's advice we went off into the village to ask the headman for permission to sleep beside the waterhole. We could not find him. One man told us, 'The headman is asleep,' another said he was, 'in the fields'. Something in their voices suggested that he was most likely drunk. One young guy, with a beaming smile, approached. His smile exposed black, rotting teeth. 'I am deputy head man, you are welcome,' he said. The man only looked about eighteen. He helped us choose a suitable spot for the night.

As we worked, children called, *'Wzungu, Wzungu,'* from the bushes. We waved. The man gave us the strangest of looks.

'You do not care that they call you *Wzungu?'* he asked.

'No, why should we?' I asked. 'After all we *are* white men.'

'To us, friend, *Wzungu* means GREAT FAT WHITE PIG!!!'

'Did you hear that?' I said to Tim laughing. 'All these weeks, all the way from Mombasa, hundreds and hundreds of kids and those thousands at the football match.'

Soon, he and the girls disappeared and left us to finish putting the tents up in the fine dust. I even managed an all-over wash in the cold pool, my first for days. I did not use soap, as it would have polluted the water, but it still felt incredible. Now, with tingling body, I was ready for the ultimate, glorious sensation: to slip into the cool fresh underpants I had saved especially.

As we cooked, no matter how hard we tried we could not stop one praying mantis after another committing suicide in our candle flames. We flicked them away and moved the candles continually, but they were really, really keen. *'Ooh wow, what's this then? Cor, light, let's have a closer look.'*

Burning off one antenna just seemed to inspire them more, back they came probing with the other, *'What IS this? OUCH!'* and they plunged headlong into the liquid wax. In the end we decided to blow out the candles, have an early night and let the remainder live another day.

Small animals came sniffing about the camp, as they often did, in search of cold pasta or the final squidged piece of Cadbury's Dairy Milk.

Unable to sleep, I crawled out into the sand and had a pee into the bushes. The sky was high and clear. From the village children sang happy songs. I looked about me, the waterhole, the stars, the tents and bikes, listening to those excited voices. It had been quite a day; bandits, soldiers and now this lovely place. I had to say out loud, 'You are really here Andy, you are really here. Don't *ever* forget it.'

Dawn air was still and cool, but after twenty minutes the dry heat was upon us again. Small birds chirped in the trees over the pool. Piping hot tea and hunks of stale bread, layered with the last of the jam, soon got us moving.

We were keen to clear the hills before we stopped for lunch. This meant we did not eat until nearly four o'clock, which was a bit stupid really. We had ploughed up and down in the heat, really hurting.

The silence of the bush was suddenly broken by a violent rush of wind which bent the tall grass and strained the branches all around us. I looked back up the road. Right behind us was a black curtain of cloud. It filled the sky and was rushing down towards us. A devilish swirl took my hat off and sent it rolling down the road. Now the grass lay flat under its force. The air was alive with menace. Turning back west the sky was still perfect, untouched. I retrieved my hat. Behind us thunder roared and a waterfall of sheet rain dropped from the cloud and seemed to be approaching like a speeding truck, metre by metre, wetting the road in an advancing line.

'I've never seen anything like it,' exclaimed Tim.

No time to lose. Jumping on the bikes, we yelled as we rode the wind like surfers. Bent low, legs pumping hard, we kept in front. Ahead and above, the sky was still bright and cloudless, the road dusty and dry. Behind, the black sheet was closing, falling water snapping at our wheels. We pumped harder but still it came on. The air smelled sweeter, fresher, invigorating. I put my head down and concentrated on squeezing every bit of power through the pedals. *'Come on, catch me, catch me!!'* I thought, as the storm propelled us on.

The road began to twist through thick woods. Village people sheltered from the approaching onslaught and exclaimed, *'EEEIIIIYYYY'* as we zoomed past. I rounded the bend and my heart sank. Up ahead in the sun was an army check point. Two soldiers stood in the middle of the road studying the approaching drama. *'Don't make us stop. This is too much fun'.*

We were approaching very fast, flat out. Tim was just behind me. Seconds fell into slow motion; the soldier on the right was sharp, he summed up the situation in a flash – The storm is chasing them down the road. From twenty metres away I saw him smile and flick his left hand, ushering me through. His mate standing beside him was slower. He was still thinking, *'What the hell's this?'* He had not seen his partner's wave. I passed the STOP sign in the road. The slow guy was surprised, *'He's not stopping!!'* he thought, *'Oh, great.'* The automatic weapon swung off his shoulder. A finger covered the trigger and the line of the barrel engaged my chest.

'Jesus!' I ducked, swerved and skidded to a stop a metre from him. He held the rifle steady and stared into my eyes. The spell was broken when Tim piled in behind me and the torrent piled in behind him. The shock of the water took my breath away. The soldiers turned and ran for their hut, not even bothering to check our documents, as we stood there and let the deluge wash over us.

Rain at last, there would be rejoicing in the villages tonight. Only five kilometres along the road we found Rufunsa, (which was indeed much further). The usual crowd gathered, a smart young man asked if I had seen rain. I was still wearing my waterproof jacket and my hair was drenched. I was incredulous.

'But surely you've just had a big storm here, in the last few minutes.' Heads shook. We looked around, the ground was fine dust, light, white and very dry. Looking back east the sky was magically cloudless and serenely blue; as usual.

Rufunsa was a scruffy town of white-washed breeze-block and corrugated iron roofs. Men hung about idly, women and children queued to use the hand pump and ferried jugs of cool, clear water to their huts. The pump was fine for pulling water up from the water table, but it was not practical to use that water to feed the fields. Tim stood guard over the bikes whilst I went in search of diesel or kerosene for the stove. There was no garage, but I found a dark, uninviting bar named *The Struggling Restaurant And Grocery*. I could see why.

The evidence of years of fighting and outrageous Saturday nights was everywhere: all the windows were broken; my feet stuck to the floor as I walked in; the essence of stale beer, tobacco and marijuana hung heavy in the air; torn beer posters were falling off offensive red paint. This business was someone's pride and joy. UB40 music whammed out of one speaker '... *don't go and leave me alone* ...' The only customers were two youths swaying in perfect rhythm, barely moving a muscle, inside the music.

A fat woman in black, with a wonky eye, did not answer my question. She silently poured diesel from a gallon can into my bottle. The can had been the only item on the shelves behind her – the beer was stored out of harms way in the back room. She spilled the fuel all over the wooden bar, before returning to her stool and her warm bottle, not thinking to wipe it up.

A few kilometres beyond Rufunsa we camped in another game reserve and, once again, did not get eaten.

Something was rustling about in the bush nearby. Big, black ants scurried over me, biting indiscriminately. I was sitting cross-legged in the sand scribbling my diary entry for the day. Actually, it could be any day in Zambia as they were all filled with a confusion of unconnected thoughts whizzing about my head.

Hours and miles slide away on rough Tarmac beneath me. My legs pump along on their own. If I let them stop now they won't start again. They are totally separate from me, into their own rhythm. There is some very grave news I ought to tell them: They are beyond exhaustion, without fuel. They shouldn't work. Disloyally, I keep quiet. Let them get on with it. They take me up over long hills and down through valleys and villages. I don't ask them to. Truck drivers wave. I have no strength to raise an arm in response, I can only nod. Still my legs pump. Throat parched, tongue swollen and lips cracked. Sweat pours off my forehead, flows through eyebrows, stings eyes.

The flesh of my back and chest is slimy and itching and arms are encrusted with salt. I stare but don't see. My face is ashen and fixed in a grimace, no one can see. Tim's way behind, or is he way ahead? I don't remember. Legs plough on through fields and bush. I lean down, fiddle with the water bottle, take a squirt. Throat and mouth are eased for a few minutes. Legs keep the rhythm. The sun beats down on my hat. Dust, always dust.

I let my mind rescue me from this and take me to safety; to where life is easy and tamed: Beside a glowing fireplace in a country pub, with my brothers, Gordon and Colin, laughing loudly, smooth, woody pints flowing, laughter growing; to a long, tearful, good-bye with Cassie on a Surrey street, neighbours peeking from behind chintz curtains (maybe one day I'll be back there with her); to a black and white movie, Peter Sellers, curled up on a Sunday afternoon; to gentle waves lapping over me in warm shallows; to Sunday papers in bed and a bowl of muesli, Greek yoghurt and grapes ... WAKE UP! Pull yourself together! Concentrate! You're here remember!

Through it all, legs pump on. Thank God, the sun is dropping behind distant hills. Nothing can stop the sunset. Falling faster, growing larger, deepening amber. Find water and let's finish this. We wander off into bush, heading nowhere. Another hour to make camp. At last I can lie down. With my mind I can push blood to every muscle. Sinews in legs twitch as each unwinds. Tea and the radio are a comfort. Clouds cross the moon. In the wind hovers the dull thud, thud, thud of drums in the night.

To stop lions prowling around outside I put the usual cotton wool in my ears and concentrated my mind on soft, warm breasts.

The next couple of days became a tired slog. The heat was taking its toll. If we had not bought food in Malawi, we would have been in serious trouble. There was none here to buy. (And how I regretted not buying the perfumed bubble bath.)

We stopped for water at a tiny village. Three pretty women and a man sat quietly, in the shade of a rough thatch hut. They were each in their early twenties, but looked thin and tired. The women wore deep red and black wrap-around dresses. They were well groomed and showed a certain self respect. We were given permission to draw a little water from the well. While I filtered the murky water, Tim admired a new born baby. The sun was incredibly hot and I knew I was close to heat exhaustion. I could not concentrate on the filtering and found myself sitting doing nothing, not even thinking. I roused myself and carried on pumping. Each time I filtered half a litre of water I gulped it straight down. It was depressing to feel no relief. I had no choice but to clean the filter and start again. It took ages.

I was so tired I was not able to speak to the people. They generously offered us slices of over-ripe pawpaw, crawling with flies. I passed, feigning illness so as not to offend them. Pawpaw was a rarity in this drought, they needed it more than we did anyway. Tim was stronger and played with the baby enthusiastically. One of the women asked him in broken English,

'You have name for my baby boy? We don't have name now.' Tim felt honoured. For some reason he was feeling very British and suggested the name Charlie, after Prince Charles, the patron of I.T. Tim had to write it down for them and repeat the pronunciation many times, in the end they settled for *Chaiyee*.

I wondered what trick of fate, or luck, had caused this little person to be born here, in this desolate nowhere, in drought, instead of New York, where you can pick up a phone any time, day or night and shout, *'I'M HUNGRY!!'* and someone at the other end will say 'Oh, okay, I'll bring you something to eat right away.'

As we neared Lusaka we came across rather too many gangs of young lads, who had clearly lost all hope; drunk on local brew or stoned on local ganja. They were a pain in the neck and difficult to escape from.

Tim was suffering from a virus now and cycling like a slug: every turn of the pedals a tortuous effort. It was terrible to see him like that and I could do little to help, except offer moral support.

We camped on a football pitch outside a village primary school, a welcome change from rough bush. Children and blabbering drunks crowded round and asked endless questions as we put up the tents. 'Where ...? Are you married ...? Do you want a smoke ...?' We had already spent an hour chatting, getting water from the well and negotiating the camping spot with the headmistress and were in no mood to entertain these people further. I struck up a deal: If I photographed the crowd would they leave us in peace?

I took one photo; the camera did not flash and no one moved. They needed evidence that the photo had been taken. I lowered my aim into the sea of black faces close to Tim, as he lay exhausted on his mat. This time the camera flashed; the crowd screamed and cheered and ran off in all directions. Within two minutes Tim was asleep and did not stir for thirteen hours. I had to eat all his dinner as well as my own; *'By God, it was hell out there, Carruthers.'*

Tim recalls in his diary: 'Another long, hard day, camped in school grounds. I was exhausted and went to bed. Hope I'm not developing malaria. I could do without that.'

The kids started to arrive for school at six-thirty the following morning. Some had walked many miles already to be there. They studied us from a distance. Looking immaculate in their uniforms, they lined up outside the wooden school house to sing the African Anthem. The girls wore light blue blouses and dark blue skirts, the boys light green shirts and dark green shorts; none wore shoes. The headmistress, Ruth Chizaza, had an impossible job. She was charged with educating three hundred and sixty children, aged between four and thirteen years. At Ruth's disposal were two classrooms and one other teacher. They had no pencils and no paper. The children came in three shifts, each of four hours. This still meant that sixty pupils would have to be accommodated in a tiny classroom built to hold twenty. Inevitably, most students were given unsupervised jobs outside the classroom. We watched them wandering about, gardening or sweeping up.

At the age of thirteen all children take a basic examination. The top 30% are allowed to carry on to secondary school. For the majority, the future holds nothing but work in the fields, drunkenness or a life of crime on the streets of Lusaka. In a total population of seven million, the majority are under twenty years of age and only three hundred thousand people are in paid employment.

The Zambian people are made up of refugee tribes who, over the centuries, have fled the might of the Zulus and other great warriors. These people are not great fighters or great workers. Many seem content to just hang out and let it all happen without them. Kenneth Kaunda had once said of his people, 'If by next year, all

Zambians choose to be as lazy as they are now, I would willingly step down as President, because I don't want to lead people with lazy bones.' They did not change and he did not step down. Many childrens' futures are decided at the age of four. Those appearing less able are selected, by their fathers, to tend goats or cattle; never attending school. We left in a state of depression. Tim was on his last legs as we struggled the last sixty kilometres into Lusaka.

> Again **Tim recalls** in his diary: 'Very weak today, didn't think I
> was going to make it. No energy at all. This is a good section
> to have behind us. I couldn't do all that again. I couldn't
> push one more pedal, yet I just had to, for miles and miles.
> Not happy.'

We stayed for a couple of days at the *Anglican Missionary Guest House*. It was a comfortable haven. With masses of sleep and good food, prepared by the housekeeper, Tim was soon back with it. A young student priest, a local boy, was also staying there. We ate together on the first night. He was still in the first year of his studies; idealistic and full of himself.

'You may call me Father,' he said, not that we had asked. It came to pass that we, henceforth, did avoideth the jerk altogether.

This was posh suburbia, but gunfire from the street outside kept me awake at night. The mission supported a sort of vigilante patrol. The officers arrested drunks and druggies from the other side of town then brought them back to stand outside my window to argue with them. Once that commotion had died down they called in the prostitutes to shriek and cackle.

The latest craze around Lusaka was stealing expensive Japanese Land Cruisers from aid workers and government officials. As the cars stopped at the lights, (locally known as robots – take a left when you see the robot. *What?*) villains pulled the drivers out, jumped in and drove away. A senior policeman had been shot dead in such an incident, just the day before we arrived. White travellers, waiting at the bus station at night, were generally taken away by the police and locked up for their own protection.

From the guest house, we cycled into town to buy some

supplies, but found nothing we could use. It was a bizarre marriage of Eastern Europe and the Wild West. Wide, tree-lined boulevards bristled with shops, but none had much for sale.

Apart from food, one key item we needed was pure alcohol, to clean the heads on the tape recorder. The tapes for the BBC were getting pretty muffled. I asked a doctor's receptionist.

'No, we don't have pure alcohol', she said, 'try the nightclub next door.'

I did try elsewhere. Dr. Hussain, a Pakistani from Lahore, cornered me for half an hour in his surgery and poured out his views on religion, women, travel and cricket.

'What do you think of the proposed changes to the LBW law?' I would have been delighted normally to hold a discussion with him but was concerned that Tim might be fighting off the lads outside.

I emerged empty handed.

Tim was furious, 'Where the hell have you been?!'

He was surrounded by five or six shady looking characters. The bikes were not locked and would have been difficult to defend if the lads had gone for him. This, he felt, was looking increasingly likely. We skedaddled. Several youths shouted to us as we passed in the street, 'I wan your bike man,' or, 'Youm on ma bike.'

We collected letters from the Post Office. The little man at the poste restante counter was well on top of his job. He kept a little book of all the names and everything was neatly sorted and piled. He even smiled. There was a letter from Cassie.

We needed somewhere safe to read and found a café that would let us bring the bikes inside, and even though they were close to us we still locked them. We ordered a big pot of tea and a plate of chips each and cracked open the news from home.

At the end of an amusing letter about our friends' love lives, Cassie said, 'Let's wait and see what happens when you get home'. Well that sounded hopeful. It was something at least. Leaving Lusaka, not a moment too soon, we passed through sprawling, stinking shanty towns, the result of the drift from the declining rural villages.

Men were breaking large white rocks into pebbles and piling them into neat pyramids, like the onion pyramids of Tanzania. These, though, stood four feet high and stretched three hundred metres down the side of the road. A man said with all sincerity, 'Yo wanna buy rocks man?'

'Oh, thank you so much' I thought, *'I need a few rocks. Just fling a ton in my back pannier old mate!'*

One hundred kilometres along the road towards Victoria Falls, we stayed with a Dutch couple on a huge flower farm. They grew carnations, exporting them to Europe and North America. This year the flowers had died and the business was at risk. Peter and Anna-Maria were about our age, both were blond, tanned and healthy looking. They had met us on their way back from Lusaka and invited us to spend the night.

The British had built a railway up from South Africa in the 1950s, to transport the copper, Zambia's one export, from the mines in the north-west. When the line was finished, many engineers stayed on and cleared great tracts of bush on either side of the railway. Here, unlike most of Zambia, the soil is fertile and they had built up successful cattle ranches, maize plantations and assorted farms. Bantu villagers provide the labour and in return are supported by the farmers; far more efficient than the small, individual plots surrounding the villages in which we had stayed. Far more efficient for foreign businesses to make money that is, but it often robs the people of their land, and the mono-cropping eventually degrades the soil and demands tonnes of pesticides to keep the bugs away, just to give us cut flowers. Peter and Anna-Maria flew tulips to England daily.

That morning, Peter and Anna-Maria told us they had left their red Toyota pick-up in a Lusaka car park. One of the farm boys stood guard in the back with a baseball bat. Through the morning Peter and Anna-Maria had come back with armfuls of groceries and spare parts for a pump. With the lad now sitting on a pile of goodies and his masters away, the hoodlums had moved in. The lad was able to hold them off for a while, slashing out with his bat but was soon overwhelmed. The entire load would have gone had not the boy guarding the neighbouring pick-up waded in with his axe. A couple of wild swings and murderous shrieks had sent the baddies running.

We left late next morning, sleeping in after too much good

food and drink. We tried to keep a low profile as we stopped for chai and to post a letter in Mazabuka, the birthplace of the author Wilbur Smith. Human contact was to be avoided. We had been told that the local hospital had taken a blood sample from every visiting patient. The authorities were staggered to find 85% of samples came up HIV positive; many with AIDS. Many faces in the crowd had the appearance of rotting away; we assumed this was through AIDS related disease, but it could have been leprosy. It was a spooky place.

People looked vacant and ghostly. There was none of the cheerful hope and laughter we were used to.

Condoms were being distributed by aid agencies and their usage encouraged, but they were not yet generally accepted. It occurred to me that the long term picture for African people was very bleak. Millions would die from AIDS. Any attempt to reproduce, to restock the population, would obviously require sex without the use of condoms, therefore exposing the healthy people to the risk of infection, a particularly nasty form of Russian roulette.

We covered the last five hundred kilometres in Zambia, from Lusaka to Victoria Falls, in just four days. The lure of hamburgers, cold beers and hoards of western travellers to hang out with, was irresistible. Great white farms lined the road and small aircraft sprayed insecticide. Before reaching Victoria Falls, the farms disappeared and we had another dangerous encounter.

One morning we were zipping along through the bush; me in front, Tim behind, when something caught my eye. Just ahead and to my right was a snake, fluorescent green and six feet long. Its graceful, muscular curls were side-winding quickly across the road towards me; we were on collision course.

I instinctively jerked away, swerving the wheels a foot to the left and the serpent passed behind me. At the same moment I yelled, *'Snake!!'*; as much out of alarm as to warn Tim. I turned in my saddle to watch, everything happened too fast; Tim's bike and the snake met ... With a sudden, *'HHHuuuuuuHHH!'* Tim's feet were off the pedals and up around his ears. The chunky tyres rolled over the body and in a flash it was gone. I saw the snake shoot into the undergrowth. Both parties were shocked but unharmed by the encounter.

The snake would be slithering back to *Mrs Snake* and the little snakes.

'Hey you'll never guess what just happened to me ...', he would say, '...Yeah, *wzungus* on bicycles ... honest ... look at these tyre marks!!'

The soldier at the next checkpoint confirmed it as a Green Mamba.

'Much deadly snake', he said, with a wicked grin, 'He bite you and, for you my friend, the day is over in half an hour.'

13 The heart of the matter – Tim

Six years before the discovery of Lake Malawi and eighteen years before the historic encounter with Stanley, Doctor Livingstone had been obsessed by one particular objective above all others, to forge a route across Africa. His intention was to start in Luanda (Angola) on the Atlantic coast, press on into the interior, continuing east to meet the Indian Ocean on the opposite side of the continent. He set off in November, 1853 on a journey that was to take him through six thousand kilometres of largely unexplored country crossing the territories of what are today Angola, Botswana, Zambia and Mozambique. Accompanied by his trusted native guide Sekeletu and twenty-seven Makalolo porters they endured fierce tropical sun and torrential rains. For months the party survived on the most basic native food, deficient in proteins and vitamins. It took almost twelve months to walk approximately two thousand five hundred kilometres to Linyanti (northern Botswana) and the party forged on east into the wilds. For twenty-five days Livingstone was laid-up with cerebral malaria which left him nearly deaf, half blind and miserably weak.

The Doctor was resting in his tent one morning writing his journal when he was disturbed by gunshots and shouting from the surrounding bush. He emerged from the tent to find his party had been surrounded by a group of hostile natives. Shots were fired at them and a rush of tribesmen threatened to overwhelm the group. Staggering angrily towards the natives grasping a revolver, Livingstone thrust the weapon against the ringleader's stomach forcing him to back down. The leader shouted an order to his warriors who melted away into dense green bush as quickly as they had appeared. Once more the explorer's incredible courage and self-belief had saved the party.

Whilst approaching Lake Dilolo, through a complex of sluggish streams, the Doctor suffered his twenty-seventh bout of fever and took such heavy doses of quinine that he started vomiting blood.

Only when the Doctor had recovered sufficiently, was the party able to continue at a leisurely pace along the banks of the Zambezi. On the night of the 15 November, 1855, Livingstone slept on Kalai Island near the confluence of the Chobe and Zambezi rivers. The following morning he had intended to strike north but decided, on a whim, to take a canoe to *'Mosi-oa-Tunya', 'The Smoke that Thunders'*. Clouds of spray appeared like moving columns of smoke from a raging bush fire as they moved forward. The fragile wooden canoe, expertly paddled by natives, carried the explorer to an island perched on the brim of a great chasm. Crawling warily to the brink, and deafened by the endless thunder of the waters, Livingstone peered into a huge, mist-filled rent in the earth's crust. He saw for the first time the awesome display of power which he named Victoria Falls in honour of his sovereign. The Doctor recalls the event in *Missionary Travels: '(Mosi-oa-Tunya) ... had never been seen before by European eyes, but scenes so lovely must have been gazed upon by angels in their flight.'*

The Zambezi above the Falls is a tranquil river, 1700 metres wide, passing through an archipelago of beautiful islands before plunging with stunning power into a great gorge 110 metres below. The water, falling sheer into the chasm, explodes at the bottom forming driving mist which billows upwards hundreds of metres above the Falls. Sunlight catches mist in a series of brilliant rainbows which straddle the gorge.

> **Andy recalls:** 'As I stood on the brink of the Falls, gazing in awe at this natural wonder, a shiver ran through my body. I could almost sense the presence of the great Doctor in whose footsteps we were now treading almost a century and a half later.'

Livingstone continued his journey east along the middle Zambezi, a thousand kilometre stretch of slow moving water fringed by beautiful evergreen shade-trees. The party travelled by zig-zagging from one village to the next along well-beaten tracks. Livingstone was now close to collapse, passing brick dust urine and suffering severe pain from prolapsed piles. Despite his appalling physical condition he found the strength to reach his objective. The party arrived at Quelimane on the Indian Ocean, on 20 May, 1856. The transcontinental journey had taken two and a half years.

'You cannot enter Zimbabwe,' said the black female immigration official. 'You must go back to where you came.'

Andy and I exchanged exasperated glances.

'What do you mean go back?' I said, aghast. I thought pleading might work, 'You've got to let me in – I'm cycling to Namibia. This is the only way I can go.'

It was the first week of March and Day 215 of the expedition. We were standing in a modern, brick-built immigration post having ridden the bikes across the Zambezi bridge, a 300 ft high jigsaw of black iron arches spanning the deep gorge and seething river which separate Zambia from Zimbabwe.

'You are not in possession of a valid onward ticket as proof of your intention to leave Zimbabwe,' she told me, as if quoting from a government manual.

Little Miss Efficient wore a crisply ironed, white short-sleeved shirt, dark blue tie, matching skirt and sensible, prison warder shoes. She was far too keen – obviously new to the job.

I was at a loss as to what to do next when Andy came to the rescue.

'There's obviously been a little misunderstanding here which we can sort out in a moment,' he said adopting his best smooth, soothing business executive mode. 'My companion and I are travelling together on behalf of a British charity. I have all the necessary documentation which validates our visit to Zimbabwe and indicates that we shall be here for a maximum period of three weeks.'

He produced a wad of official looking documents, letters of introduction from embassies of several African countries and a letter from Intermediate Technology; all telling anyone who might be interested what good solid chaps we were. Andy showed her a ticket from Cape Town to Rio de Janeiro, dated for two months' time (mine was waiting for me in the Varig offices in Cape Town). He even fished out a letter from his mum. *Little Miss Efficient* gave all the documents a thorough inspection before speaking to me again.

'You are most fortunate to have a friend who is so well

prepared,' she told me. 'Otherwise you would not be entering this country. Have a pleasant stay.'

The town of Victoria Falls was a blessed relief after the past weeks of struggle in the harsh Zambian bush. Andy and I were exhausted, having punished our bodies over the past fourteen days. We had covered eleven hundred kilometres through the most demanding country and were badly in need of rest and nourishing food to build up strength.

We pedalled to the camp site in the centre of town and started to unload the bikes. Two heads appeared from a shabby, purple tent a few metres away in the shade of a tree. Both heads had identical long, blond hair and huge, bushy, blond beards.

'Hi,' said one. 'You must be the mad Pommie bastards cycling across this shit heap. We've bin hearin' a lot about you blokes. My name's Growler, this is Taupo.'

Growler and Taupo looked as if they had just stepped off a longboat in a Norwegian fjord following a spot of recreational rape and pillage. Andy and I struck up an instant rapport with these two larger than life Kiwis.

'Sounds like you blokes are out on a mother of a trip,' said Taupo.

'We're on a bit of a wander ourselves.'

'How long have you been away?' Andy asked.

'Must be about four years,' said Growler. 'Jeez, and we've raised some hell along the way,' he chuckled.

'How did you hear about us?' I asked.

'We met up with two Canadian babes back in Harare,' said Taupo.

He pointed out a smart silver mountain tent. 'They're here now, camped over there.'

'You blokes are famous,' said Growler. 'Everyone's heard about the Pommie cycle boys.'

'Yeah', said Taupo with a grin, 'we thought we had a chance with those two chicks but all they talked about was you blokes. Makes me wanna puke.'

'Tell yer what', said Growler, 'let's go out, drink a shed-full of beer and you blokes can tell us what yer secret is.'

We promised to join Growler and Taupo later for a small aperitif.

We found Annie and Macy, whom we had met in Northern Malawi, lounging in their tent, caught up with some travel gossip, and invited them to join the soirée. Locking the bikes to a tree, Andy and I headed for the famous *Victoria Falls Hotel*. I remembered the words of Klaus, a big, beer drinking Swede we had met in Malawi.

'If you get to Victoria Falls', he had said, 'you must check out the buffet at the main hotel. All you can eat for $10. It's the business.'

The thought of tucking into this buffet had kept Andy and I going over the past few days.

We walked through the town past modern low-level buildings with flat roofs and brash neon signs. There were international banks, car hire companies, a hotel and casino and to our delight a Wimpy fast food restaurant. Cheeseburger and chips was a delicacy we had not sampled since Perth. In fact the town looked very much like small town Australia.

The *Victoria Falls Hotel* looked like an English country mansion nestling serenely amongst glorious pink, yellow and purple bougainvillaea. Manicured lawns were highlighted by sculptured marble fountain and long ornamental pools. Tall palms swayed in a cooling breeze. The whole place oozed class, much too smart for the likes of us. I looked at Andy and laughed. As usual, we were hardly dressed for the occasion. A valiant attempt had been made at cleaning ourselves up in the communal washroom at the camp site. We had shaved off ten days' thick stubble, put on rather pathetic, crumpled glad-rags and run combs through unruly mops of hair. It was a good effort but we still looked exactly what we were ... two scruffy, grimy, weather-beaten cyclists.

'They'll never let us in here in a million years,' I said to Andy.

'Of course they will', he said confidently, 'after all we're British!'

Two minutes later we were seated in a luxurious cocktail lounge listening to the loud conversations of cigar smoking American and red-faced South African business men. I nervously ordered two large Gin & Tonics from a waiter, immaculate in his white tuxedo and matching gloves. He eyed me with a little distaste but made no comment.

'Well so far so good,' said Andy. 'At least they haven't kicked us straight back onto the streets.'

I wondered, as I tucked into my third plate from the sumptuous buffet, if this was as near as I was ever going to get to becoming a *lounge lizard*. It lasted ten days.

The day we chose to leave Victoria Falls was dark, dirty and grey. After another soaking outside the post office, we managed to pedal the bikes out of town at 3 pm. under leaden skies. *'So much, for the early start,'* I thought. The moral of the story was, clearly, not to go out on the town with two Antipodean Vikings the night before setting out to cycle eighty kilometres through the African bush.

The final stage of the journey was planned to take us west, touching Botswana before entering Namibia. We had to cross the Caprivi Strip before riding south west to our finishing point, Swakopmund, on the Atlantic Ocean. Another sixteen hundred kilometres lay ahead of us over the next three weeks.

Having left behind the comfort and civilised atmosphere of Victoria Falls, we soon found ourselves pedalling through thick bush on a good quality, sealed road. I retreated into the comfort and security of my thoughts.

Here we were again, back out in the middle of it all. *Great!* No sense of time, free from hassle, free to do as we wished, no constraints. It was like a game without rules. We made it up as we went along. No one had control over us. Total freedom of mind and action.

I remembered part of a William Blake poem from the dim and distant past:

> *'In every cry of every Man,*
> *In every Infant's cry of fear,*
> *In every voice, in every ban,*
> *The mind-forg'd manacles I hear.'*

Had we managed to break free of these shackles? Were we truly free at last or was it a temporary illusion? We had seen so many things, been to so many places, done so much over the past months. We had changed, moving far away from the conventional lives followed by most people. Even the most hippie of the travellers we met thought we were unusual. When all of this was finally over could we possibly go back to the lives we had lead before? Would any of it make sense or would our lives become trivial and meaningless? Despite the warmth of the sun these thoughts sent a shiver down my back.

One hour after starting we entered Zambezi National Park, famed for its prolific wildlife. I tried to force childhood images of savage carnivores from my mind. The bush was strangely hushed. Not even bird song broke an uneasy silence. There was a sense of expectancy and I waited uneasily for some event over which I would have no power of control.

'I don't like it,' I said to Andy.

He looked at me questioningly. 'What do you mean?'

'I'm not sure but let's be careful ... it's a jungle out there.' I tried to keep the grin off my face.

Cruising along fifty metres behind Andy, I was lulled by the gentle whirring of my freshly oiled gears. Up ahead a huge, dark shape drifted from deep bush into the road. My eyes widened in astonishment. Andy continued pedalling away, head down, unaware he was about to cycle into several tons of bull elephant. A shout died in my throat. I was too far back to warn him and watched in sickly fascination as he rode on.

Instinct caused Andy to look up from his handlebars at the very last moment. The bike skidded across the road as he rammed on the brakes, stopping within touching distance of one of the most dangerous of animals. He stood quite still looking up at a mountain of grey flesh. For many seconds the great bull peered at him with small rheumy eyes; time briefly suspended. The huge beast swung his trunk majestically, flapped his tattered ears and set up a cloud of white dust.

At last, the bull turned his head away as if to dismiss this puny creature in his path and with a few ponderous steps was swallowed by the bush.

I pulled up beside Andy, who was staring intently at the spot where the elephant had just disappeared.

'I told you it was a jungle out here,' I said breathlessly.

'Bloody hell,' he murmured.

We covered the eighty kilometres to the immigration post on the Botswana border in three and a half hours. This was not really surprising as a couple of litres of neat adrenaline were still coursing through our bodies.

'Many apologies,' said the muscular soldier at the border post. ' Border is much closed now. You give documents and rest until morning when border is again open.'

A shout just died in my throat.

We were in a compound thirty metres square containing two concrete huts, all enclosed by a tall wire mesh fence.

I did not wish to argue with a beefy soldier in full camouflage smock and webbing with an AK 47 assault rifle slung over his shoulder.

'Okay,' I said, handing over the passports. 'Whatever you say.' I did not know why he needed our passports. There was no way we were going to lift our bikes over a three metre fence and sneak across the border in the dark, dodging elephants, lions, hyenas and whatever else was out there.

The soldier gave us a thorough inspection, taking several covetous glances in the direction of the bikes.

'You must sleep here,' he said, pointing to a small patch of flat grass by the side of the immigration hut.

We laid out flysheets, unrolled sleeping bags and made ourselves as comfortable as possible. I tried to settle down and get some sleep but found it extremely difficult. Squadron after squadron of mosquitoes kept up a remorseless, high-pitched whining bombardment reminiscent of Luftwaffa Stukka bombers. The more repellent I sprayed on the more they enjoyed it.

A band of hippos came wallowing nearby, on the muddy banks of the Zambezi. Great, deep 'Ho Ho' Ho's' reverberated through the still, muggy night. Soon it was the turn of lions whose mournful roars carried from deep in the bush. The lions had only just packed up when the singing began. Drunken, raucous army songs in native tongue drifted through the open window of the guards' hut. The boys were relieving the boredom of another long, lonely night in the middle of nowhere with bawdy songs. This racket was accompanied by a full chorus of cicadas rubbing their back legs together with glee at our misery and discomfort.

I gave up any pretension to slumber and watched a thin sliver of bright moon drift out from behind a dirty rain cloud. Small, dark shapes flitted overhead, bats, silhouetted by lunar light. My mind turned to the coming days. Tanzania and Zambia had been rugged and inhospitable but we knew the Caprivi Strip was going to be our toughest test yet.

A narrow corridor of Namibian territory on the northern edge of the Kalahari Desert, the *Strip,* separates Botswana to the south from Angola and Zambia to the north. It provides a vital trade route from Namibia to Zimbabwe and to the rest of central southern Africa. This corridor, five hundred kilometres long by thirty wide, was created by treaty between Britain and Germany in 1890. The name came from General Count von Caprivi, the German Chancellor at that time. Through this area flow two of Africa's greatest rivers – the Zambezi and the Okavango. The *Strip* had only recently been opened to non-military traffic following years of guerilla warfare.

I was roused from a restless sleep by the gentle prod of a rifle butt just before dawn. It was the beefy border guard from the night before.

'Border is open. You must be travel,' he ordered us brusquely.

My eyes felt gritty and sore as we packed up our meagre camp. I was covered in livid, scarlet mosquito craters and it felt as if roadworks had started inside my head. Later that day we discovered the loss of a knife and headtorch.

'Oh, I wonder who stole those then?' I asked Andy.

'Well, it wasn't me and it wasn't you, so it must have been the hippos,' he replied.

At the tiny settlement of Kasane, the border crossing into Botswana went with a minimum of hassle. We rode along a rough, sealed road through light bush for twenty minutes until a young, official looking chap stepped out and flagged us down. He wore a freshly laundered, crisply ironed orange boiler suit and vivid yellow construction helmet. He might have stepped out of an oil exploration commercial.

'Excuse me my gentleman,' he addressed us politely. 'We are having veterinary check point.'

'That's a new one,' said Andy. 'So what do we have to do?'

Boiler Suit pointed to a shallow pit by the side of the road filled with a bright green chemical.

'You must be dipped in there,' he said.

I took a long, hard look into the green, festering pit.

'Dip ourselves in there? You must be joking mate!' I told him, flabbergasted.

'No joking', he said solemnly, 'we are killing animal pests.'

'You'll be killing cyclists as well if we have to swim about in that lot!' said Andy.

'No swim!' he laughed. 'Bicycle wheel and boots!'

This was rather a strange request but Andy and I duly wheeled the bikes through the pit and paddled about for a while in green stuff.

'This is enough,' said *Boiler Suit* after a couple of minutes. 'Now, you must give me cheese.'

I looked at him, puzzled, 'You want us to give you cheese?'.

'Yes.'

'Well, we don't have any cheese,' said Andy.

'Then give me fruit.'

'No, no fruit.'

'Ham?'

'No.'

'Bread?'

'No, we don't have bread either,' I told him. 'Why do you want these things? Is it to stop the spread of disease?'

'No', said *Boiler Suit,* 'it is for my dinner.'

A few kilometres past the green pit, the Tarmac petered out as we entered our fourth game reserve, Chobe National Park. A sign warned:

NOW ENTERING GAME PARK –
DO NOT LEAVE VEHICLES.

'It doesn't say anything about cycling,' I said to Andy.

'No', he replied, 'and we won't be leaving our vehicles, so we're all right.'

We found ourselves on a rough road made of sand and gravel, running through dense bush. I could see no further than a few feet into the thick barricade of dark green mopani trees and tangled bushes that pressed in on both sides. The going was tough, our thick knobbly tyres sinking into off-white sand. By noon the temperature had risen above forty degrees Celsius; the sun beat down on our khaki bush hats from a cloudless, pale sky. The water bags had been filled at the border and we were carrying twelve litres each, in the hope that this would be sufficient for two days. We had been sweating heavily, however, and drinking regularly to prevent dehydration so that our water supply was fast running out. More had to be found before the end of the day.

At last we came upon a brown, stagnant water hole in a small clearing.

'Brilliant!' shouted Andy.

We stopped to filter water, brew up, and refuel with cheese, bread and jam (okay, so we had lied to *Boiler Suit*). We slogged out another twenty kilometres before I called to Andy.

'How far is it to the Namibian border?' He turned in his saddle to reach the map case which lived under a couple of straps on one of his rear panniers.

'Oh, bollocks!' he cursed venomously. 'The bloody map has dropped off the back of the bike.'

'Great, that's just what we needed,' I said, trying to control my frustration. 'We've just lost the knife and a torch and now we've lost the bleedin' map. We're not having one of our better days are we?'

'Well, we're not here to enjoy ourselves,' said Andy with a rueful smile.

'Now ain't that the truth,' I replied. 'Come on, let's go back and look for it.' Despite myself I managed a tired smile.

It was then, as I mounted my bike, that I discovered a needle sharp, three-inch long acacia thorn had pierced the thick rubber of my front tyre. It was completely flat.

'Oh, dearie me!' I said, or something quite similar!

Andy recalls: 'I was a little peeved at having lost the map case but, worst of all, the calculator and statistics had also gone. All those delicious figures I had lovingly nurtured every night for the past months had been taken from me. I felt like a mother who had lost her infant. I left Tim to fix his puncture and back-tracked for twenty kilometres searching the road all the way to the water hole where we had brewed up and had last studied the map.

I hated expending vital energy going back over ground I had already slogged across. Despite many false alarms, which turned out to be rocks or leaves, the map did not appear. On my return journey, tired and fed-up under the burning sun, I was joined by a lone, black vulture. He circled high above for a full half-hour before deciding I was probably too fit and healthy to drop down dead in the dirt. He gave up his vigil and glided off in search of a more promising titbit.'

At the end of a long, hard and difficult day we emerged from the claustrophobic confines of Chobe National Park to be greeted by the wide, slowly flowing, Chobe River. Here was the border village of Ngoma, gateway to Namibia and the third country we were to ride in that day.

From Ngoma to Katima Mulilo, the start of the Caprivi Strip, is a distance of eighty kilometres. After a night camping in the bush outside Ngoma, we found ourselves riding along on sand and gravel through sparse veld.

From time to time we saw people walking by the side of the road, out there in the middle of nowhere heading for unknown destinations in the bush. Barefoot young men dressed in tatty slacks and grubby T-shirts watched us warily, many of them with squints or casts in their eyes. Eye defects are common in Namibia, with many people suffering from river blindness but unable to afford medical treatment. There was a general feeling of distrust towards us from the native people. With the exception of the children, people were not as welcoming or open as those we had met in other countries.

We stopped for a drink of water and before long we were surrounded by small, inquisitive black faces. They gave us and our bikes the once over and one little boy spotted Andy's rear view mirror clamped to the handlebars. The young lad peered into the mirror and saw a strange face appear. He let out a high pitched wail of fear and fled to hide behind his friends. His buddies were intrigued by this. A game developed. The children crept up, one by one, peeked into the mirror, recoiled in fright at the sight of their own reflections and ran away in fits of giggling terror. It was twenty minutes before they allowed us to continue on our way!

A few kilometres along the road, I wondered whether the sun had finally succeeded in frying my brain.

'Andy, am I seeing things, or is that a sledge up there?' I asked.

'Well, unless we both had LSD with our tea this morning, I think you're right.'

Coming towards us, fairly flying across the sand, was a large wooden sledge drawn by a big white ox.

We stopped in amazement. Andy started singing softly, 'Jingle bells, jingle bells, jingle all the way ...'

It was clearly a family outing. Dad held the reins, mum sat by his side holding baby, off to see the in-laws no doubt. Despite our waves, they paid us no attention and the odd vision soon became a distant speck.

'I've seen it all now,' said Andy.

'No you haven't,' I told him. 'There's a polar bear selling ice cream just down the road.'

Three days after leaving Victoria Falls a storm blew in from the west. It had been humid and sticky all morning, making pedalling uncomfortable, strength sapping work. Dark, ominous clouds rolled slowly in choking a clean blue sky. The air became heavy and oppressive. When rain finally arrived it came with great ferocity. We rode into a black wall of water. Big, heavy droplets totally drenched us in a matter of seconds. The sand road was transformed into a river of deep, clawing grey mud. We struggled on whilst purple-bruised skies unleashed a relentless torrent of water.

Within a couple of kilometres our bikes began to seize up. Great clods of mud stuck to the tyres, jamming the gears and clogging the chains. Mountain bikes are capable of handling most types of terrain but thick mud was proving too much even for our trusty steeds. We stopped to clear the worst of the sludge.

'How far is it to Katima Mulilo?' I asked Andy.

'I don't know,' he replied. 'I lost the map if you remember.'

'Well, we can't ride much farther in this,' I said. 'The bikes are totally clogged. What do you think?'

'We can either call it a day now and camp up in the bush or try and ride on a bit longer and see if anything turns up.'

The prospect of putting up the tents in this deluge and spending the night soaked through did not appeal.

'Okay, I'm for going on for a while,' I said.

'Suits me,' he replied.

Slogging on we tried to negotiate a way through the quagmire, dodging cascading streams of water and collapsed drainage ditches, half a metre wide. After an hour, through perpendicular rain, I spotted a sign.

HIPPO LODGE

ROOMS, MEALS AND BAR.

5 KM

We stopped the bikes and looked at each other. Without exchanging a word, we turned down the small track which lead to sanctuary. An hour later, having just enjoyed a steaming hot shower, we were sitting in the *Hippo Lodge* drinking cold Windhoek lager and tucking into succulent rump steaks.

I looked across at Andy and grinned, 'Who needs heroes?'

The following morning I woke to the sound of rain hammering on the thatched roof of our room. The road would be impassable. There would be no cycling today. After a leisurely breakfast, I took a walk around the grounds of the *Hippo Lodge*. It was ideally situated on the banks of the Zambezi, with a clear view across three hundred metres of water to the bush of Zambia on the other side. The gardens were ablaze with purple, yellow and red blooms from a thousand exotic flowers. The lush, emerald green lawns had been nourished by heavy rains.

Hippo Lodge had been tastefully designed; the huts fashioned from local wood and thatch. I settled into a comfortable wicker armchair, in a thatched gazebo, to watch the broad backs and twitching ears of a group of hippos wallowing fifty metres away in the muddy waters. I sipped tea from a china cup and put my feet up for an hour or more, content with my own company.

Presently, a herd of a dozen elephant emerged from the bush and entered a clearing on the other side of the river. A small calf played by the side of its mother, tossing leaves into the air with its tiny trunk. The herd leader, a big old bull, backed himself up against an acacia tree and rubbed his backside up and down the rough trunk, relieving a troublesome itch before leading the group back into the bush.

Using a hose, which I had found in the gardens, we set about cleaning the bikes. Keeping them in good working order was a high priority.

Our maintenance session revealed a broken spoke in one of Andy's wheels. This was difficult to replace because the freewheel had become jammed. Good fortune smiled upon us in the form of Healie, a white garage mechanic employed by the local Toyota dealer. Healie, we discovered, had a workshop of his own at home.

Andy recalls: Healie took me back to his workshop in Katima to use his vice. He poured two stiff rum and Cokes and we chatted whilst I worked on my bike and he tinkered with a troublesome carburettor.

'You have a great advantage travelling by bike,' said Healie.

'Why do you say that?' I asked.

'Because you guys have seen Africa as no white or black has. The blacks tend to stay close to their villages whilst the whites race past everything at a hundred k's an hour. You guys are just out there all the time, seeing and feeling everything.'

Meanwhile, back in the bar of the *Hippo Lodge* I got talking to Adri and Jannie, two South African road engineers.

'Man, what are you doing in this God forsaken place, eh?' asked Adri in the thick, nasal accent of the Afrikaaner. He was the boss, a big, bull-necked man with heavy jowls and a raw, sunburned face.

'I'm riding a bike to Swakopmund,' I told him.

'Ah, Swakopmund', said Jannie with a wistful look in his eye, 'now there's a place for drinking a few beers, eh.' He was a wiry little man with bored, muddy-brown eyes and the skin of a withered prune.

'What are you guys doing out here then?' I asked.

'We're supposed to be building a road between here and Rundu,' said Adri. 'But we haven't got very far with it.'

'What's the problem?' I asked.

'It's like everything else in this tin pot country man – half-arsed and crap,' Jannie snapped. 'The government wants a road built but doesn't want to pay for it. They use cheap kaffir labour who keep knocking over the bleedin' levelling pegs. The materials are cheap and the schoolboy German planner doesn't know his arse from his elbow. They get what they deserve – a real shit job. I'd bet a thousand rand the road falls apart a year after it's built.'

'Suits us', said Adri, grinning, 'coz we're the boys who'll have to come back and mend it. How about more beers eh?'

Katima Mulilo is the regional capital of the Caprivi Strip, a pleasant town surrounded by lush vegetation and abundant wildlife. It was also an important garrison for South African troops during a recent bitter war.

Namibia, under its former name of South West Africa, had been under the control of South Africa since the early part of the twentieth century. The whites owned and developed the land, mines and commerce.

The blacks were restricted by labour and pass laws and herded into reserves. World opinion denounced this illegal regime but South Africa maintained its grip. In the 1960s a war of liberation was mounted by SWAPO guerillas (South West Africa People's

Organisation). The fighting escalated during the seventies and eighties. SWAPO set up guerilla bases inside neighbouring Angola (who also opposed South Africa). From here they conducted raids into South West Africa. More than ten thousand South African troops and some twenty one thousand troops of the South West Africa Territorial Force were stationed along the border with Angola. These forces carried out a number of full scale invasions of southern Angola aimed at wiping out SWAPO guerilla bases.

South Africa's determination to hold on to South West Africa was due, partly, to fear of having another hostile Marxist regime on its borders. The black governments of Zimbabwe and Mozambique were already heavily anti-South Africa. The prospect of losing the fantastic natural wealth of the country was, undoubtedly, another major factor. Namibia is rich in uranium, copper, lead and zinc. It is also the world's premier source of gem diamonds. These were all mined by South African and multi-national western companies using a black labour force.

It was probably not the activities of SWAPO or the pressure of international sanctions which forced South Africa to grant Namibia its independence. White Namibians were becoming dissatisfied with the effects of war on the economy and the exploitation of the country's mineral wealth by foreigners. The war was becoming very costly in terms of human life and damage to the country.

Finally, in March 1991, South Africa granted Namibia independence as a Republic. An election was held which had an incredibly low turn out. In some areas only 5% of the electorate voted. A government was formed under Marxist president Sam Nujoma, the former SWAPO leader. Shortly after taking power, Nujoma was reported to have advised the coloured people that if the white man had something they wanted then they should go out and take it.

The blacks now have political control but whites have extensive commercial power and the business expertise which the government desperately needs. It remains to be seen if Namibia has been given real freedom or simply a crippled economy which is totally dependant upon South Africa.

We stopped in Katima town centre to stock up with provisions.

The next stretch across the Caprivi Strip would mean surviving for a week or more in the wilderness. This would be our last chance to buy food before we reached Rundu.

It was possible to buy soya mince, jam, biscuits, peanut butter, chocolate and corned beef, all imported from South Africa. These were paid for in South African rand, still the currency of Namibia.

By the time we had messed about paying bills, oiling chains and shopping it was mid-afternoon. Fortunately, the first section of road was sealed and we made good progress covering eighty kilometres before dusk through sparse bushland.

Our reserves of strength and stamina had been built up over the months so that we were now cycling farther each day than at any other time. It was interesting to reflect on the early days of the expedition in Australia when we had struggled to cover seventy kilometres in a day. Now we were disappointed if we did not complete a hundred kilometres each day. Often we managed much more.

Even more amazing, was the fact that Andy and I were still getting on after all these months together. In almost eight months we had only spent three weeks apart, whilst in Kenya. We now worked well as a team, planning and organising everything together without a cross word between us. The secret to the success of our partnership was space. When I was tired or niggled, Andy naturally backed off and vice versa. Gone were the scenes of confrontation that had been so destructive in Australia. I enjoyed Andy's company but was also content to spend many hours each day riding alone, wrapped in my own thoughts. I am essentially a social animal who thrives on human contact. The trip had taught me I could never have survived such an experience alone. There would have been too many days trapped inside my head lost in pointless introspection.

I had experienced some unforgettable moments which had been all the better for having had Andy there to share them. I also needed a companion to bounce ideas off. Part of my inner strength to continue came from the comforting knowledge that I had a tried and trusted friend on hand at all times.

As the sun dipped below the veld we pulled the bikes off the road and found a campsite concealed by stunted trees and thorny green bushes. I sat cross-legged on the sand and cooked up spaghetti, chilli beans and bully beef whilst Andy stretched out on his sleeping mat to attend to the new *'Captain's Log',* his daily ritual of recording facts and figures.

The following morning we continued pedalling west on the sealed road. The tar turned to sand as we entered Caprivi Game Park. Once more it was hard, physical work pumping the pedals to drive the bikes through thick sand under a pale blue sky. There was a total absence of wildlife despite the dense bush. Perhaps all the game had been shot or frightened off during the recent years of fighting.

By early afternoon the temperature had risen to forty-five degrees Celsius and we had run out of water. The twenty-four litres we had carried from Katima was all used up. I watched Andy lick the last precious drop from his water bottle as we stood under the patchy shade of a spindly tree.

'You could say we're in the brown and smelly stuff,' I said.

'You're not wrong there,' he replied. 'It's not going to be much fun out here without water. We'll just have to pray for a miracle.'

As we stood there, pondering our predicament and putting our faith in mindless optimism, I noticed a thin plume of dust moving towards us from the west.

'It's some type of vehicle,' I said.

This was a rarity. We had been passed by only a handful of vehicles since leaving Katima the previous day.

Within a few minutes the dust trail had almost reached us. Andy and I stood in the middle of the road frantically waving our arms. A bright yellow Toyota Land Cruiser skidded to a halt, enveloping us in a cloud of choking white dust.

The driver's door flew open and out stepped a priest in flowing purple robes. He was white, in his fifties with iron-grey hair and steel-rimmed glasses. From the other side of the Land Cruiser appeared two young black nuns, splendid in grey-blue habits and white wimples.

'Good afternoon to you,' the priest greeted us. 'My name's Father Heinrich. May I introduce sister Mary and sister Ruth.'

'Nice to meet you,' said Andy, looking stunned.

'Now how may we be of assistance?' he asked.

'Have you any drinking water you could spare?' I asked.

'Water! Lord above we can do better than that,' he said. 'How about cold Pepsi?'

From the back of the vehicle he produced an ice box and we gulped down chilled Pepsi and re-filled our bags with fresh, cold drinking water. Heaven!

'Where are you going?' he asked.

'We're heading for Rundu,' I told him.

'It must be mighty hard work riding bicycles out here,' said Father Heinrich.

'Yes', Andy agreed looking over at me, 'it does have its moments.'

'Well, we must be going,' said the Father. 'We're on our way to Victoria Falls for a holiday.'

He pulled the Toyota back onto the sand, shouted, 'God be with you,' and roared off east towards Zimbabwe.

'Amazing!' I said, looking at Andy in wonderment. 'You didn't tell me you had a direct line to the *Big Man.*'

14 Sauerkraut and Cream Cakes – Tim

We toiled on the sand throughout our second morning out from Katima. Constantly switching back and forth to avoid ruts, we searched for the easiest ground to pedal through. I rode ahead, Andy a hundred metres behind when a huge articulated lorry, similar to the road trains of the Nullarbor, hammered towards me. Enormous wheels sprayed sand, dust and gravel in all directions. I ducked my head to avoid a shower of debris but was caught on the fingers by a flying stone. Pain shot through my hand and I swerved blindly into the side of the road through billowing clouds of dust. I hit a boulder the size of a large medicine ball and went sailing over the handlebars to land on my nose in sand and gravel. I lay by the side of the road for many seconds, too shocked and winded to move when Andy drew up.

'Are you okay?' he asked showing concern.

'No problem!' I replied clutching bleeding fingers to my chest. 'I just haven't quite got the hang of steering this thing yet.'

Later that afternoon the village of Omega appeared unexpectedly from the bush. Turning our wheels off the main road, we headed down a rough dirt track towards the centre of the village. We never missed an opportunity to refill the water bags and the possibility of buying bread to supplement the evening meal.

At seven am a shimmering heat haze had begun to distort the air above the bush. Tired and filthy after a long spell of isolation, we broke camp for our sixth day on the Caprivi Strip. We had covered more than four hundred kilometres from Katima and I was on my last pair of underpants. The last clean T-shirt had been donned two days before and was now little more than a filthy, stinking rag. My socks were about to walk off into the bush to die quietly by themselves. Washing and shaving were luxuries we could ill afford so we were both now sporting swarthy beards.

By now we had left the game park and crossed the slow moving Okavango River. The nearer we got to Rundu the more the road managed to deteriorate.

There was a lot of activity on this section of road. Road diggers and heavy machinery were busy doing something, although I found it difficult to see exactly what. Huge yellow bulldozers constantly trundled up and down scraping off the top layer of sand, pushing it to the side of the road. The exercise seemed quite pointless. No sooner was the sand pushed aside than it was washed back by rains and rutted again by trucks. Nobody was actually getting around to Tarmacing the surface. This was probably because the South African engineers conducting the operation were permanently resident in the bar of the *Hippo Lodge* back in Katima Mulilo. While they drank beer and enjoyed a prolonged absence from their wives, the black workers drove continuously up and down the road, keeping it clear.

Riding on ahead, I failed to read a sign which was written in German or Afrikaans.

Andy recalls: 'I realised that this sign pointed to the new sealed road we were looking for and that Tim, riding a few hundred metres ahead, had missed it. It was more than a little frustrating to know we were wasting time and energy on this terrible road when we could have been gliding along on smooth Tarmac. It was incredibly hot. I was physically drained and struggling along the worst road in the whole of Africa. For the second time since leaving Sydney (the first being before Border Village on the Nullarbor) I had to admit this was not fun. When I finally caught up with Tim I told him, as calmly as I could manage, that all that time and effort had just been wasted. I also knew we needed to fill up with water. There wasn't likely to be any on the new road. We passed a small cluster of huts on the way back but, for some reason, I was not my normally assertive self and didn't insist on stopping to find water. In his usual optimistic way Tim was confident we would find water before Rundu. We didn't.'

A new tarred road provided blessed relief at six pm. A sign informed us Rundu was still forty kilometres away. Andy looked across at me.

'There's seven-eighths of bugger all out here,' I observed.

'Yes', he replied, 'you could say that. I certainly don't fancy spending tonight and tomorrow morning out here without water.'

'Let's take a break, cook up some grub and go for it tonight,' I suggested.

'Sounds like a good idea,' he replied.

By now we had both used up most of our energy resources and were starting to feel light-headed and weak. With the last of the fuel and water, I cooked up pasta and soup and brewed a couple of mugs of tea. By the time we put our sore backsides into the saddle again the sun was fast disappearing. A cold wind had sprung up, replacing the heat of the day and putting a chill into our bones.

Andy set a fierce pace, determined to reach Rundu that night come what may. We belted along side by side, riding west into the setting sun, concentrating on keeping the rhythm of pounding legs. After an hour we were riding in the dark. My mind and body had become numb, shut off to pain and thought. There was only the road, the darkness, and the rush of the wind. Nothing else existed.

As we neared Rundu, my mind snapped back to awareness as we narrowly missed riding into a huge yellow bulldozer. It had been working on the road and was parked without lights, sticking out into the road. The next hazard was a pedestrian, whom I avoided by a whisker as he walked down the centre of the road in pitch darkness.

At 8.30 pm totally exhausted, we crawled onto the forecourt of a smart petrol station on the outskirts of Rundu. My cyclometre read one hundred and forty-two kilometres. Andy approached the petrol pump attendant to ask him where we could stay.

'The camp site is burned down,' was his reply.

Too tired to explore this oddity, we found the police station and were given permission to camp on the lush, green lawns. I crawled into my sleeping bag and made a short entry in my journal:

'31st March

This is wild. This is now. This is Africa. It doesn't answer any questions, it simply is. This week has been the very heart of the whole expedition. Out in the middle of the bush, in the heat and sand. Pure pain. Survive this and we can survive anything!'

I drifted into sleep with a big grin on my face. We had broken the back of it. The Caprivi Strip and *'Darkest Africa'* had been overcome. Next morning, as we sat in front of the tents relaxing and brewing tea in the sunshine, a black policemen wandered across to talk to us.

'Hello my friends,' he greeted us. 'You are wise to have chosen the safest place in Namibia to put up your tents.' Peter was a tall, elegant detective in his early thirties, dressed smartly in grey suit and paisley tie.

'You have very nice bicycles and much equipment,' he stated. 'May I ask from where you have travelled?'

'We've ridden all the way from Kenya', I told him, 'and we're heading across to Swakopmund.'

'You are to be saluted,' he said with a big friendly smile. 'I would like to be with you on such a journey.'

'Why don't you join us?' I joked.

He seemed to take my proposition seriously.

'Unfortunately, I have a disability that makes this impossible,' he said. I could see regret in his dark eyes.

'We have had many problems here in Namibia in past years,' he told us. 'I was in the army, stationed at Katima for two years fighting against SWAPO.' He rapped his right leg with his knuckles, making a dull, hollow sound. 'I lost this leg.'

'How did it happen?' I asked, hoping he would not take offence at such a direct question.

He appeared not to mind my prying.

'I was travelling in a Landrover when it was hit by a rocket' he said without emotion. 'The driver was killed and I survived with only one leg. It troubles me no longer, but riding bicycles is not possible,' he said with a grin.

Andy changed the tack of the conversation. 'This is a very big station, is there much crime here in Rundu?'

'Oh yes', he replied, 'there is much for us to do here. I am working on a very serious case at this very moment. I have twenty-four people locked up under investigation for murder.'

'There are twenty-four murder suspects locked up here?' I asked in amazement.

'Yes, they are locked up only fifty metres from here,' he said.

'What, you've had twenty-four murders here?' exclaimed Andy.

'No, just one. It is an interesting case,' said Peter. 'A black driver was operating a large digging machine on the road to Katima. The same road as you must have travelled. (I remembered the roadworks and large yellow bulldozer we had nearly crashed into in the dark the night before). This man, he lost control of his machine and crashed into a Toyota pick-up filled with villagers. It was a terrible accident. All eight people in the Toyota were killed immediately. When the news of the accident spread, the friends and families of the dead went looking for the driver. When we arrived we found his body, mutilated. His eyes were pulled out, his ears torn off and his testicles removed. A most horrible sight. We arrested many suspects.' Peter shook his head and murmured, 'These people simply cannot take the law into their own hands.'

'Wow!' exclaimed Andy. 'When did this happen?'

'Yesterday afternoon,' he replied.

'That can't have been more than a few hours before we rode past those roadworks,' I said. I noticed Andy's sunburned face had drained of colour.

We took a much needed rest day in Rundu. I strolled around the town, leaving Andy in a café indulging in a favourite hobby – stuffing himself full of cream cakes. I walked down a wide main street full of pot holes, past shabby shops selling cheap clothes and hardware. There was a mixture of black, white and coffee-coloured people speaking a mixture of languages. Blacks and whites spoke Portuguese or German. Some whites spoke Afrikaans whilst many blacks spoke their own native languages including the unusual clicking language of the Kalahari Bushmen. Rundu was a half-way house, a place where the diverse races of Namibia mingled on their way across the Caprivi Strip.

Back in our safe camping site we were joined by Mike, a lone South African cyclist. He was slight in build with short-cropped, brown hair and wore fancy, wrap around cycling shades.

'I'm from Jo'burg,' he told us. 'I'm cycling east across Namibia to Zimbabwe.'

'We're headed the other way', I told him, 'west to Swakopmund.'

'I'm going to Victoria Falls, then all the way up to Egypt ,' he continued as though he had not heard me. 'By the time I've finished, I'll have seen everything there is to see in Africa.'

'Oh no' I thought, 'we've got a 'Been There Done That' here'.

We had come across a few of these characters, travellers who were only interested in bragging about the number of places they had seen. For the next hour he kept up a non-stop monologue on the subject of 'Mike's Travels'. Andy and I rarely got a word in. The final straw came when he started talking about Britain.

'Well of course', he said, full of himself, 'Britain's a Third World country.'

'What!' roared Andy. 'You don't know what the hell you're talking about.'

'You only have to look at the Gross National Product to see that Britain is a spent force,' said Mike.

'Bullshit!,' said Andy. 'Have you ever been to Britain?'

'Actually, no,' said Mike.

'Well', continued Andy, 'until you've been to a country and seen it first-hand I don't see how you can comment.' Neither Andy nor I thought of ourselves as being particularly nationalistic but we were certainly not going to sit by in silence, whilst this arrogant South African rubbished our country.

Mike sank even lower in our estimation after he offered to change our excess Zimbabwe dollars for South African rand. He did not have enough rand on him and promised to pay us the balance in the morning. We never saw him or the money again.

There was something about such long distance, solitary cyclists I did not care for. They were generally loners, totally wrapped up in themselves and their own achievements with little time for anyone else. It confirmed my earlier suspicions that being trapped inside your own head for too long is not healthy.

We covered the two hundred and seventy kilometres, south

west to Grootfontein, during the first two days of April and revelled in the luxury of an excellent, flat Tarmac road. At the end of the first day, we came across a transport cafe in the middle of the bush. A white, German speaking couple had set up shop in an old coach and were doing a roaring trade serving greasy fry-ups and chip butties. We pitched the tents by the side of the coach in pouring rain and eagerly tucked into piles of junk food. We had not had a sniff of burger and chips since Victoria Falls. A huge German Shepherd dog, who patrolled the premises, became a firm friend when we shared our feast with him.

The following afternoon on the outskirts of Grootfontein, Andy turned in his saddle towards me, excitement written all over his face. He pointed to a scrawny, stunted piece of vegetation by the side of the road ten metres ahead.

'Do you know the significance of that bush there?' he asked.

'Yes', I said. 'It was the sight of a famous battle between Count Otto von Bratwurst and an army of three foot tall Kalahari bushmen.'

'Close,' said Andy. 'It is, in fact, two thirds of the way around the world – ten thousand kilometres and exactly eight months from leaving Sydney. This means we're still bang on target to reach the coast of Chile within the year.'

I looked at him with admiration.

'That's amazing Andrew', I said. 'Just how do you do it?'

As we rode past *'das kino'*, on the outskirts of Grootfontein, we were overtaken by a couple of young white lads on new mountain bikes. The cinema was showing *Robin Hood,* starring Kevin Costner. We were back in civilisation.

We pedalled on past *'das rathaus'* and *'die kirche'*, weaving in between gleaming Mercedes and BMW's.

'Güten Tag meine herren, möchten sie etwas zu trinken?' asked the burly landlord of the *Nord Hotel*.

'Zwei biers bitte,' I replied, trying to recall my schoolboy German.

All the people in the bar, black and white, were German speaking. We were served weinerschnitzel, sauerkraut and apfel strudel by a big, hearty girl in traditional Bavarian dress and drank cold lager from heavy litre steins. I felt we could have been in a bar in any small town in Germany.

Namibia was annexed by Germany in the last minute scramble for colonies towards the end of the 19th century. The indigenous tribes, the Herero, Nama and Ovambo, fought to keep their independence and in 1904 rose in rebellion against the German colonial authorities who responded with a campaign of genocide, which wiped out some 60% of the native population.

The period of German colonisation came to an end in 1915 when the colonial army – the *Kaiserliche Schutztruppe fur Deutsch Sud-West Afrika* – surrendered to a South African expeditionary army fighting on behalf of the allies. Namibia still retains a strong German influence as could clearly be seen in Grootfontein.

We found the majority of whites here to be aloof, arrogant and serious whilst the black people were surly and suspicious.

> **Andy recalls:**'I had a conversation with Michael, a young black lad, whilst he was waiting for a bus and I was fiddling with my bike. He was a tall, bright lad of about fifteen. We chatted for twenty minutes. He told me there was still apartheid in Namibia, despite the new black government. He could not get the same quality of education, housing or employment as white people. The government had told the people apartheid was a thing of the past. He thought this was a lie to encourage foreign aid and investment'.

The road from Grootfontein to Omaruru consists of three hundred and fifty kilometres of straight, flat road running south west through featureless bush. We were now flying along, covering one hundred and thirty kilometres each day, with the scent of victory in our nostrils.

Part of our Saturday routine was to stop in the bush, brew up, and listen to sport on the *World Service*. I had already celebrated England victories in the five nations rugby tournament. Whilst England were scoring tries at Twickenham, I was frightening baboons in Zambia, dancing around the bush in my underpants to the accompaniment of *Swing Low Sweet Chariot*. In the hotel in Grootfontein we had tuned into the Oxford versus Cambridge

Boat Race. Today in the Namibian bush it was the Aintree Grand National.

My chain snapped on a long, slow climb out of Usakos, one hundred kilometres south-west of Omaruru. There was no warning, just a pinging sound and the sudden release of tension on the chain-wheel.

'We could have done without that,' said Andy.

'Yes', I replied. 'I'd hoped we'd get another twenty or thirty k's in tonight.'

The sun was beginning to dip behind the hills to the west as the chain broke twice more and we spent the best part of an hour fiddling with chain links and pins.

'There's not much point in going any further tonight in the dark,' I said, once we had fixed the chain.

'You're right, let's camp here,' said Andy. 'The only problem is it leaves us with a hundred and fifty k's to do tomorrow if we're going to reach Swakopmund. That's a hell of a long day.'

'At least we'll be finishing in style,' I replied.

We pitched the tents amongst dusty green thorn bushes, cooked up pasta and cheese for supper and lay outside on our sleeping mats under a clear, star-bright sky. I was on the point of dozing off when I was startled by a huge roar a few metres to my left. I was up and out of my sleeping bag in an instant, turning to face the danger, ready to fend off the rush of a charging lion or leopard. Instead, it was a big daddy bull that appeared from behind a thorn bush. Having vented his anger and proved who was boss, he wandered off into the darkness. Andy, who was still in his sleeping bag, was clutching his sides helpless with laughter.

'That's the fastest I've seen you move since they called last orders in the *Malt Shovel*,' he said, gasping for air.

The following morning we were on the road by 7 am, an early start essential, with such a long stretch ahead of us. The first twenty kilometres continued up-hill against a stiff head wind, making progress slow.

Eventually, the road levelled out to run arrow-straight across the desert, west towards Swakopmund. To the left, an endless line of telegraph poles faded into infinity. To the right was the

Windhoek–Swakomund railway, by the side of which ran a huge metal pipe-line raised on stilts, two metres above the desert.

The landscape changed from the familiar, featureless bushland into real desert. The vegetation gradually disappeared, until we found ourselves riding through a barren moonscape of sand and boulders, stretching away in all directions.

Hour after hour we pedalled on under a cruel sun, eyes shaded behind dark glasses, heads covered by bush hats. Every ten kilometres there was a sign – Swakopmund 130 KM ... 120 KM ... 110KM. Psychologically this was tough, as each ten kilometre stretch seemed to take an eternity and each sign looked the same as the one before. The desert, the straight road, the strong headwind, the pipeline and the thirst were unchanging. A desperate tiredness had crept through my whole body.

To cope with this ceaseless torment, I shut my mind to road signs, desert and exhaustion and allowed my imagination to whisk me away. We had promised ourselves three weeks off after completing this African leg of the expedition. I experimented with images in my mind. I was drinking cold lager, watching rugby in the sunshine of Pretoria, with my old mate Chris *'Zouga'* Morton. I was heroically fighting alongside the Welsh Borderers of Rorke's Drift, against a black mass of four thousand rampaging Zulu warriors. I was lying on the beaches of Cape Town soaking up the sun's rays. On the top of Table Mountain I gazed down on the Cape of Good Hope where Indian Ocean meets Atlantic.

'Just a few more hours,' I thought, *'and the pain will be over and all these things will be yours. Keep the legs pumping, keep the rhythm, put your head down. Not long now.'*

We pedalled on through the fierce heat of the midday sun, stopping every few hours to brew up in silence. Wrapped in personal battles against heat and exhaustion, neither of us had energy for talking.

The worst of the afternoon heat slowly passed and was replaced by cooler air. An eerie white sea fog rolled towards us, across the desert, drifting in from the coast. I welcomed the cool blanket of mist which indicated how close we were to our goal. Still struggling against a headwind, we took it in turns riding in front to shield each other. Five kilometres and change over; hard physical graft up front, blessed relief cruising behind. Another sign materialised through the mist:

SWAKOPMUND – 10 KM

I shook my head in disbelief. Ten kilometres more and we would have ridden across Africa! Almost five thousand kilometres in thirteen weeks, surviving everything this wild continent could throw at us. We were so close now, I could smell salt air.

We pedalled into the centre of Swakopmund at 9 pm, fourteen hours after hitting the road that morning. Neither of us talked as we rode slowly through the dark, quiet streets lost in our own thoughts. Reaching the sea-front we rode out along the ancient wooden pier through an eerie shroud of sea-mist. Black fishermen, in woolly balaclava hats, sat with their backs to us as we passed. Coy lovers stole kisses in the shadows. White surf crashed angrily beneath our wheels as we reached the end of the pier. Breaking with convention we hugged each other. Standing side by side, we stared silently out into the infinite darkness of the Atlantic Ocean.

SOUTH AMERICA

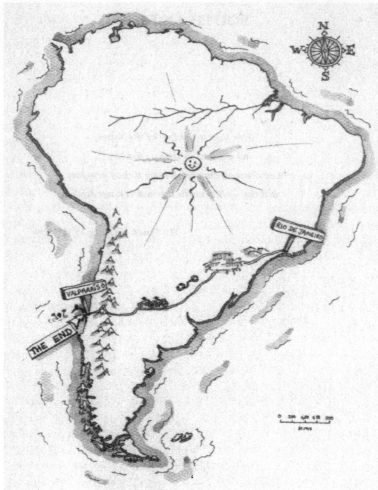

Now that is the law of the jungle
as old and as true as the sky;
And the wolf that shall keep it may prosper
but the wolf that shall break it must die.'

Rudyard Kipling 1885-1936

15 Hottest spot north of Havana – Andy

Fear must have shown in my eyes. With sun bleached, blond hair I was a prime target. We stepped out of the back street hotel. It was dark. I looked left and right. Gangs of youths lurked in shadows. We had taken ten paces towards the neon glare of the plaza, a tantalising hundred metres away, when the lads closed in. One grabbed my right wrist and held it tight, staring into my eyes; he smelled and looked decayed. His eyes showed no fear, shame or guilt, such traits were long gone. His was a life of survival like a wild animal. If I had been wearing a watch it would now be his. His left hand shot in and out of my back pocket and found nothing. I swore at him, shook my arm free and strode off. The lads jeered. Our first taste of downtown Rio de Janeiro.

We had been in the country two hours; flown in from Cape Town, one marvellous city to another. After finishing cycling in Swakopmund, our African mission complete, we had switched off. We had been capable of nothing but sleeping, sitting and eating, seldom leaving the guest house. After a week, we had roused ourselves sufficiently to travel down to South Africa. It wasn't an easy decision to make. Should we go or not? In the end we felt we could have no real view of the politics of the country unless we saw it for ourselves. South Africa, for me, oozed evil. Whatever people said about reform, reality could not be pushed out of sight. The whites were living the high life; the blacks were down-trodden, resentful, broken spirited. This is not the way the world was meant to be. Black is not inferior to white. Only a few people from each race seemed to really believe this, the rest just muddled along ignoring the gross insult of it all. *'We built this country'*, say the whites. *'Before we came there was nothing'*. The history of the black South African tribes before white men showed up, though, is full of honour, courage and justice. The history of the white man in South Africa is full of greed, self importance and damage. Now that the black man has taken his rightful place in the world, after so much oppression and deprivation, there must surely be a taking of revenge; it's the way of nature.

Over the final days in Cape Town I had been pre-occupied with the words of the dour Scotsman at Balladonia on the Nullarbor, with his beautifully rolled R's, *'... Australia and Afrrica urr fine lads, but Sooth America, thut's wherre you'll end yrr days'*. As the plane started its long descent, far out over the Atlantic, I went to wash. In the mirror I saw an unusual sight. Was it stress and apprehension? We must be nuts! Cycling across South America? We were going to die. We knew virtually nothing about the continent. We had never met anyone who had even crossed it by bus let alone by bike. All I could imagine were bandits, drug dealers, endless jungle and bent policemen. Our luck could not hold out. We were going to die.

I returned to my seat and we planned how we were going to get ourselves and the gear safely to a hotel. I studied Tim as we talked, Yep, it was in his face too.

Against our instincts we had ventured out. We could not ignore our hunger any longer. Tim and I had been in many wild places in the world; Rio had its own elite reputation and its own air of menace. We were in one of the most dangerous places in town, at night, feeling extremely foreign.

Between the hotel and the street café, five hundred metres away in the cobbled plaza, I was hassled another three times whilst Tim, with his dark complexion and swarthy looks, passed for a local. Every hawker came running. We could speak no Portuguese but understood the offers of chewing gum, peanuts, big wooden ships, pens and cigarettes. We dismissed them all. I was so defensive that I even refused to buy caramels from a friendly lady in a wheelchair. I hated myself instantly. Tim told me off, 'She's got no bloody legs Andy! And she's selling not begging!' I was able to clear my conscience by buying some and paying extra, when she returned half an hour later. We had often given a few coins to needy people we had met in Africa, but this atmosphere was far more aggressive. Later, we were approached by two little cuties with big brown eyes. They were perhaps seven and five, around the same age as Lauren, Holly and Dulcie, my nieces. It was eleven o'clock, but these two were not snuggled up in bed, safe and warm with cuddly pink toys. They had to sell an armful of leather bangles before they could sleep, driven, no doubt, by some master hiding round the corner. Selling to drunks and tourists, in this wild city, was all they knew of life. Already they were well acquainted with blackmail. They talked and snuggled up to us, just as if they were still children. The little one lent her head into the comfy hollow of Tim's elbow and closed her eyes, exhausted. Soft black curls fell across her cheek. She let out a little whimpering sigh. It was pitiful. The older girl chattered away in Portuguese whilst playing with my fingers and comparing the size of my hand to hers. We bought four bangles and wore them for many weeks afterwards. We also gave the girls some extra cruzeiros for themselves and when they had gone, a teenage boy came up and demanded to know how much money we had given them; we pretended not to understand.

Over the next few days we gradually ventured further and further from the sanctuary of the hotel. Before stepping out we hid our money, passports and watches in the hotel room, behind the wardrobe.

In well hidden money belts we carried just enough cash for our immediate needs, plus ten dollars in a pocket, to give to a serious robber should we meet one. Our jazzy African shirts gave us away, so we began wearing plain T-shirts. I even contemplated dying my hair black but, seeing more and more blond Brazilians, decided to stick it out. We quickly learned the rules of the city: don't look people in the eye, ignore all shouts and greetings, don't look lost especially when you are, don't open a map in a public place, don't carry or wear anything worth stealing, walk confidently as though you have somewhere really important to go.

As our confidence increased and we started to blend in, the fear must have left our eyes because the bad guys left us alone.

We succumbed to the tourist sites; riding the cable-car to the top of Sugar Loaf Mountain, to view the magnificent Rio bays. Cloud enveloped the mountain summit, only occasionally dispersing to reveal the awesome statue with Speilberg eeriness. A mile or two from downtown, yuppies rode $500 mountain bikes up and down cycle tracks on Copacobana Beach. *'At the Copa, Copacobana, the hottest spot north of Havana ...'* goes the song. When we saw Rio it was about 8,000 kilometres south of Havana. The beach lay just across the road from the city's high-rise office blocks, hotels and shops. Crowds of workers joined the young tearaways and mulatto (half Indian) girls during lunch hour, flopping on the sand or dodging deadly surfers crashing through the shallows.

The beach was alive with volleyball tournaments, head tennis athletes, sun-lovers and body-lovers. Macho men strained at pull-ups and briefs at beach gyms whilst girls giggled and whistled. Voluptuous mulatto girls paraded in near-invisible costumes. Playful rogues slid about in the soft sand selling things that no one wanted: hot beers, dubious pre-cut mangos and melted ice cream. Litter was left where it fell; someone else could worry about that tonight. Children ghosted through the crowds sneaking unattended towels, flip-flops and T-shirts. People danced all afternoon to the rhythms of samba music, in private parties, under giant umbrellas. The beach was a microcosm of Brazilian life. These were fun people; so much sun gave them a coating of overwhelming *joie de vive*.

A skinny American in his forties, with a pony tail and a deep tan, came at me out of the sun and thrust a camera in my hand. 'Photograph me with this chick's aaase!', he ordered, though he probably thought it was a request. Surf crashed in the reflection of his dark glasses. 'These girls have the best butts in the whole world', he preached, turning his companion around; her behind was barely covered, 'and I should know, I've been *everywhere.'* he continued. I reluctantly took the snap of the guy and the young girl, or at least part of her. 'I love these chicks so much', he shouted.

'I'm buying a house down here ... *FOR CASH!!'* With that he took the camera and strode off. I had not spoken one word to him.

A gang of lily white bodies wandered along the beach. The bodies held great beer bellies and blue tattoos. 'Pipe-cleaner' legs dangled beneath. Colourful long shorts magnified pale, unhealthy skin. Tim struck up a conversation as they passed, 'Is there a ship in port?' he asked.

'How can you tell?' the lads asked.

They were Royal Navy, on exercise, (they needed it too). They sat down beside us on the hot sand. For some reason I had assumed that our sailors would be kept fighting fit. These poor guys, it seems, were cooped up in the depths of the ship for weeks on end, without exercise or even a sniff of the sun.

'I ain't touchin' these girls, not me', said one sailor in a thick, nasal Birmingham accent. 'They've made us watch that many films, about all them diseases, ya know, I feel sick just looking at women.'

During the day, the faces in the crowded streets of downtown Rio told the history of the country. After nearly five hundred years of European settlement half were of pure European stock: Portuguese, Italian, German and Spanish. I had now seen so many blondes that I stopped looking out for them. About a third of the people looked of mixed race, Indian with European. There seemed to be a white professional class, driving big American cars. The rest were black; descendents of slaves taken from East Africa, Kenya and Tanzania, probably passing through Mombasa. All appeared to knock along in harmony. Only later in Amazonia and the southern mountains did we see pure Indians.

Bedraggled children were everywhere; not part of anything yet at the centre of everything. There are perhaps two hundred thousand of them surviving on the streets of Rio. Some hustle on the streets but go home to their families at night. Others have either been abandoned, or have left of their own accord. For these children the street is their only home and its pickings their only hope of survival. Without family support or guidance, it is hardly surprising that their moral values have become distorted. The police treat them like vermin, not people. There is said to be a programme of routine culling, by *Death Squads,* to keep the numbers down. If the unlucky kids are not murdered they may be jailed along with adult prisoners. Jails are regarded as places of punishment and abuse, not of child care. At a street café we invited two small boys to polish off our spaghetti bolognese and salad; they washed it down with a slug of sugar from the glass container on the table, all the while checking us over to see if we had anything worth stealing. The waiter shooed them away.

As they ran across the street I noticed one of them held a clear plastic bag stuffed with bank notes. It looked a king's ransom but those low denomination notes were almost valueless.

Steep mountains of rounded volcanic rock, some heavily wooded, surround and penetrate the city. Bare granite contrasts with smart shops, lush parks, a jumble of skyscrapers and silvery beaches. In other great cities of the world it is the rich who inhabit the cool and security of the high ground. Here the rich live on the beach front. On Rio's hills are the *flavelas*. Shanty towns controlled by Mafia-like organisations, where police and city officials do not, or cannot, interfere. If you live on the hill you are safe. A stranger will be spotted and dealt with quickly, perhaps killed. Prostitution, drugs and gambling empires are protected with AK47 assault rifles. Inter-hill conflicts, with forces of hundreds of men, are common. The men of the *flavelas* are better paid and better armed than the police, who just let them get on with it.

> **Tim recalls:** 'Despite its problems, Rio was a wonderful, vibrant city. Having to watch our backs (and our fronts) every moment added spice to the place. We loved everything about it. If your lot in life is to be poor, some say Rio is not such a bad place to be poor in. Cities like Calcutta, New York and London cannot offer the bonus of sublime climate, endless beaches or astonishing beauty. This is, I suppose, the simplistic, patronising view of the voyeur with dollars in his pocket. I doubt the street kids of Rio know or care what life on the streets of New York or Calcutta is like. With no shoes, no families, no school and no food, I doubt they wake up in the morning sun and say 'Oh, it's great to be alive!', I doubt they go skipping off down the muddy hills cheerily singing 'Always look on the bright side of life ...'

We left the bikes with a contact, the boss-man at the BP Investimentos Office, and flew up to Manaus in the Amazon. 'We can't come to Brazil and not see the Amazon,' we told ourselves, even though funds and time were short. When looking at a map of the whole of Brazil, flying from Rio to Manaus seemed a short distance; in fact it is as far as from Los Angeles to Miami.

It is easy to see why industrialists were blasé about forest clearance for so long; Amazonia is unimaginably vast; a seemingly endless ocean of green. A great area of cleared forest looks like a postage stamp when viewed from two thousand feet. Size, though, is deceptive.

Our mission to Amazonia was significantly less noble than saving the rain forest. We hired a boat and the services of three locals and went for a lazy chug down the river.

Snoozing in hammocks on the little river boat was spiced up with the odd adventure or two. After a long hot trek through the jungle one morning Dudu, our Indian guide, encouraged us to freshen up with a swim in the river, a small tributary of the Amazon. Tim and I stripped down to underwear, jumped off the boat and splashed around for ten minutes in the rust coloured water, feeling the grime and sweat fall off and our bodies cooling luxuriously. Dudu stayed aboard. We climbed out to a lunch of spaghetti, rice and fish, served on a trestle-table on deck. 'This afternoon I can teach you to fish for piranha if you want,' said Dudu as we ate.

'Great', said Tim, 'where will we go to fish, out into the main channel?'

'No, no', said Dudu nonchalantly, 'we can just fish over the side here.' Our mouths dropped. Piranhas, the stuff of James Bond movies; fish that eat elephants in two seconds flat and suck the bones clean. Dudu laughed.

He was twenty-two years old, short and powerful; life in the jungle had hardened his body. The jungle was his place. He knew it and we did not. This gave him confidence and a permanent grin. Although he had been exposed to very little schooling, he spoke his own Indian language, Portuguese, English, French, German, Italian and Danish, all picked up over the years from tourists.

The next day Dudu warned us, 'Must not pee while swimming here. You will bring fast, biting fish.' This fish, he claimed, would zoom to the source of the urine and start biting its way into the body in a frenzy.

We scientifically named it the *willy fish* and went swimming with our legs crossed. The following afternoon Dudu took us off into the swamps in a leaking wooden canoe, I sat at the back paddling as Dudu perched at the front navigating, paddling and showing us the Amazon's secrets. We were swallowed immediately by the sunken forest. Without Dudu we would have been hopelessly lost. For hour after hour we zig-zagged though a maze of thick-trunked trees and saplings, growing out of the metre deep water. Deeper and deeper into the flooded jungle we went. Dudu pointed out and named countless plants, spiders and creepy-crawlies. Monkeys barked as they chased and frolicked, leaping from branch to branch. Purple fruits, like big grapes, fell intermittently from the canopy, landing in the water with an eerie *ploop*. Water seeped into the canoe through ill fitting seals of black goo and we took it in turns to bail. We kept fingers out of the water as they would look quite tasty to a snake, piranha or even a *willy fish*. I wanted to know more about the rain forests from the Brazilian view point. Dudu was happy to have an audience.

Dudu told us as he paddled that he thought that by tu-tutting the Brazilians, the wester nations are throwing up a smoke screen, and that it is the North American and Europeans who, having destroyed their own forests, now destroy Amazonia to produce their coffee tables and hamburgers, destroying the complex food chains and interrelationships bewtween planys, trees, insects and birds. As he was talking I thought, *'Dudu must be a damned good navigator,'* every tree looked the same. Turning round I could not even make out where we had just come from. We had been out four hours and the sun was starting to set when Dudu stopped the canoe and shinned up a dead tree tilted at an angle of seventy degrees. From thirty feet up he could see above the low canopy. After a minute or two he came down looking worried and proclaimed 'We are completely lost!'

Tim turned round and we smiled at each other. We were both thinking, *'Yes, this is what we want! Adventure!'*

'If we don't find our way out in the next thirty minutes we will be staying out here all night,' Dudu added, looking genuinely worried. We had been scooping water out of the canoe, with a plastic plate, all afternoon. There would be nowhere dry to lie down; and what about the snakes and lost insects? Everything around here stung or bit. This was all the inspiration we needed.

Lost

Dudu found a tangled mass of creepers and vines, twenty metres wide, which he insisted was the way out. The canoe stuck fast on a bed of clinging greenery and could not move forward or back. By grabbing the vines and pulling with all our might Tim, Dudu and I were able to move it an inch, then another, and another. It seemed hopeless but gradually we eased through. Dudu found a further three such barriers; some contained spiky plants which had to be grabbed, other plants stung like nettles. Early qualms about touching a tree trunk for fear of spiders were soon lost. We had to get out. Actually we did have to get out, to lift the canoe over a fallen tree. We stood on the rotting tree and, huffing and puffing, pulled the vessel across, as the bark crumbled beneath us. Tim and I loved it. Dudu shouted encouragement as we heaved through impossible undergrowth in the gloom.

'This would have been easy if I had brought my machete!' called Dudu cheerfully. There was no polite answer to that.

At last we found a clearing where moonlight broke through the canopy; this was the channel we were searching for. Once in the narrow channel it was a half hour paddle back to the boat and by heck it was a beautiful sight. After dinner we sat chatting all evening on deck. I asked the obvious question, 'Why does the Brazilian Government allow the destruction of the rain forest?'

'They need the money to pay off loans,' said Dudu. Loans handed out by pushy American and British banks in the '70s and '80s.'

Many of those projects were under researched, inappropriate, and only designed to supply cheap goods for the West. They now spend more on servicing loans than on education or health.

I asked him what could be done.

'First we must sack the President. There is much corruption, so much money disappears. We must also control the use of the forest more than we do. The western banks should let us off some of our loans, they were the mistakes of the past but they will destroy the future for everyone.'

After the trip up to the Amazon we returned to Rio, vowing to come back someday. In the evenings, whilst Tim serviced the bikes and went to the movies, I sat alone quietly drinking beer and watching people. The city buzzed with countless bars and clubs. Girls cruised up and down the Avenue Atlantica, the three kilometre strip next to Copacobana Beach.

'Darling, I love you, you are very beautiful,' they would sidle up and whisper, as I drank icy glasses of Chopp beer at friendly street cafés. All looked stunning, dolled up to prowl the bars and the aptly named *HELPE*' disco. 'You don't want me darling? OK but I still love you.' One sent a little note via the waiter saying, 'You are alone I am alone, just buy me one beer darling.' Beautiful as the girls were, they were not hard to resist. I stuck to an amusing game of cat and mouse. 'Darling I will be your girlfriend for the whole week.'

'But my wife will suspect me,' I protested ... 'but I have a wooden leg ... but I prefer older women ... but I have no money.'

'I don't want money darling, I just want love.'

One German guy had hit the papers by going with a bar-girl in Rio and waking up two days later minus a kidney. It is said that unscrupulous transplant surgeons will pay about $20,000 for a healthy kidney. No thanks, babe!

16 Two scabby dogs on the road to Iguacu – Andy

After so much sun, it was ironic that when we eventually cycled out of Rio it was pouring with rain. Future visits to Worthing or Brighton in December would remind me of that morning in late May on Copacobana Beach.

The night before we left I had spoken to a journalist in the hotel bar. He had just come back from Bolivia and Peru and warned strongly against cycling across the Paraguayan Chaco, a nine hundred kilometre desert.

It would mean a major change of route, but once again we considered our mums and looked for an alternative!

The Andes form the backbone of South America, stretching nearly eight thousand kilometres from Tierra del Fuego in the south to the Caribbean. The only alternative pass over the mountains, available to us in winter, was in Argentina. We decided we would cycle across southern Brazil, southern Paraguay and central Argentina. We could, we hoped, cross the Andes between Mendoza and Valparaiso, Chile. Since the war, Argentinians are not noted for their hospitality towards Britons but we guessed they would be marginally safer than drug runners.

'We've as far to go now as from Morogoro to Swakopmund.' I told Tim. It was a long way. There were four and a half thousand kilometres to go. Our first goal was Curitiba, eleven hundred kilometres away, mostly along the coast. The proportion of distance covered against distance still to go would increase dramatically each day from now on. After the hard core endurance of Zambia and the Caprivi Strip, we felt we could achieve our mission. The hardest was surely behind us. I was glad, however, that we would cycle over the Andes mountains in midwinter as the grand finale.

Weird people were doggedly jogging, surfing and playing volleyball in the rain as we cycled along Ipanema Beach on a Saturday morning. I had thought such eccentricities were unique to the British. Our biggest worry was how to get through the suburbs without having our kidneys stolen. We need not have worried. The army ensured our safe passage. Hundreds of stern young men in green capes, fingers on triggers, lined our route along the shore.

Tanks stood at every intersection and at the entrance to every tunnel. They were taking no chances with these cyclists! The illusion was shattered when a speeding motorcade of motor cyclists, armoured cars, jeeps and a coach with blacked out windows forced us off the road and showered us with spray. They were either carrying a great politician or a major criminal; most Brazilians would say there is no difference!

The first day out of Rio was a bit of a balls up. After escaping, with the help of the army, we sped into the wind through misty beach resorts, heading west. Union Jacks flew proudly from our panniers. Day-trippers hooted and waved encouragement.

It was not long before we found our communication skills seriously lacking. The map was very basic, it showed neither villages nor minor roads. When we came to a three way junction, each road looking equally important, we sought help from a lad walking along the beach carrying a surfboard.

'Boa tarde,' (good afternoon), I said and in some sort of Portuguese asked, *'Donde este estrada para Santos?'* (Which way is Santos?). Santos was a mere six hundred and fifty kilometres away. It was like asking somebody in Margate, 'Which way to Durham?'

The young man rabitted on, '*@#?II <!~/ < @@*'> #+ *&!'. We listened intently.

'Uhm. Er. *Obrigardo*' (Cheers mate) I said.

'Did you get any of that?' Tim asked me.

'Something about cabbages, I think.'

We did not have a clue so took the road that continued along the coast. This quickly became a one in three ascent of K2. At the summit we planted a flag, then whizzed down the other side to another crossroads. We asked again. Same thing. Off we went through lovely villages in swamp land. On the edge of a great estuary we came to a town. It was getting late and we asked again, *'Donde este estrada para Santos'*. More pointing, more lingo and more long hills.

As dusk came a young couple stopped their Toyota pick-up as they passed us on a hill. The girl spoke English, she had worked in Los Angeles.

'Hi, we passed you this morning', she said, 'we've been out to Itacuruca. How's it going?' We told her we were looking for a campsite. 'There is a campsite near the beach just a few miles ahead,' she assured us. Off they went, wishing us luck. We followed them up the hill in the deepening gloom. Something was wrong here but I did not know what.

We came up to a three way junction. I thought I was dreaming. I had never been to Brazil before so I knew it was not *déja vu*. It was the same bloody three way junction we had been at four hours before. We had ridden in a circle. If we had carried on we would have been back in Rio in no time. I thought of all those hills we had climbed. All that wasted effort. I didn't cry but I didn't laugh either.

To make things worse, the nearby campsite wanted us to pay $20 US each, just to pitch tents. In Africa we had paid $2 each for hotels and had obviously camped free in the bush most of the time. We told them to stuff it. I was keen to move on anyway to avoid the embarrassment of being seen by the guy with the surfboard who had given us verbal directions earlier.

We turned around and cycled back in the dark, to a motel we had passed an hour before. A sweet young girl was at reception. Tim used the phrase book to ask for a room, but she spoke English.

'We have only double beds. Would you like it for one hour or four hours?' she asked. I watched her face carefully. She didn't blink, blush or look away. I turned to Tim, 'What do you say big boy?'

'I want everything,' he said, keeping a straight face.

'You better give us the whole night,' I told her.

We filled in the form, paid $10 US each and took a key.

'Enjoy yourselves!' she called happily as we pushed the bikes across the gravel. The room was dimly lit and dominated by a big, round bed with silky, pink sheets. Mirrors covered three walls *and* the ceiling! There was a double nozzle shower and no wardrobe. They didn't have a restaurant but we could order a meal from the room service menu if we wanted. I half expected the menu to say:

Beef Steak .... 5,000 Cruzeiros

Omelette .... 3,000 Cruzreiros

Buxom Brunette .... 20,000 Cruzeiros

Small Blonde .... American Express Only

Tim slept under the sheet, I slept on it. We took care not to touch or brush against each other in the night.

We were up and off in the early sun next morning, suffering from the hills of yesterday. We soon backtracked and found our way. It was now flat and pleasant farmland. Donkeys pulled cart loads of families to church. We had refitted the bikes in Rio with new chains, front and rear cogs and bottom brackets; they sounded and felt smooth. When the bikes were in good shape everything seemed easier.

Oh, the freedom of the road, how I had missed it! We had been physically and mentally exhausted on reaching Swakopmund, but now, six weeks later, we were fit, relaxed and raring to go. In the first few days we rediscovered what a joy cycling can be. So much of Africa had been extremely punishing, toiling under merciless sun on rough and endless roads, enduring that spartan existence. Despite the hills it was thrilling to be out there, in mild sun and sea air, smelling the sweet trees, on the move again, not knowing where we would end up each night. It was during these days that I started to appreciate what we had achieved in Africa.

'Did we really do that Tim?'

'We certainly did old boy, and I'm glad, mainly because it means we won't have to do it again.'

A game of football caught my eye. Tim and I sat on a dirt bank for twenty minutes watching the action on the bumpy pitch, cut out of dense woodland. The goalposts were stripped saplings, tied together with rope to form a crossbar. I was greatly encouraged to find that Sunday League 'footie' in Brazil is just as hopeless as it is at home. No budding Rivelinos here. Both teams wore fancy kit; one was in blue and white stripes, the other in bright yellow. Three of the blue and whites played barefoot; everyone else had boots. The yellows took every opportunity to slide into tackles on these three or jump on their toes at corner kicks; as one does! We winced and groaned for them but were greatly entertained.

We had agreed not to worry too much about distance for the first few days, as we wanted our muscles to stretch and harden up gradually to avoid injury. After the 'footie' we came to a way-side café and felt no guilt in stopping for a drink and a snack.

The maps on the back of the T-shirts had been useful hundreds of times before. 'Turn around and show 'em your map,' had been heard many times each day since Sydney. Where we could not speak the language it was the only way of answering people's questions.

The café was busy with locals inside and city slickers on the veranda. Dubious looking sausage rolls lurked menacingly on a plate under a smeared perspex cover. With ice cold cokes and sausage rolls in hand, we nattered in pidgin Portuguese to a couple of guys enjoying a Sunday beer. One had his twelve year old son with him. The boy approached me nervously and I worked out that he was asking where we were going. I turned Tim around and went through the map, following the long line of dots from Sydney and told the usual story. The boy was confused but elated. It was the most amazing thing he had heard all morning. He made us feel good. Outside in the sun sat a group of big, muscular guys and their girlfriends. The girls were chic, the cars in the yard expensive. I talked to one of these guys at the bar, he also spoke English. They lived in the city of Sao Paolo and had been in Rio to support a friend, one of the guys at the table, who had been fighting for a place in the Brazilian Olympic Judo team. They had stopped to celebrate his victory on the way home. The young lad reappeared with a pen and asked me to autograph his shirt. Tim and I were flattered and obliged him.

'What do you do if it rains?', someone asked.

'We cycle anyway, we like rain,' Tim answered.

They shook their heads and laughed, *'Mucho Loco!!'* (Very Mad!!) The lad went off and brought his bike for me to look at. I gave the rusty chain a squirt of our special teflon oil and tightened the brakes. He was as pleased as punch. I wished later that I had remembered to give him one of our *Cycle For I.T.* stickers and taken his name and address.

That night we stopped in Itaguia. It was an odd, forgotten place beside a picturesque but polluted bay. We asked directions to a guest house. With our understanding of Portuguese being so poor, we should have known better than to follow directions. The mud track took us way off the road, up a hill and past two old farmers leaning over a fence, as they probably had done every Sunday afternoon for years. As we passed they stopped talking and stared, as though we had just landed from Mars. I said hello in Portuguese. They were absolutely gob-smacked. They did not know Martians could speak Portuguese. We turned a corner in the track and came to a dead end. The directions, or at least our understanding of them, were wrong.

When we found the guest house, it was like Butlins out of season, but worse. The pool looked like a laboratory experiment of diseased green mould. The table tennis table had no balls and we had to fight tooth and nail to be given two single beds instead of one double. That was two nights in a row we had been mistaken for gays. I blamed the leather bangles, bought from the cuties in Rio.

In a big hall at the centre of Butlitz a chap was singing into a microphone whilst his mate played the Hammond organ. The whole of Brazil could hear it. Classic *pub singing* caressed our ears.

'NNNNyyyeeehhhryyyoorrrrrrraaIllyyyAAhhhAANNNoorrrrAA WWWWHHOOOOOOOOOaaagggHHHHHH NNNggggnnnniii'.

Total drivel. It is the same, whether it is in English, Welsh or Portuguese. Better than I could do of course, but still drivel. The audience cheered and clapped after each number. There were three adults and six children. We made a speedy exit. Later, when all the fun had died down, it was safe to come out of our room to eat. We were the only customers in a room that could have held the *Spruce Goose*, Howard Hughes' giant white elephant of an aeroplane. Sonia was a bubbly waitress, though with her pudding bowl haircut she looked a bit school-teacherish. She told us, 'I used to work in the back office but he moved me out here. He said the people would like me.' We liked her.

'Uma Uva!' I said to Tim, out of the corner of my mouth.

A stooped, over-dressed chap swanked out of his chalet, put a Freddie Mercury tape on the player and plonked himself down at our table. I thought, *'This is Sunday night in Butlitz buddy, you don't need the flowery tie and Brylcreem'*. A little later another guy, Sonia's 'sweetheart', as she put it, dropped in; no doubt to check on her behaviour.

Sweetheart thought we were trying to lead his girl astray, and treated us with suspicion. He cuddled and touched her at every opportunity to mark his territory. I don't know what he took us for, we were just chatting. The guy with the tie and Brylcreem, Nino, was a sad, lonely chap, about our age, whose wife and kids had left him. He lived here in Butlitz (could life get any worse?).

They were interested in our trip and as the evening went on and the beer flowed, we got on to the subject of the millions of children dying every week, part of the reason for our being there.

'I'm not any more special than one of those kids,' said Sonia, 'I could have been one of them, so could any of us, it's just luck.' We all nodded and murmured agreement.

Nino took over, 'I do feel sorry for them and for the street kids in Rio but it doesn't help me in my situation does it?'. He went on, 'I still have to go to work every morning and find my own food and live with my pain and my past, don't I? I don't live in their world, I live in my world, you know. Where is my future going to roll up from eh? Who's looking after me?' Everyone was a bit shocked at the outburst but it was a good point.

'Well maybe that's right,' said Tim, 'but at least you've had the opportunity to make your own choices, you can't deny that. If it hasn't worked out for you that's a pity, but you are in control of your own life. At least you can take responsibility for your own mistakes. Those dead kids can't do that.' He was not convinced.

'Look at it this way Nino,' I said. 'By the time we reach Valparaiso, assuming we make it, about thirteen million children will have died needlessly since we left Sydney. Thirteen million, that's about three deaths for each pedal stroke we've made, all preventable.'

Tim broke in, 'Compared to ours their lives were pretty simple: they were born; they knew the warmth of their mother; they knew love. They were just starting to learn about fingers and shapes and a load of other interesting things when ... Buuumph ...' his hand sliced horizontally through the air '... it ends. For no reason. And the kid thinks, 'Oh! was that it? So that was life was it? What's all the fuss about?''

'It's nature,' said Nino, 'if they don't die we'll be over populated,' though his voice was losing conviction.

'Yes' I SAID, 'I've read that if the growth continues by the year 3500 the total mass of human flesh will equal the mass of the earth and by the year 6000 it will equal the mass of the known universe.' Yet they say that the planet can only sustain 2 billion people. It'll all end in resource wars. We are screwed. The survivors of humanity will be farmers and conservers, not the businessman and consumers.

'Well maybe, my friend,' said Nino scoffing. 'You are full of numbers. I shall wait and see, but it still won't help me will it?'

Nino rounded the evening off by insisting that Tim and I went back to his chalet. It would have been very rude to refuse. In Nino's room the Butlitz furniture had been replaced with selected remnants of the family home: pine wardrobe, china figurines, orange standard lamp and a photo of the wife and kids. Nino was buoyant but it was a sad scene. He presented us each with a small, polished pebble and told us, 'You are my very best friends'. We thanked him, and ran for it.

Everyone we had met on this journey had been doing the same basic thing, in different ways. They were trying to provide for themselves and their families as best they could. Everyone has problems: health, money, careers, partners, families, self confidence. We all have them. Some problems, though, are even bigger. Some things arc a problem for the whole of humanity now and to come. The easiest thing to do is to let our own problems consume us and forget the other boring stuff – that's okay, it doesn't matter, concentrate on you, things will be all right, don't worry, everything's great, really it is, it's fine, oh yes, believe me, it'll all work out for the best.

The next day we felt fitter. Just as well because the hills kept on rolling. In thick, lush forest we went around, over and through magnificent mountains. The long climbs brought their reward in cool descents with whoops of satisfaction.

Each valley brought a whitewashed fishing village or a weekend resort for the rich of Rio. Hundreds of under-used yachts rested in secluded coves. Little green islands floated in the bays. It felt like Spain or Italy. From each village we were faced with another slow, grinding ascent. We climbed ten or fifteen long hills each day.

This really was perfect cycling. Blue ocean in sweeping bays, deserted beaches and lush forest in warm autumn sun. We stopped on a beach where kids in school uniform, white shirts and blue shorts, played volleyball. The girls were much more nimble than the boys and were winning easily. Each point was followed by shrieks, cuddles and high fives. Water, sand and sun were perfect. We gave in to temptation and cycled no further.

As the afternoon washed away, a mangy mongrel befriended us for the chance of cheese roll. The dog met me as I climbed out of the surf. He showed no emotion, not even a wag, but walked with me across the beach. My buddy! Hot sand moved under my feet, squashing up between white toes. The dog kicked sand up behind as it waddled along. Tim looked at the mongrel but said to me, 'Hello, scabby dog, have you been swimming?', I looked at him silently, then at the dog. He went on, still looking at the dog, but with a quick glance up at me. 'Do you want some lunch scabby dog, or are you going to have a sleep in the sun first?' There was, of course, no answer. The dog just looked at us both, confused. This kind of schoolboy humour kept us entertained for weeks. Pathetic, eh?

In the hills we met our first South American cyclist. He was a real star. Nelson was an ecologist from Venezuela and had ridden his mountain bike from Caracas, down through Amazonia and around Brazil, a distance of five thousand kilometres. A bushy moustache lay across his top lip like a wild caterpillar. Long raven-black hair squirted from beneath a battered white cycling helmet. He sported a yellow and green striped vest with a Brazilian emblem on the front. I was surprised to see his bike equipped with all the latest Japanese and American gadgets; a cyclo-computer, fancy lights, cow horn handlebar extensions. 'Where did you get that gear?'

'Caracas of course. Do you think we are cannibals?'

He was going to speak to the Ecology Summit in Rio. Whilst Nelson's colleagues from around the globe arrived by jet, he was keen to make a point by arriving by bike. He was tanned, sleek and hairy and looked the part. Nelson gave us dates; we gave him peanuts. In one water bottle he carried pure honey. Solidarity. The crucial cycling hours of the afternoon slipped away as we chatted, swopped stories and laughed.

It was surprising to see the coast so developed; we had expected something very different. One little town, Mariessa was the place to be. We had come across it only a few miles after leaving Nelson. Here cool dudes and hot babes did the weekend from Sao Paolo in Ford Escort XR3is. They surfed all day and squashed into throbbing, smokey bars all night. I almost fainted in the heat and jam of bodies. These bright young kids of Brazil spoke excellent English, most had studied in England or the States and were merchant bankers or something similar. They were truly cool, man. *Ya bebbee*. I had come to Brazil expecting blow-pipes, but found beach bunnies. (Not that I was complaining, not really).

We realised that in the five days since leaving Rio, we had still been in holiday mode. We were not covering enough distance each day to keep on schedule and were too easily giving in to the dreaded *'couple of quiet ones'* at night. This was just not good enough. Here, in Mariessa, we gave ourselves a severe talking to and jumped into expedition mode. In the morning, hung over and gasping from passive smoking, we defied the people of Mariessa by cycling up their mammoth hill and out of town – it nearly killed us though. It was a good start to our new regime.

I know why no one knew the way to Santos: no one goes there. It's a hole. The roads were clogged with trucks and industrial plants vomited on everything. What a stinking mess! Pele was born here and played his club football here. It is surprising that, having climbed out of poverty, he hung around.

Beyond Santos, we stopped to calm our nerves. We were tired and the road was nasty; the worst we had experienced in the entire journey. Lorries thundered about, seeing how close they could get to us. We were continually diving into the long grass beside the road to escape being splatted. The café sold delicious, milky coffee and cold meat pies that would have excited Marks and Spencers. A crowd gathered to watch us eat pies. A cameraman on his way back from a news assignment dropped in for a snack and filmed us. That night we were on national TV, 147 million population! We did not watch it but I should think we looked as though we were riding across South America on plastic bar stools. *'Good evening, and here is the news: Today two cyclists ate pies ...'*

The guy got us to repeat something in Portuguese, God knows what! The crowd went crazy with laughter. Over the next few weeks several people said the Portuguese equivalent of, *'Saw you on the telly, you were really funny'*.

We left the Atlantic Ocean at Peruibe, and headed for the Pacific. The coastline from Rio had been deceptive; we had felt the illusion of going south, but had in fact been travelling almost due west. After ten days on the road we were back in the groove. The hills had been good for us. Legs, backs, arms and bums were now hardened.

The land was cultivated, open bush for camping was gone. People in farms were scared of us or, at least, didn't understand us. They would certainly not allow camping in their fields. One farmer, though, had seen us earlier, on the road, and feeling unusually charitable, allowed us to sleep in his out-house. The soft, warm smell of cow dung permeated the tea, the vegetable curry and the sleeping bags and lived with us for days!

Our road soon joined an even bigger, busier road, the main route from Santos and Sao Paolo to the south. It was unbearable, an endless procession of bike-eating trucks. This was worse than ever; no fun and very, very dangerous. Shrines to dead travellers, built by grieving loved ones, dotted the verge. Vases on marble blocks held dried-up flowers. Crosses were draped with rosary beads, constant reminders to us that we should be somewhere else.

Tim recalls: 'One stretch had earned seven shrines within one hundred metres. The hard shoulder was our only protection. This kept disappearing and starting again on the other side of the road. We tried to keep our nerve as we repeatedly crossed four carriageways in the fog to stay on it. It was a bit worrying to find some lorries used the hard shoulder to overtake on the inside, thus forcing us to stop and pray as they crashed by with inches to spare.'

Curitiba was still a day and a half's ride away on this road. The chances of being zapped were high. Tim shouted to me above the roar of the traffic.

'This is crazy. I didn't come to Brazil to cycle on a motorway.' (This was not a happy soldier). I was foolishly keen to push on carefully down the main road. My priority was keeping to our schedule. Tim was insistent, safety was more important. He took the lead in working out an alternative. I gave in eventually and agreed to follow his plan. Although we would not arrive in Curitiba until we had slogged for another seven days over the mountains, he was right.

In England and Australia I had felt frustrated that I was doing most of the thinking and making most of the decisions. Through Africa, Tim had gradually taken more and more responsibility for planning, making lists, thinking ahead and dissecting problems. This decision to leave the road and go off into the mountains was significant. Gradually we had become equal partners in the planning department.

We decided to take a three hundred and sixty kilometre detour, through the mountains and up the Serra do Mar (The Great Escarpment) on dirt tracks. The relief was instant. Not only had the road been hell, the route from Rio had been decidedly unadventurous. We needed something difficult. For the first time since leaving Rio we felt we were in the real Brazil. Once again we were in the silence and peace of dense forests and farmland; no trucks, no cars. The red dirt was clogged with rain and made the going slow and hard. Armed with bagfuls of bananas, bread, cheese, vegetables and little smiles we set off into the mountains!

The people, we found, were very shy. They were of mixed race with strong Indian appearance. None waved or spoke. Here there were no happy, big eyed, bare-foot kids, running along beside us shrieking and grinning. A group of children were playing on the track outside a wooden shack as we approached. They saw us and ran off screaming and crying. As I passed the blue, peeling building I could hear little sobs coming from inside. Tim has that effect on some people!

Tim's right-hand pedal chose this afternoon to start disintegrating; three million turns and repeated coatings of desert dust were too much for it. The thing squeaked, ground, and chomped with every turn. We both found the noise psychologically unbearable; it seemed to make everything more difficult. I had the advantage of being free to cycle out of ear-shot and live with the sweet, smooth whirr of my own gears. Tim would have to live with it until he could find a bike shop in Curitiba. After covering fifty kilometres from the busy road on the dirt, we started to look for somewhere to sleep. There were no obvious camping spots and we were encouraged by a name on the map, Sete Barras. We did not know if this was a tiny village or a big town. Hoping that it wasn't the group of huts we had already passed on the track, we decided we had nothing to lose by pushing on for another ten kilometres to see what would happen. Miraculously, deep in the forest, where it had no reason to be, we found it; a proper town, with paved streets, drunks, litter and all. Finding somewhere to sleep, however, took a further expedition. I asked a café owner, a shopkeeper, a bank manager, two women in the street and a group of kids, 'Pour favor, donde este es pension?' In convoy the kids led us towards the Sete Barras guest house, along cobbled streets and down a very steep hill. Three of their bikes were without brakes and could only be stopped by crashing into conveniently placed bushes. The kids knew this before they launched themselves from the top, but it didn't seem to be important until the very last milli-second before impact.

The landlady was an ancient Oriental. As I had found the place, Tim took responsibility for organising a room and a meal. This sort of teamwork was now happening without need for discussion. He found himself negotiating, in Portuguese, with a woman who spoke only Japanese. Much fun was had by all!

Many Japanese retire to Brazil. After a lifetime squashed into Japanese cities they must be attracted by the space. The same is happening in Australia. An Aussie farmer in Victoria had remarked to me, 'I hear the Sahara Desert's quite spacious too. Know what I mean?'

The Japanese lady was small to start with, and her round shoulders and curved back made her about half our size. Tied back hair and a large forehead exaggerated her ball-like appearance. Tim's mime of hungry cyclists had been good, much too good. The lady watched him, pumping up hills in hot sun, struggling through sand and mud, she nodded knowingly, turned and shuffled off to the kitchen barking orders. The two local boys must have cursed us for they spent ages bent over a big, old cooking range stirring and chopping to the old lady's commands. We waited. The dining room was in the cellar but was bright and cheerful, fluorescent lights glared at orange table cloths and yellow glossy walls. Rows of bed sheets hung from the ceiling drying, giving the appearance of a Chinese laundry. We waited. We relived the events since breakfast and agreed we could very easily have lost our lives that morning. We waited some more. The TV showed the only Brazilian made programme we had seen, a soap opera which went out for two hours every night. I did not understand a word but easily followed the plot, just like soaps back home. Being so distanced from it I spotted that every single scene involved people arguing, we called it the *Constant Conflict* show and watched avidly.

Eventually, a lad brought out big bowls of chunky vegetable soup and hunks of bread.

'Great, just what we need!' I said.

The lad went back and reappeared with two more plates, piled with chicken, then two more piled with potatoes and spaghetti. 'Good job,' said Tim, 'this'll do us.' But no. Dishes kept coming: beef steaks the size of Tim's thighs, tomatoes, kidney beans, lettuce, hot bread, onions, boiled cabbage and sliced, buttered carrots. Each plate overflowing. Soon the big table was totally full. Plates of chips and rice were piled directly on to the green salad and beans. Before us was the equivalent of three or four meals each. The Japanese lady came out smiling with a big jug of iced water and asked if we were enjoying the meal. We nodded and made enthusiastic noises. She stood watching us eat for a while then offered to peel some more spuds.

We ate every last morsel, of course, but it took about two hours. We also paid a hefty bill, but then it was a hefty feast. We sat recovering with coffee poured from a red thermos flask, praying that the Japanese lady didn't have any apple pie or ice cream. A man approached the table; a boy stood shyly in his shadow. In Portuguese the man said, 'I want my boy to meet the famous cyclists.'

Tim recalls: 'We greeted the boy and the father wandered off. The lad had no questions to ask and stood there highly embarrassed so, revelling in the celebrity status, I took him upstairs to see the bikes and the kit. I talked him through everything; the gears, the frame, the strange handlebars, the knobbly tyres, the cyclometer, the water filter, the tents. The lad puffed out his chest and touched the black bike, eyes full of awe.'

I must have picked up a bug from the feast, for the next day, even though the track became firm and the sun mild, I found I was having to cycle with my cheeks clenched and struggled to keep up a decent pace. We cycled through wide banana groves where unseen men whistled and sang as they worked. On thick trunks, bunches of bananas hid under wide rubbery leaves. Chickens ran free among palm trees on brittle, bleached fronds. We balanced precariously on plank bridges to cross creeks.

Our first serious action in these mountains was a five kilometre climb up a one in four hill. At the top were *Los Caverna De Diabo,* the Devil's Caves. I could see why they were so called, the climb was sheer HELL! We still refused to get off and walk. I kept telling myself, 'It's good practice for the Andes, it's good practice for the Andes. I diagnosed my stomach problem by carefully studying the symptoms (don't ask). I had a dose of Giardi. I must have drunk some unfiltered water. We had been carrying a supply of antibiotics and instructions, ripped out of a medical book, for just such occasions. I worked out the course myself and got on with it.

Unfortunately, we spent the next few days, while I was meant to be recovering, struggling over the most challenging hills of the entire journey so far. The idea was to climb the one thousand metre escarpment, from the coastal plain to the inland plateau. We huffed and puffed our way up the stony track to the top. The rear wheels often lost traction in the loose gravel and slipped away beneath us. Above the clouds we looked down on gently rounded peaks, carpeted in lush green forest, jutting out of a mystical blanket of whiteness. It was magnificent, worth every drop of sweat. Joy turned to despair as the track proceeded to swoop all the way to the bottom of the escarpment, leaving us to climb again. I have always loved cycling up hills for the sense of achievement and the reward of the zoom down. This track, though, followed a steep-sided river valley, taking the easiest route over a series of bluffs pushing in from the side. It became a roller coaster ride. At the base of the eighth ascent of the same escarpment I was getting a bit cheesed off. In four days we had climbed the equivalent of Kilimanjaro, over nineteen thousand feet, and we were still at sea-level! For only the third time on the whole journey, I thought, for a few minutes, *'I am NOT having fun!!!'*. I felt weak from my bug, a vicious gremlin was inside my knee jabbing me with a rusty nail with every turn of the pedal and, not for the first time, we were out of water. The gravel continued to spin away beneath the tyres. I pushed my weight back in the saddle and weaved across the track searching for solid ground. The top seemed a hundred miles away. The temptation to stop and rest nagged me but I resisted. I turned to my old friend *The Owl and Pussy Cat* for a distraction ... in a beautiful, pea green boat (puff) ... stars above ... (aaah) ... for a year and a day ... (oooh) ... a piggy-wig stood ...' – it didn't help. Waves of nausea flowed through me. My eyes stung with sweat, I could find no power, my face screwed up into a grimace. I hated this hill but I was *not* going to get off and walk. There was only one thing for it; as in Malawi, the final resort: Kipling's *If* – 'If you can trust yourself when all men doubt you (uugh) ... and not make dreams your master ... (phoo) ... If you can force your heart and nerve and sinew ... (nngh) ... each unforgiving minute ... (eergh) ... you'll be a man my son.' – It never fails. You don't dare give up when you're saying that.

Eventually a remote, sleepy village appeared out of the forest. We bumped over the broken tarmac of a wide dusty street in search of a place to rest. People sat on benches looking vacant and there was no movement except for a scabby dog licking its groin. The café did not sell proper meals, so we made do with a big pile of sausage rolls each. In the corner sat an old television. As we ate, the lad came out from behind the counter and switched it on. There we sat, miles from nowhere, in a village with nothing, watching live football, Sweden against France, beamed in by satellite from Europe.

Flat, open ground for camping was a rarity in these mountains. One night we slept in a derelict hut, watching out for spiders and snakes that may have been sheltering under the broken floorboards. Another night was spent on a sloping bed of pine needles in thick forest. It was comfortable but cramped; if I moved I bumped into one of the trees or bushes which surrounded us.

> **Tim recalls:** 'There is something special about sleeping in a ditch, the ultimate travelling experience. I used to dream about living in a ditch one day.'

Tim was thrilled that evening when he realised a ditch was our only option for a flat camping spot. Even then there was no possibility of pitching tents in the tangle of undergrowth. If it had rained we would have been soaked and the nearby stream would have risen to wash our kit away. Vaguely aware of the potential threat from dangerous Indians and the man eating Puma I was startled by a friendly dog who stumbled across us.

'Hello scabby dog', said Tim from the shadows, 'did you get a surprise?' He went on, 'Do you like sleeping in ditches scabby dog?'

It was a cat however, that gave us trouble that night. A little black kitten, a domestic pussy-cat, who also lived in the ditch. He was only a few weeks old and very hungry. He gulped down two bowls of milk that I made up from our powder supply and was overjoyed with his new friends. We named him Pele. He snuggled into my sleeping bag, sheltering from the cold and drizzle. Rather than sleep, Pele chose to spend the whole night purring in my ear and kneading my chest with his claws.

We could not possibly take him with us so, to escape in the morning, we had to trick him. When we were ready to go, Pele followed us to the road, mewing. Leaving the bike, I picked him up and walked back to the bottom of the ditch, put him on a log and sprinted off. He stood forlornly as we rode off up the mountain. I think he believed we were all going to settle down and build a life together, there in the ditch. Tim was seriously tempted.

We cycled on through the hills and made lunch and a brew in the well-groomed gardens of a plaza. This was the remote town of Iporanga.

Forested mountains towered all around. Shops lined the road opposite the plaza. People were going about their business, not taking much notice of us. The buildings were dirty grey concrete cubes. A crowd of denim-clad workmen drank beer outside the bar, whilst women bargained for mangos or plastic bowls and cloths piled on trestle tables on the pavement. It had a quiet order to it. Near to us a simpleton, wearing a grey boiler suit and a dodgy grin, swept leaves with a witch's broom. Rock music suddenly blared out from somewhere nearby; a shop or perhaps a car? It was so unbearably loud that we found ourselves shouting to be heard. With amused expressions, the locals watched as I walked around the square, trying to find the source of the noise. At last I came across a metre high speaker, concreted into the ground. Three others were placed in the corners of the plaza, each exploding with Guns 'N' Roses. This was official, municipal pandemonium. I decided I must be getting older and town councillors getting younger!

If we had been cycling through these mountains in 1541, we would have surprised Alvar Nunes de Vaca, and three hundred of his closest friends on their trek across the continent from the Brazilian coast. Alvar was already a veteran of a ten year expedition in which he and his men walked from Florida to the Spanish garrison in Mexico City. (When he got there they said, 'Yeah? And what do you want?' which had been a bit of a let down.) The King of Spain then sent him off to discover a legendary mountain of silver and a white King, who was said to wear European clothes and ruled over a wealthy Indian nation in the Andes. The objective was to kill the King and nick the loot. Alvar was a clean shaven aristocrat, the youngest son of a nobleman. His troops were bearded, hard men, stinking and covered in sores from months at sea. A dangerous band of adventurers, armed with fine swords and long spears. They wore a rag-tag assortment of inappropriate heavy clothes and armour. Alvar found the Indians of the Great Escarpment of the Brazilian coast to be friendly and willing to trade chicken and corn for beads. On reaching the Iguacu River half the force built canoes and continued west by water. The remainder cut their way through the forest.

Thirty kilometres north of Curitiba, the nasty dirt track gave way to friendly, smooth tarmac and a friendly, fat café lady. She treated us to free hamburgers and milky coffees. Later she said goodbye with hugs and kisses.

After the hardship of the mountains, Curitiba, a busy modern city, was a fine spot to rest for a couple of days. Throughout our journey across Brazil we had found the standard of living, for the majority of people, was far higher than we had expected.

Here we visited cinemas and watched the latest American films. These were in English with Portuguese subtitles, the locals, therefore, felt free to talk loudly to their friends throughout. As soon as one showing had ended, the movie would start again immediately. This encouraged people to drop in at any time and sit there until the same piece of action came around again. Throughout *Basic Instinct*, *Fried Green Tomatoes* and *My Own Private Idaho* there was an extraordinary procession of comings and goings. Many people seemed determined to come in to see the grand finale, sit there for two hours to see why it happened, then rush out before seeing the end a second time. We seemed to be the only people to watch a film from beginning to end. After each absorbing movie, I had difficulty remembering where I was, England, Australia, Africa? I had to adjust my mind to the correct language and adopt the relevant state of self defence before hitting the street.

We had a team haircut and I found a cobbler to stick some new soles onto my faithful trainers. A smart shopping mall was jammed with foreign goods. Supermarkets sold everything a man could desire. The city was dotted with leafy plazas, each with a frenzied market selling piles of bananas, mangos and pawpaw or cheap cotton clothes. At night, in front of the magnificent, floodlit cathedral, a kaleidoscopic flower market emerged; a thousand neon lights lit crammed pots of blues, whites, reds and yellows; blooms in all shapes and sizes. Through my window I could hear its clatter and laughter till dawn.

The mark of civilisation, as we had discovered in Rundu, Namibia, is the existence and quality of cake shops. Only in Paris have I tasted better pastries than those dripping cream slices I scoffed in the park in Curitiba.

A quiet, pleasant road now headed west across the plateau towards Iguacu Falls, the spectacular cataracts which lie at the junction of Brazil, Paraguay and Argentina, over eight hundred kilometres from Curitiba.

The drought that was taking so many lives in Africa would have been welcome here. The three great rivers which cross this region – Rios Iguacu, Parana and Paraguay – had been swollen by heavy rain, causing extensive flooding. Many roads had been closed and many lives lost. Far ahead of us, Western Paraguay had been officially declared a disaster zone.

We cycled through the town of Uniao da Vitoria, where the Iguacu had burst its banks. Hundreds of wooden roofs bathed incongruously in the muddy stream. At this point the river was a kilometre wide; five times its normal size. We had planned to follow the path of the Rio Iguacu to the falls then cut southwest, following the Rio Paraguay. We were taking pot luck with the flooding. Roads were said to be closed, but we had no choice but to find out for ourselves.

We were climbing a ten kilometre hill, heads down, slowly, slowly. As we neared the top, a car carrying two men crept along behind us on the hard shoulder. I waved it past but it stayed there, matching our pace. *'Who are these guys?'* I thought, *'bandits or flashers?'* At the top of the hill the car pulled past and stopped. The two men jumped out and ran up smiling and waving, *'Perhaps they are flashers!!'*

They were just jovial reporters eager to fill a few minutes of radio time. They were clean-cut young guys dressed in leather bomber jackets who obviously revelled in their media image.

Neat little moustaches made them look older than they were. The interview went out live. We talked in English while one of the chaps asked the questions and the other translated for us. They asked the usual questions; what were we doing? Where were we from? Did we like Brazil? Did our legs ache? and so on.

Our Portuguese was improving at last so we were able to answer some questions directly. 'Yes, we are mad, ha, ha', 'Yes, we like Brazil',

'You have a very beautiful country, er ... *Senoritas este mucho lindo'* (the girls are very beautiful), etc., etc.

When the interview was finished, the microphone was packed away and the pair prepared to leave. The translator thanked us and shook our hands. 'You are correct', he said, 'Brazil is a very beautiful and it is a very wealthy country but we, the people, are very poor.'

Because I knew he wanted me to, I asked 'Why is that?'

'Because our President is a fucking crook.'

The land was now open cattle country on gently rolling hills, reminiscent of Wiltshire. We were able to make fast progress on a good road, covering a hundred and twenty kilometres or more each day.

Little towns popped up every eighty kilometres or so. They were always set back five kilometres from the road so we missed most of them, though we stayed in one or two. A certain Mr. Oak of Olive Tree was our friend for one night. We were in a small, tidy town with low buildings and the usual serene plaza with swings for kids and benches for people watchers. He had a Portuguese name, of course, but he translated it to Mr. Oak of Olive Tree. He was in his fifties, wore a black leather jacket and was in need of a shave and a good night's sleep. He walked up and introduced himself as we were tucking into our meal in a bar. Mr. O. of O.T. spoke slightly less English than we spoke Portuguese and was steaming drunk. When we had eaten, Tim uttered those dreadful words, 'Just a couple of quiet ones,' and we joined him and his friends for a beer. Mr. Oak of Olive Tree stood and gestured that we should watch him, he had something to tell us. He didn't need language, he was a mime artist:

'*Him,'* said Mr. O. of O. T., (Meaning 'this'); he was holding the collar of his leather jacket.

'Me Argentina,' (I bought it in Argentina) … then began an elaborate mime describing a beautiful woman …

'Long head,' he said (Long hair) … he leant towards Tim and mimed long hair on Tim's head. He swept back the imaginary hair and whispered loudly in Tim's ear …

'Wool Wool, sheep, sheep,' (Don't ask me). Tim and I were confused but nodded encouragement. Mr O. of O.T. mimed a helicopter, spinning his finger in the air above his head, then grabbed his own earlobe and shook it.

'Him, him,' still shaking his ear, *'New York, Miami, Dallas, No?'* He laughed loudly and clapped himself.

I thought, *'Hmm, Good one. If we are playing charades, I give up.'* We laughed and nodded. The others around the table slapped our backs. What jolly good fun we were all having. This was all very encouraging for Mr. Oak of Olive Tree.

'Cerveza, cerveza!' he called, (Set them up barman).

The barman, a young, fresh-faced engineering student called Roberto, brought the beers to the table. While he was there, he took the opportunity to sing the first few lines of his favourite Elvis Presley song, though not quite the way I remember them, '…And I can't stand falling in love with you…', and so on. He brought the house down. This was Mr. O. of O.T.'s cue to start a new mime.

'Him,' … *'Me Argentina,'* … a beautiful woman

'Long head.'

I butted in: 'Don't tell me, don't tell me'.

He pulled back my imaginary long hair and whispered

'Wool, wool, sheep, sheep …'

'Him, New York, Miami, Dallas, No?'.

It is incredible how one man can be so funny, isn't it? We and the others were in fits, though not necessarily for the same reason.

'Cerveza, cerveza!' Oh No.

'Come, come!!' He made me stand up, beside him …

'Him' … *'Argentina,'* … *'Long head'* etc … etc … etc … etc.

And so it went on, time after time, each bemused explosion of laughter just encouraged him more.

When, at about three in the morning, Mr. Oak of Olive Tree

was leaving he insisted on paying for our meal and all the beers. We protested but he was adamant; we were his friends. When he was gone Luis, the proprietor, told us, 'Do not worry, he can afford to pay your bill, he is the town lawyer.'

As we staggered out, Roberto, the waiter sang, "Maybe I wouldn't love you quite too much as I could have ..."

The next morning as we soothed our aching heads, we tried to make some sense of it all. 'Well, I tell you what Tim', I said philosophically, 'You'd never hear Perry Mason tell a joke like that.'

'True,' Tim replied.

Before leaving town we went to a backstreet laundry to collect our washing. The bespectacled, old German owner, the image of Laurence Olivier's Nazi dentist in *Marathon Man*, said there would be no charge for the washing if one of us would play chess with him; no one else would play. While Tim exchanged bishops I played with the grandchildren and sucked on a jug of maté, the smoking herb tea, sucked from a kind of pipe. With smoke streaming through green leaves it looked and tasted like a witches brew. They played on the counter, breaking off occasionally, while the old man served and gossiped with jolly women. National pride was maintained with an honourable draw. For once in history it was England 0, Germany 0.

Brazilian warmth was repeated many times in the little towns. People went out of their way to welcome and help us. We happily gave interviews for more local radio stations and school newspapers. A teacher in one town warned us, 'You must be very careful in Argentina, it is not like Brazil, you know.'

One character, though, reminded us of the other side of Brazilian culture. We cycled up to a police checkpoint, a solid square building, painted bright yellow, to the right of the road. We were used to being ignored or waved through at these checkpoints. Here we were stopped by a fat guy in dark glasses and pristine blue uniform. Before he even opened his mouth I suspected he was the big, ignorant bastard make of policeman. The glasses gave him away, definitely insecure, probably a potty training problem. He questioned us in Portuguese. We did not understand everything, but listened hard and answered what we could using our phrase book.

'Do you have permission to be on this road?' he asked.

'We don't need permission,' I replied defiantly.

'Yes, yes you must have permission,' he went babbling on for a while.

I just smiled at him.

He asked, 'Have you been working in Brazil?'

'Nas,' we said (No).

'You have many dollars?' He continued, still in Portuguese.

'Nas,'

'Yes, many dollars.'

'Nas.'

He said something like, 'You have been working in Brazil, that is not allowed. You do not have permission to be on this road. This is very serious for you. I will have to arrest you.'

'No entiendo' I said, (I don't understand). I knew exactly what he was on about.

'Do you have dollars?' he asked.

'No entiendo.'

'Sim, muitos dollars, dollars.' (Yes, many dollars.)

'No entiendo.'

'Sim, Sim, you have many dollars!!'

'No entiendo.'

Tim recalls:'We were not going to give in or be intimidated by this fat bully and he realised it. By staying calm and polite and pretending not to understand we totally flummoxed him.'

The *'No entiendo'* thing worked brilliantly. So well, that we just got on the bikes, gave him a wave and rode off. He threw his hands up, swore and went into his hut to await the next victim.

Warm rain storms caught us many times on the way to Iguacu. I don't mind cycling in the rain, it is certainly preferable to forty-six degree heat, or an air conditioned office!

… In 1541, alerted by the incredible roar of the Iguacu river and the alarming increase in the speed of the current, Alvar Nunes de Vaca ordered the canoes ashore and investigated on foot. Had he not been so cautious, his force would have been swept over the Iguacu Falls. The Iguacu River was nearly two miles wide here as it dropped sixty metres over a series of rock steps, in two hundred different falls. As they looked out from spray soaked, virgin forest they were the first Europeans to see this spectacular sight. The volume of water was immense and the noise deafening, punctuated by the shrieks of blue and green parrots. Spray fell like heavy rain. Swarms of white butterflies fluttered playfully around the Spaniards' heads as they did around ours.

Alvar and his men continued from Iguacu, to join the garrison at Asuncion, in Paraguay and in 1543 pushed on to the foothills of the Andes. In the jungle they came across the female warrior tribe of the Amazon. What a nightmare: Imagine: a gang of wild, half naked women, armed and dangerous, chasing you through the jungle! ('It was a bit like the El Rave Up Disco in Benidorm on a Saturday night,' said one conquistador later). Alvar found the Amazon women friendly, welcoming and willing to trade beads for gold, which is pretty suspicious.

The force went onward in search of the white King and the silver mountain, but their route was blocked by swamps and fever hit the troops. They were forced to retreat and the mystery of the mountain and the white King remained unsolved.

Iguacu Falls was a major landmark for us. We celebrated the end of the first stage of the journey across South America and marvelled at the spectacle of the Falls. It was all very satisfying. We had cycled nearly two thousand kilometres from Rio de Janeiro in five weeks. The hills and mountains had slowed us down badly. We were now in early July. It was tight, but if we kept at it we could still cover the final two thousand five hundred kilometres, to Valparaiso, in the next five weeks. We had to finish by 10th August to meet our objective: to cross the three southern continents within one year. Ahead of us lay Paraguay, Argentina and the Andes and winter was fast approaching.

17 The Lost Jungle – Andy

I had at last mastered the Portuguese for, *'I not much Portuguese speak do'*. Now we entered Paraguay and had to start speaking Spanish.

It was Saturday lunch time; streams of cars and pedestrians choked the bridge joining Brazil to Paraguay. People were off on mammoth shopping expeditions. Those returning to Brazil had armfuls of cigarette cartons and cases of beer, portable hi-fi's or bottles of whisky. Was Paraguay having a closing down sale? Apparently this was normal. A generous tax system meant luxury goods were one third cheaper in Paraguay than in Brazil. People were allowed to cross the border with no immigration or customs formalities. The Brazilian officials did not even bother stamping our passports as we left their border. In *Ciudad del Este* (City of the East), on the Paraguayan side, we actually had to go in search of the immigration post. I found a bored looking man behind a desk in an unlit office. I insisted he give me a stamp in my passport; I did not want some keen young policeman to check our papers in a few days time, only to send us all the way back to the border. He grudgingly gave me a stamp. Tim went in for his, whilst I guarded the bikes from the group of youths asking impossible Spanish questions.

We squeezed the bikes through the crowded market which spilled out onto the main road. Stall holders and shoppers alike disregarded the buses and trucks which sped by on their way to Asuncion. These people were truly prepared to die for a bargain. Each shop seemed packed full of the same sort of stock, mainly Japanese electrical goods. One guy hurried through the crowd scaring people with a fake snake. Money changers stood out in their uniform of cheap leather jackets and calculators and we had no trouble doing business.

'What do you know about Paraguay?' Tim asked as we climbed

out of town.

'I've been thinking about that myself', I said. 'I know England beat them 3-0 in the World Cup. And wasn't it here that a referee shot a footballer dead for arguing?' We bumped over sleeping policemen on the hard shoulder, placed there to prevent undertaking (overtaking on the inside). It's such a waste of policemen though!

'I thought that was a goalkeeper who shot the ball after someone had scored,' said Tim.

'I think they had the eighth biggest navy in world at one point', I continued, 'even though they are landlocked.'

Tim was impressed. 'That's a good one. All I know is that it has a dangerous sounding name, which means it probably isn't.'

'Oh, and it's meant to be full of Nazis', I recalled, 'so we better watch out for dachshunds again.'

It would be a short journey through Paraguay. We were to cut south west, close to the Brazilian border, following the course of the Rio Parana. It should only take three days to reach Encarnacion, three hundred kilometres away. There we would cross into Argentina: land of Malvinas fanatics and cheating footballers.

The land was flat and featureless, as was the asphalt. The map showed no towns along the road to Encarnacion. We had been told by the British Embassy in Asuncion, 'Nobody lives out there, it is virgin jungle, take everything with you.' So we carried supplies for four days. I insisted on carrying ten litres of water from the hotel. 'We don't need that!' Tim had laughed.

'Yes, we do!' I said, adding in my best *Hill Street Blues* accent, 'Listen, it's a jungle out there.'

There was surely some mistake. We could see no virgin jungle at all; only large tobacco farms and neat fields stretching to the horizon. Past houses, villages and farms I carried that water; ten litres of water is not light, I can tell you.

As evening approached, we kept an eye out for somewhere to camp but all the land was cultivated and offered no possible sites. We decided to follow a dirt track and cycled five kilometres off the road to a wooden farm building. The people were friendly but very wary. They were Guarani Indian with thin faces and fine features. Using the new Spanish phrase book, we asked the young man at the door if we could put a tent up in their yard. He asked us to wait and walked off. A little while later he reappeared with his brother of maybe twenty years. He was still wet, having been disturbed in the middle of his bath in the back yard. There was much debate between the two boys and a much older man who seemed to hold no authority. In the end the wet brother told us, *'No! el patron no permiso'* (the owner does not allow it). I asked if I could speak to the owner. It turned out the owner was a Japanese businessman living in Asuncion, three hundred kilometres away. They were afraid this man would punish them if he found out that we had camped on his land. It seemed ridiculous, we would do no harm and leave no mess, but there was no budging them. This had recently been Indian land, now they were scared of a foreign, absentee landlord. The dry brother told us there was a town only eight kilometres along the road where we could find lodgings. We set off in the dark, not pleased. Despite the empty map, we did indeed find a town with a cheap hotel, not eight but twenty eight kilometres away. The big fat manageress came out to greet us and found me pouring a bag of water into her flower bed. She gave me one of those big-fat-lady funny looks.

'Agua Braziliano,' (Brazilian water) I said, as if that explained everything.

'Ah gracias, gracias, senor.'

'You see Tim, I told you we'd need it.'

After a late start the next morning we faced a filthy day. The townsfolk gathered to see us off and worriedly pointed to the sky as though showing us a UFO, but it was only rain clouds. The weather was grey and miserable, our first real taste of winter. An unyielding, icy wind blew up from Antarctica, chilling our bones and slowing progress to a crawl. The desolate landscape moved past forlornly. After a few hours my ears had dropped off so we had to find shelter and warmth. A village appeared and we dived into the café shack. For a luxurious hour we sat lazily sipping steaming mugs of coffee and listening to the *Voice of America* on the radio. I savoured a month old copy of *The Times,* given to us by the lovely ladies at the British Embassy in Asuncion. It was an enormous treat. Before we finally discarded the paper we would each read it twice, cover to cover, soaking in the news from home. Asuncion had been on the original route, before we decided to avoid the Chaco and the Bolivian drug farmers. We had zipped over to the Paraguayan capital on the bus, before leaving Brazil for good. The bikes had been left to rest for two days in Iguacu Falls, whilst we had collected post and arranged cash advances on credit cards. The cost of all flights, equipment, food and accommodation had come from our own pockets throughout the journey. Our pockets were now empty. Things had been dramatically more expensive than our original research had shown, particularly in Australia and Brazil. We had overrun our budget and the first task, when we eventually got home, would have to be to find some way of earning a big wad of dough to pay off the overdrafts. That was something to worry about later though; now was for cycling. I had virtually nothing left in the world except the bike and the gear I was carrying and I truly would not have swopped it for anything.

Outside the peaceful café, in the littered village street, a bus disgorged its passengers. People filed in and were soon talking noisily, drinking cokes and tucking into mountainous, greasy hamburgers. We got up to leave and were stopped at the door by a small lady handing out leaflets. We took ours, thanked her and talked amongst ourselves as we prepared the bikes to leave.

'Oh, you speak English!' she said, surprised.

'Yes, we are English,' Tim told her. It was a treat to talk to a native English speaker. Apart from the ladies in the Embassy we had met no other foreigners for over five weeks.

This was Irene Fostervold, an American missionary; her husband Rolf joined us on the wooden verandah. They were happy, gentle people with leathery, weather-beaten skin and both wore well lived-in denims. Rolf sported a head of long, silver hair and shaggy side-burns.

We chatted for half an hour. As we stood there, the passengers climbed back onto their smelly bus. Whilst the driver waited for stragglers he revved noisily and various men and women chucked empty cans and wrappers out of the windows.

'They haven't learned about pollution yet,' said Rolf.

The Fostervolds had travelled widely and understood the difficulties of life on the road. They had driven to this place from

California in a jeep, with their baby son, who had nearly died of pneumonia in the Andes. The couple had worked here, with the Guarani Indians, for thirty-two years.

Missionaries have been involved with the Indians in Paraguay since 1609. The Guarani had fled the Portuguese who had invaded their homelands in Brazil after Alvar Nunes de Vaca had pioneered the area. Over sixty thousand Indians were enslaved or murdered and only four thousand had reached the safety of the Paraguayan jungles. When the Spanish Jesuit Missionaries arrived they improved the lifestyle of the Guarani enormously; the Indians became skilled farmers, blacksmiths, artists and musicians yet maintained their reputation as fierce warriors. Over a few short years, they had grown so strong that they even attacked the Portuguese in southern Brazil. This growing power worried the Spanish Government who closed the missions and withdrew all support.

Long before this, Alvar Nunes de Vaca had recruited a force of Guarani Indians for his expedition in search of the silver mountain. Another Indian army had fought with the Spanish in the first ever attack on the Incas. By 1800, though, the Spaniards had reduced the Guarani to servitude.

'When we first arrived', Rolf told me, 'we had to cut our way through the jungle to reach the villages, there was not even a track.' I looked around me. 'But it's just farm land.'

'Yes, I know, terrible isn't it. As soon as this road was built, ten years ago, the Government sold the land and it was gradually cleared.'

'How could so much jungle just disappear?' I asked.

'They did it almost totally by hand,' he said. It seemed impossible, an incredible amount of manual work; hundreds of square miles, maybe thousands. 'They sometimes used machines to pull out big tree stumps, but they did it mostly by hand.'

Unable to stand in the way of 'progress', Irene and Rolf had helped paid farm labourers. Rolf warned us, 'A motorcyclist was shot and killed here a few months ago, at the bridge about ten kilometres along the road. The men pulled up along side the bike as it went along and shot the man twice. The police found the murderers hiding out in a shack near the river, Brazilians. They still had the motorbike with them. We get many Brazilians living in the hills near the river, they are forever causing trouble.' I could not really see how we could defend ourselves against such an attack and it seemed unlikely to happen again, but we promised to be careful.

Tim recalls: 'Irene was very motherly, she showed me photos of her son's wedding in America, the one who had nearly died of pneumonia. She gave me a tape of Paraguayan harp music and invited us back to the house for a meal. Unfortunately, it was seventeen kilometres off the road so we had to decline. This was often our conflict, whether to stop with friendly folks or push on. This was not normal travelling, we had set ourselves a target and had to keep moving.'

The poor weather continued for the next two days. We spent an uncomfortable, wet night in a muddy field with tents flapping and bending. My run of victories in spoofing was becoming embarrassing; it was Tim who found himself walking three kilometres in heavy rain to find water, while I wrestled to put the tents up in the southerly gale. The wind next morning was crushing; it shot up from the south and sought to stop the bikes dead. We were reduced to thirty kilometres all morning, each metre hard won. Tim and I had been together for eleven months, near enough all day, everyday. Amazingly, we were still able to find new topics of discussion to pass the hours on the bikes and in cafés. As we slogged south Tim piped up, 'Do you know how they used to select people to work for the Chinese Civil Service?'

'Well, it's funny you should say that ... No.'

'They used to put you in a room on your own, gave you a desk, a pencil and a load of paper and told you to write down everything you knew.'

'Everything!?' I considered this, 'It would take a life time.'

'Everything about everything you know. Imagine, you could start with any one subject, say ... lamp posts: you could waffle on for thousands of words describing different styles; telling funny stories about dogs; where you've seen them; recounting films... Singing in the Rain...'

'Easy Street ...' I added.

'Yea, then you could start on geography or Peruvian poetry.'

'I don't know about Peruvian poetry,' I said.

'It doesn't matter, no one would have the time to read it anyway.'

'I think it's a trick,' I said to Tim after a while. 'I bet they would come in after an hour to see what you had written, and if it was all lamp posts and Peruvian poetry they'd kick you out and you'd have to get a job in Sainsbury's.'

A few more minutes sailed by in the wind before I came up alongside Tim and said, 'I think I would write: I KNOW NOTHING. And if they didn't like it, well stuff 'em.'

'Yeah, Yeah,' Tim enthused.

A wise man might write: I know nothing, but there is insufficient paper to write what I have seen and heard.

At the border town of Encarnacion we scoured the markets for essential warm winter clothing. The centre of the town was a bustling market; again everyone seemed to be selling the same things. There was one addition, we were continually pestered by lads selling musical condoms. We didn't get to find out when and how they played their tune or what tune they might play, maybe Bob Marley's *Get up Stand up*, or Queen's *I Want to Break Free*.

An unfenced railway line ran through the middle of the town, crossing the main street; we did not actually see anyone get splattered but it must have been a regular event. Shopkeepers used watering cans to damp the dust in the street and dreamily washed everyone's lower legs and shoes. After three hours of miming to giggling girls, (who probably thought we were trying to buy musical condoms), we had secured woolly mountain shirts and the only two pairs of gloves in town.

After dark the town was deserted. Policemen warmed themselves over braziers on street corners and eyed us suspiciously. Litter and cardboard boxes, abandoned after the market, danced around in the flickering shadows to the whistling of the Antarctic wind. No doubt, this country would once have been warmer and calmer. Those were the days when it had been protected by jungle.

18 A little Argie bargie – Andy

'That's all very well, but what if they don't like Ozzies either?' asked Tim. We were planning how best to handle ourselves whilst crossing Argentina. The objective was to reach the Chilean border, high in the Andes, without having our throats slit. That was two thousand kilometres away. There were bound to be a few bitter people about. People who had lost a son or a brother or who had, themselves, been damaged by the Falklands War. It would not take much for someone to hear that Brits were about and run us down or shoot us, way out in the grasslands.

It had been more than ten years since the Falklands War. A blink of an eye in human terms. The hurt, the humiliation and the anger would still be there. Britain had only resumed diplomatic relations with Argentina two years before. An official from the British Embassy in Buenos Aires had given sound advice when I phoned him from Brazil. 'Be something else', he had said. 'Don't be British and you should be all right. I'm usually Swedish.'

'Oh yeah?' I was intrigued, 'Do you speak Swedish then?'

'No, but neither do they.' We laughed.

We did not feel comfortable with Swedish, or with American; the Americans were mistrusted here, as in many parts of the world. Canada was a possibility but it is too close to America for its own good. Australia was the obvious choice. We could talk about Oz knowledgeably if we needed to and route maps printed on the back of the T-shirts seemed to confirm that we came from Sydney. We just hoped they liked Ozzies. We had been told to expect a full body search at the Argentine border. So we hid our Union Jacks, sprayed some deodorant and changed our underwear. 'You never know', said Tim, 'we might get searched by Gabriella Sabatini's little sister.'

'You never know,' I agreed.

Our efforts were sadly wasted. The guard was a big ugly bloke and fortunately, did not feel like giving us a full body search, nor did he search bags. As he stamped our passports he was interested to know why two British people wanted to cycle through Argentina. That was a tough one to answer; we had been wondering the same thing. 'Enjoy your journey in Argentina,' he said with a big, perhaps even genuine, grin. That was a good enough start.

We cycled away from the border post and into the town of Posadas where we were greeted by a big, blue and white sign proclaiming *'Las Malvinas son Argentinas'*, (The Falklands belong to Argentina).

'Oh, they seem to be perfectly reasonable about the whole thing,' I said to Tim. The irony is that the political arguments were the same now as they had been before the war. Despite the loss of over a thousand lives, both sides still claimed sovereignty. In fact, those arguments had barely altered since Captain John Strong first set foot on the Islands in 1690 and named them after Lord Falkland, the First Lord of the Admiralty.

I felt somehow disloyal to the men who had fought so bravely to retake the islands from the Argentinian invaders. They might, understandably, be disgusted with us for entering the country which had been our enemy such a short time ago. The war had cost the lives of two hundred and fifty-five Britons, with over seven hundred wounded, many seriously. However, our presence in Argentina in no way condoned the behaviour of the previous Argentine Junta; it was merely necessary if we were to achieve our own objective.

'Don't mention the War,' we agreed and kept a very low profile. For the first five days we hardly spoke to anyone. We were extra careful not to be spotted when sneaking off into the forests to camp. One night a pair of bedraggled farm workers stumbled across us as we unpacked the panniers at the side of a field. They were absolutely insistent that we were not going to stay there in their mud. We did not argue, we were after all just visitors, but I was furious as I repacked the bags. Eventually we tucked ourselves away, deep in a forest, where long straight avenues of pines spread out in every direction providing no place to hide properly. We set up camp and listened to a radio play whilst watching the clouds through swaying pines. A schizophrenic faith healer and his troubled wife recalled their life on the road and how one rainy night, in the corner of a field, in northern Scotland, they had buried their newborn baby. In our heads we were there.

Only when our supplies ran out would we have to test the safety of our Aussie identity. We knew it was the young farm lads of this region, *Corrientes,* who had been taken away to form the bulk of the conscript army that was ordered to defend the Falklands. Most were illiterate and did not even know where, or what, the Falklands were. They had been given virtually no training and their clothing provided totally inadequate protection against the South Atlantic weather. Large numbers of Argentine soldiers had died from exposure rather than British bullets. Many had sat, terrified, in cold wet bunkers for weeks, waiting for the British to come. They had to resort to killing sheep to stay alive.

Despite the terrible conditions many fought bravely, giving the British a run for their money. Only extreme courage and tenacity won the day for us at Goose Green and finally in the mountains around Port Stanley.

Many of the *Corrientes* farm boys did not come back. Of those that did, some were severely mentally disturbed but received no psychiatric treatment. It was clear that a pair of Brits, even harmless cyclists, would be far from welcome here.

At one point a convoy of military trucks passed us, carrying troops.

'STICK IT UP YOUR JUNTA!!,' I called, when I was sure they were well out of earshot.

We rode over a series of low, rolling hills, covered in pine plantations and *estancius* (cattle ranches). Blue skies, warm sun, golden fields and a tail wind made life rather pleasant.

My thoughts wandered again towards home. I had expected a letter from Cassie to be waiting for me in Rio, but none had come. I had not heard anything since the *'wait and see'* letter in Lusaka. This did not stop me wondering how I could organise things to accommodate both our needs when I got back. Compromise and a cheaper, more meaningful lifestyle were required, (perhaps we could live in a tent on Shepherd's Bush Green). There were many unanswered questions though, not the least of which was, 'What about her current man?' It was all a bit unsatisfactory trying to organise one's love life from a bicycle saddle in the middle of South America.

It was Sunday morning, there had been no towns and very few villages in the three hundred and fifty kilometres we had covered from the border in three days. We were heading southwest, aiming eventually for the city of Santa Fé, one third of the way across the country. From here we would head due west to Cordoba and Mendoza, which lay at the base of the Andes.

The vast majority of the population was four legged, although there had been a surprising number of waving car drivers. Supplies ran low and afflicted as usual by *cyclists' bonk,* we were forced to leave the road and go in search of a settlement where bread and cheese might be bought. We slogged down a sand road and came to a neat whitewashed bungalow with two youths sitting on the verandah. Tango music blared from a transistor radio. Using the phrase book I practised my Spanish quietly for a minute then went for it, addressing the surprised youths, 'Excuse me, can you please tell me where I can find a shop?' Incredibly they did not laugh or look confused; they actually understood me! They nodded and replied in their own language that there was a shop just up the track; and I even understood them! I almost jumped for joy. All those weeks of struggling with Portuguese, so similar, had prepared us well.

'*Nos Australianos,*' I told the family who had assembled outside their shack of a shop to study us. To our relief they liked Ozzies. The father had a brother in Australia, who had emigrated there in the 1970s to escape the brutal dictatorship. They opened the shop for us and we restocked with goodies; a hunk of cheddar, juicy slices of ham and enormous tomatoes. Gratefully we accepted a bag of oranges, on the house. I suspect that had we been British, we would have found the shop irretrievably closed.

Unsure of our route, the father said in Spanish, 'Be careful in Brazil, many bad people, they are not like us. I would never go to Brazil.' Kenyans and Tanzanians, Malawians and Zambians, white

Australians and Aboriginals, Argentines and Brazilians, British and Argentine, British and German, Protestant and Catholic, Serbs and Croats, blacks and whites; they all say, *'They are not like us'*. We are better, they are worse. They are not worthy. They don't love their kids. They don't want to sleep safe and warm. They don't deserve a chance to learn and prosper. They don't want to be in control of their own future. They don't want to live peacefully in the land they love. *'Not like us.'*

We cycled round the corner from the little shop, had a lazy lunch on a grass bank, and listened to the British Grand Prix on the radio.

Herons and swooping hawks accompanied our ride through the farm land. We took full advantage of the north wind to bang out some good distance; over a hundred and sixty kilometres one day. When the weather changed, as it certainly would, we knew we would have to struggle into the icy head-wind blowing up from Antarctica. These were kilometres in the bank.

We came to a crossroads where the tarred road went off to the left and took a long loop towards Santa Fé, whilst straight ahead a sand and gravel track took a shorter, more direct line to the same town. What would it be, the long tarmac route or the short sand track?

'Always take the less travelled road,' said Tim.

Before venturing onto the track, we stopped at the isolated petrol station which stood at the junction, to refill the fuel container with kerosene. The tall, skinny boss-man was surrounded by a crowd of mechanics, pump attendants and hangers on, far too many people to be profitable. He looked at us curiously. *'Nos Australianos,'* I proclaimed. *'Ah, Australianos! Habla Alemania! Serra serra!* Swiss, Swiss, no?' I listened carefully and asked him to repeat it. In the end I worked out that he thought we lived in the mountains, near Switzerland and spoke German. We were quite happy with that. He wanted to know all about our journey and was really enthusiastic. He asked some good questions, which was refreshing: were we not frightened to be in strange countries alone? Did we not argue with each other? Where did we find food? How did we persuade our families to let us go? Had we ever seen a kangaroo or a shark? Were people in Africa starving? Had we seen anyone with AIDS? Did we not have wives and children? Who won the cup in 1954?

'Tim has many wives and children!' I told him. 'Four wives in Australia, nine children in Africa and a fiancee in Rio!' This tickled them.

He was surprised to hear that we were going to take the fork onto the dirt track and not stay on the road. He was concerned about punctures and lack of food. For good measure he added, *'Peligroso, peligroso, Policia y bandidos'* waggling a long oily finger, (Danger, Police and bandits). As usual we laughed it off and trusted our luck.

We cycled off, on soft sand, in cold drizzle. The weather was starting to turn and the day was fading. The road was raised on a causeway, five metres above the plain. Land on either side was marshy and the sloping banks too steep to negotiate. When we did eventually spot a dry field, we had to make several journeys, laboriously carrying bikes and bags down the bank and over the fence, ducking out of sight as a pick-up sped past leaving a plume of dust as it went. We were soon snuggled up in our tents, fighting the bitter, frosty night with a big pan of corned beef stew.

Sand pulled at our tyres. A cold southerly wind chilled hands and ears and again made progress very slow. The bush on either side was grey and depressing. Icy rain hit us with sharp splinters. We tried to smile and just got on with it. By late morning we had reached Santo Jamie, the only town on the track. We needed to get out of the wind for a while and slurp some hot coffee. As we searched for a café I noticed, in a side street, an immaculate 1920s car, with spoked wheels, white walled tyres, long sweeping wheel arches and a black canvas roof. Beside the car, one foot on the chromed running board, stood a *gaucho*. He saw me and adjusted his pose, putting one hand on his hip, adjusting his big black hat to the back of his head with the other and pushed out his broad chest proudly. Red baggy trousers, tucked into high boots, fluttered in the wind. A pleated white shirt contrasted with the short black jacket and black, Pancho Villa, moustache. Goodness knows what he was doing; probably a failed actor on the run from a loony bin.

Further along the bedraggled street we spotted a little huddle of school children, all wearing long, white laboratory coats. We found a cafe that had no real food but did have masses of deafening music, sweet cakes and milky coffee. More lab-coated children walked past, studying the bikes then peering inside at us. It was eleven in the morning but all the shops were shut and the streets deserted except for this scattering of white coated children. Where were the grown-ups?

'It's obvious', I told Tim, 'there is a secret laboratory nearby run by the evil Pancho Villa. All the scientists have been injected with an experimental drug which has turned them into children. To produce the drug they use the bodies of the towns-people who have been systematically whisked off the streets and liquidised. We better leave Santo Jamie as soon as possible, just as soon as we've finished another plate of cakes.' He gave me a cold stare and said, 'Andy … Shut Up!' just like Suzanne used to.

For the umpteenth time on the journey, we found ourselves miles from nowhere, waterless and with dusk approaching. In Australia and Africa we had been in burning heat, now we were in freezing rain. After eight hours exposure each condition requires equal respite. We plugged on for another five kilometres then another and another over the dreary scrub land, hoping for a building or a stream. When the stream came it was stagnant. When the building came it was a police post. We chose not to involve ourselves with either.

Ten minutes later I heard a car approaching from behind and made space for it to pass. It threw up a shower of gravel as it roared by. The car was a big old Chevrolet, shiny black, with a wide, flat bonnet and long boot. It was the kind of vehicle Ronnie Reagan used to drive in his heist movies, or in which Michael Caine was kidnapped in *The Honorary Consul;* the setting for which was in nearby Corrientes. The three men in the car looked suspiciously like robbers on the way to a job.

Twenty metres up the road I saw heads turn in conversation. They made a decision. The car skidded to a halt and was slammed into reverse. It screamed back towards us much too fast and in a clatter of gravel on metal, skewing to a halt blocking the road.

There was no time to think much more than, *'Oh, shit. Here we go.'* Out jumped three very serious looking guys in dark glasses and denims. All moved with the confidence and lithe coordination of sportsmen.

'Ola!' (Hello), said the wiry one with the black beret and droopy moustache. He was acting super-cool. That is easy to do if you are wearing dark glasses, on a dark day, at dusk and are carrying a pump action shotgun. Another was stern and beefy, his belt carried a revolver. The third was younger, still in his twenties. Wearing a malevolent grin he perched himself on the big wide boot, feet on the shiny bumper.

We put on the usual jovial, pleased to see you, faces and gave *'Olas'* in return. The wiry one with the shotgun and the beret, spoke fast in Spanish. We listened hard but there was too much to grasp. I asked him to repeat it and worked out that he wanted to know where we were from and why we were here. He was impatient and wanted answers.

I could not work out whether these guys were goodies or baddies, police or bandits. If they were police we must say we were British, but in this region of Falklands conscripts that might be fatal.

'Nos Australianos,' I said (We are Australian). Tim glared at me accusingly. Was this the wrong thing to say?

'Documentos pour favor.' (documents please). The guy held out his hand. We leant down to pull our passports from the cloth money-belts, stashed in front panniers. 'I don't believe you said that,' whispered Tim. We were on different wavelengths. We stood and handed them over. *'These better not be baddies,'* I thought, *'Oh ... they better not be goodies either. Hmm'*

'You idiot, they're police,' whispered Tim again. My eyes flashed over the three characters for evidence. What had Tim seen? There, right enough, on the denim jacket of the guy sitting on the boot, was a silver badge.

'Gra Bretania? Gra Bretania?' said black beret, quizzically. His tone made me feel that I had just committed the crime of the century and now I was going to pay for it. He was clearly concerned that we did not know where we came from.

I do not beleive you just said that

Now the problem could only worsen. We understood only a fraction of the things he was asking. Even then we had great difficulty explaining why we had said we were Australian. I mentioned the Malvinas which only did more damage. Everyone became frustrated with the lack of communication. They wanted answers. We tried to explain about our expedition but it did not get through. Neither of us, for once, was wearing a *Cycle for I.T.* T-shirt with instant maps. They could not imagine why we were there in the middle of all of this nothingness, or why I had lied.

The guy in the black beret took the passports into the car where he recorded the details onto a report sheet. He then spent a long time on the radio. The others were silent, watching us smugly.

Black beret had clearly seen too many American cop movies; Clint Eastwood would have been awestruck. He climbed out of the car smiling, still super-cool and pointed at us in turn and said in English, 'Under arrest'. We opened our hands in a plea of innocence; we had seen too many Diego Maradona games. He turned and pointed down the road in the direction we were travelling,

'Cinco kilometres, Policia. Si?'

'*Si*' He wanted us to cycle to the next police post. They drove off, still in possession of our passports. 'Sorry mate,' I said to Tim.

'Ah, don't worry. It'll be an adventure. Anyway we need somewhere to sleep.' Our three guys and two more were chatting in the drizzle outside a concrete building eight kilometres down the road. It was almost dark now. With great courtesy the two new guys showed us around to the back of the building. Two horses grazed in the yard amid various dead cars and bits of rusty metal. There were no human corpses strung up in the trees which was encouraging. We went through the rear door of the building and were led into a small room. A harsh, unshaded bulb lit our home for the night. Rough wooden shelves covered one wall. On these were piled countless bundles of papers, each held together with elastic bands, so that they curled untidily. Dates were scrawled on each bundle 1986, 1975 and so on. These were the police records. We could always wile away the long night boning up on the criminal history of the area. We found out later that the major role of the police here was to deter and nab cattle rustlers; a job that they were said to be fantastically bad at. From the ceiling hung two saddles with thick sheepskin linings. These, and indeed the whole room, stank of horse sweat. We had slept in worse, though I preferred my tent. I lay down and could just touch both sides of the room with head and feet. By closing the door first, Tim could lie down too, which was a bonus, though it would be a little claustrophobic if we were to be given a thirty year sentence. Across the corridor was a filthy, non-flushing toilet and next to it an ever dripping cold shower, which we were graciously invited to use. Within ten minutes of entering the building, right on cue, the heavens opened releasing a torrential downpour. Some of the rain bounced noisily off the tin roof but most of it dripped through onto my sleeping bag.

We were given permission to cook our own food using their kitchen. They were not expecting prisoners that night and therefore did not have any extra food in for us, (they could have baked a cake!). We gathered, from what was said, that we would stay here and be taken into the Police Headquarters in the town of Féderal in the morning, twenty-five kilometres away. Here we would be expected to answer their questions properly.

We had had quite a hard day, grinding into the bitter head wind in the rain, on soft sand and gravel. We needed to have some tea and curl up in sleeping bags for an hour before making some snack. *No way José.*

The three in the car must have gone, for we did not see them again. The two who were stationed here stood in the doorway watching us make tea and peeking into our panniers in search of hidden cows. This meant that we could not lie down. One of them crouched down to be closer to our level.

The standing one soon became bored and wandered off. The crouching one asked, *'Donde a?'* (Where from?)

'Ingleterra,' I said. He nodded then sank into silence.

After a while he asked, *'Donde va?'* (Where to?)

I was quite friendly, but did not see the point in him asking the same questions as the guy in the black beret had done; and the same questions that we would be asked in the morning, but he insisted and went over and over the same old points again and again, each interspersed with long silences.

He was pleasant enough and only doing his job, but I think he was a bit simple and rather sad; a country copper forgotten out here in this miserable place. He was milder, older and fatter than the guys in the car. A green beret was his only concession to uniform. Faded jeans, a pale yellow jumper and a long red scarf wrapped around his neck three times did little to keep out the cold. His name was Angel and he shivered a lot. He had the defeated look of a man who was disappointed with life. Was this all there was? Living out here for the last two years being outwitted by cattle rustlers? He told us that his wife had left him. No wonder! There was hardly a spark of life in him, neither humour nor malice; either would have done.

After another long silence, the tea finished, he asked that old brain teaser, *'Donde va?'* (Where to?) This was intolerable! With a flash of inspiration I pulled out my plastic bag of documents and flicked through them. I showed him our copy of the leaflet we had once sent to hundreds of companies and individuals, trying to raise money for I.T. It had a photo and maps and looked professional. I thought vaguely that it might help to explain what we were doing and that we were *bona fide* people. The leaflet contained a photo of the three of us.

'Donde este es senorita?' (where's the girl?), asked Angel. I answered solemnly in a kind of Spanish, 'In Africa there was no food so we had to eat her.'

Angel jerked back and eyed us seriously until he saw the hint of a smile on my face and realised he had been had.

Tim produced the letter of introduction from the Argentine Embassy in London. It was written in Spanish and explained clearly what we were doing and that we were *"to be given every assistance ..."* It was only a short letter, seven or eight lines, but it took Angel five minutes to read. The poor chap was mouthing the words as he struggled with them.

I wanted him to understand about the charity and everything, so that he might just let us go free in the morning. It was slow going. My final attempt was to show him a copy of the letter from the secretary to HRH Prince Charles.

'... His Royal Highness has personally asked me to express to you his very best wishes in your challenge.'

Angel seemed impressed. *'Principe de Argentina?'* he asked excitedly. For a while I could only look at old Angel, lost for words. Oh dear. I suppose we were both being terribly narrow minded, he for not knowing who Prince Charles was and me for expecting that he would.

'No, Principe de Gra Bretania, hijo de Reina,' (son of Queen). Something here had clicked. Angel walked away into his office. I heard the mumble of his voice on the radio, probably to the headquarters in Féderal.

Perhaps things would be all right now. We cooked and ate in Angel's ghastly kitchen, rotting carrots and curdled milk lived a full and contented life in the fridge. Pans and plates with dried-on sauce were piled in cold, greasy water in the enamel sink. Two canaries chucked seed down onto the worktop from their cage in the corner. It desperately needed a woman around here, preferably one carrying a flame thrower.

When we went back to our room to settle down, Angel accompanied us. For a moment our eyes met, *'Just try it Angel,'* I thought, *'just try asking, 'Donde va?''* Fortunately, he just wished us good night and locked us in. After experiencing such freedom for months the feeling of claustrophobia and impotence, induced by being in someone else's control, was very disturbing.

After breakfast, Angel showed us his police car. Both front wings were missing. The paintwork was an imaginative variety of colours and textures. In some places it was magnolia emulsion, in others chocolate brown. My favourite was the brilliant purple gloss on the driver's door. He explained that we were going to squeeze the bikes into the boot and the bags onto the back seat. This took some doing but we managed it. Before leaving, Angel curiously insisted that he and his colleague be photographed with us. The image was of two proud, grinning oafs.

Eighteen millimetres of rain had fallen in the night; Angel had shown me his rainwater collection tube. The road was waterlogged; clinging black mud lay four inches deep. When we got out of this mess we were going to have to make our way back to the police post to pick up our route. If the track did not dry out quickly it would be a slow, sticky business.

Angel had dressed up for his trip into HQ. He looked pretty dapper in his long coat and green beret. His belt and boots gleamed.

The windscreen wipers did not work, so Angel had to keep opening his window to reach round and smear mud away with his hand. This only made matters worse and let in another blast of icy air and we all froze. I relaxed in the back enjoying the novelty of the adventure.

A white car overtook us at speed, spraying a shower of mud over Angel through his open window, I could not contain my laughter. Angel cursed and honked his horn three times. The white car pulled in a little way ahead. *'Oh great'*, I thought, *'some action. He's going to get him for speeding'*.

Angel pulled up behind, kicked open a stubborn door and got out. From the white car sprang a handsome, blonde woman in her fifties. With her smart, blue suit she wore black wellies. She waved to Angel and rushed past him, pulled open the front passenger door, gave Tim a big hug and planted a wet kiss on his cheek!!

She tried to get at me too but could not get over the seat. I held my stomach, rocking with laughter. What on earth was this all about?

She pulled me out into the mud so that she could kiss and hug me.

'Do you speak English?' she gushed. 'Oh English! I used to be an English teacher, I'm not very good though am I? Isn't the road terrible!? *Mucho barro, mucho barro'* (Much mud). We nodded. 'Do you like Argentina? Have you come from Brazil? I think it's wonderful, don't you? Do you know the Queen!! So exciting!! Anyway we must let you continue, see you later. *Ciao.'* With a kiss and a wave she was gone. Curiouser and curiouser!

About thirty uniformed officers were waiting for us outside the police headquarters. More came out to look as we unloaded the bikes. We were told to wait. It was a square, two storey building painted pale yellow. One policeman was watering the lawns with a hose. Across the road was a large plaza lined with leafy trees. Two young girls were chasing a scabby dog around the fountain shrieking and giggling.

Angel quickly disappeared. Some of the policemen shook our hands and made jokes about us amongst themselves. They seemed friendly enough. Eventually a swarthy officer came out. The men moved back to allow him through the crowd. The officer had a serious demeanour, oiled hair and a six o'clock shadow. He shook our hands and introduced himself as the sheriff. I noted that he was not wearing spurs. He started asking questions, again we listened carefully but could only pick up snippets. He was repeating the words, *'Internacional caridad? Internacional caridad?'* I could not work it out. Again we were all frustrated. Some of the men continued to make jokes, annoying the sheriff. He barked orders at one officer who scuttled off in a police car and we were again asked to wait. Shortly the officer returned, bringing with him a very small, very beautiful woman wearing an enormous red scarf over a smart black overcoat.

'Hello', she said confidently, 'I am Anna Maria, do you speak English?'

'Hello, Yes we are English,' I said.

'I am the English teacher. He is my husband,' she indicated the sheriff. 'He wants to ask you some questions which I will translate. Then he will telephone the higher police in Buenos Aires to tell them about you.' Mystified, we nodded. There did not seem to anything worth telling. 'My husband is unhappy that you told the officers you are Australian when you are not.'

Still unsure of our position, friend or foe, we were led upstairs into the large office of the Chief of Police. That distinguished person was comfortably seated behind a highly polished desk. Behind him a framed photograph of President Menem lent weight to the proceedings.

The room was crowded and smelled strongly of furniture polish and sweat, mainly our's. Two officers sat behind a second desk under the window. As the sheriff questioned us, one of the officers typed furiously, recording Anna Maria's translation of our answers. Most questions were a repeat of everything we had been asked the day before. Our passports reappeared and for the third time the details were recorded. With Anna Maria's help the formalities were soon over.

Now there was much *'Ahha-ing'*, and, *'Hhhhmm-ing'*, as things became clear. They did not really mind that we were British and the sheriff seemed to be satisfied with our explanation of our assumed Australian citizenship. He ticked us off mildly, but said he would not take the matter further. All in all they had treated us very decently. Had they been so inclined they could have been far more difficult and might well have extracted considerable pleasure from doing so. The Police Chief even thanked us for visiting Féderal and, said Anna Maria, thought we were brave men.

Tim shook his head smiling broadly, 'NO', he said, *'Nos Loco, mucho loco!'*, (crazy). This was always guaranteed to raise a laugh.

Anna Maria turned to us and said, 'Now they would like to see the letter from the Queen, and my husband wants to know at what time would you like to speak to the priest?' At that moment the blonde woman from the white car appeared at the door followed by a man carrying a video camera. She said to me, 'Is it time?'

'I haven't a clue ...', I replied, '... about anything.' I blame Angel, this was all his doing. Where was that bastard? *(Donde va Angel?)*

It took some sorting out. I am not really sure what went on. My best appreciation is that they had been told by Angel, on the radio the night before, that we were on a mission from the Queen of England to deliver an important message to the Government of Argentina. On the way through Argentina we were understood to be collecting money from church funds which would be given to people in Africa, *('Internacional caridad'* was international charity). The Police Chief was concerned that we wanted to ask for money from local people who were themselves poor. 'No, no we only raise money in England,' I assured him.

Anna Maria read out the letter from Prince Charles' office. The gathered policemen listened intently, then became confused and disappointed. We explained that we would not need to consult the priest and that we were certainly not on a mission from the Queen to President Menem.

It seems the blonde lady was a news presenter in her spare time and she was still interested in our story. The fifteen minute interview would go out as a news item to the whole region.

Standing there in the Police Chief's office, we could not possibly claim to be Australian, that would have been complicating things all over again. I could envisage a Keystone Cops scene with the sheriff, the Chief, Angel and the camera crew chasing Tim and me around the office, climbing over desks. So that night many thousands of Argentines would hear the news that they had two British cyclists in their midst. Our cover, you could say, was blown!

It did not end there, though. When the interview was finished it was after one o'clock so it was hardly worth cycling that day. When we explained that we had decided to stay the night in Féderal, the sheriff started fussing over us like a mother hen. He felt he had to find us a hotel and a good restaurant. We must be given a lift to the hotel. We had cycled over thirteen thousand kilometres to reach Féderal. How did he suppose we had made it this far if we could not look after ourselves? I was feeling spiritually claustrophobic again and hated not being in control.

After a long wait a pick-up arrived and many willing hands lifted bikes and panniers onto the back. Ten policemen piled in too. They were a friendly lot. It turned out that they were all going home for lunch. We weaved through streets of neat white bungalows, slowing down here and there to allow a policeman to jump out. We turned a corner in a residential street to be confronted by a line of fat, white geese crossing the road in front of us. The pick-up slowed but could not stop. Beautiful geese scattered left and right. The one in the middle hesitated for a moment, undecided which way to run. The vehicle hit it with a loud, sickening, thud, but the driver drove on. Looking back we saw the goose on its back desperately kicking and flapping, making a final, impossible attempt to survive. Its friends formed a circle and turned outwards, hissing, defending their buddy against further attack. After three seconds the goose died. One moment it was hanging out doing goosey things, moments later it was gone. It had died of indecision, literally of being *'middle of the road'*. Nothing was going to bring it back. The finality was very sobering. That could be us on the road at any time. Before we turned out of sight, a small boy braved the defensive cordon, grabbed a big orange foot and dragged the heavy goose off the road, wiping away a tear with his spare hand.

The driver waved as he left us amid a pile of kit outside the hotel. He worried us with his shout of, *'Hasta la vista'* (see you later). Were we meant to be doing something later?

We checked into the expensive hotel, ten dollars each. A tiny, black puppy played in the dusty courtyard at the back, getting under our feet as we, and a troop of youths put our kit in the room. They had been hanging out in the bar and seemed to belong to the place.

The lads directed us round the corner to a café. After five days in the bush we were tired, dirty and unshaven. We were still wearing shorts and smelly T-shirts, but the people in the café welcomed us anyway. We would get cleaned up after lunch. The jolly lady proprietor tested our resolve by offering a bottle of local wine with our steaks. I looked to Tim for support, 'We shouldn't really, we're cycling tomorrow.'

'Just a quiet one would be all right,' he said. I caved in. So we celebrated our interesting arrest and release in style. Old-timers in brown suits sucked on their maté and studied us. We entertained the three teenage daughters of the house. They giggled at our silly jokes. We deliberately mispronounced Spanish words using the phrase book and said things like, *'Please send an ambulance, my wife has eaten a telephone box.'* A second bottle of wine slipped down nicely.

Just as we were paying the bill the sheriff arrived in his blue Ford Cortina and whisked us off. Now what? He stopped outside a normal looking white bungalow and led us through a comfortable sitting room and into another room at the back. As we entered the room twenty children stood up from their desks and said in unison, *'Good Afternoon!'* This was Anna Maria's school, in the back room of her house. Anna Maria wanted the children to meet real Englishmen.

Tim recalls: 'The children ranged in age from ten to sixteen years. I instantly thought of the kids I had been teaching in Shropshire. These children looked just as smart, innocent and trusting. We, l am afraid, looked horrible, dirty and half cut. I wanted to go away and come back when we were respectable, but it was impossible.'

They were shy at first but soon asked very good questions about Africa and Australia, bicycle maintenance, drought and weather, all in very good English. The afternoon finished up with them each demanding our autographs. We loved it.

Later, the lads at the hotel watched the nine o'clock News with us, we were the main feature. The word was out. Two of the lads spoke English. Having heard that we were British, they immediately rounded on us, 'You killed our brothers!' said one youth.

'Your brothers?' I questioned defiantly.

'You killed hundreds of Argentine boys!' said the other.

'Not us, mate, we've killed no one,' said Tim.

I expect Argentinians would meet a similar reaction if visiting Wales or Portsmouth. Anticipating such a confrontation we had prepared diplomatic answers, 'We regret the deaths of both British and Argentine men', I told them, hoping I sounded like Douglas Hurd, 'but Argentina took the Islands by force, illegally. Countries can't do that.'

'Huh! You took them from us first!' said one.

'We shall not forget,' said his buddy.

Tim carried on, 'We regret all the deaths,' he repeated. 'The war was the fault of the politicians on both sides. They failed to understand each other. We hope they will one day find a solution which is acceptable to everyone involved.' This seemed to take the steam out of things, without being disloyal to those who had fought so bravely for Britain. One of the lads had the final word though, 'We know the truth. Mrs.Thatcher was told to attack the Malvinas by her husband because he owned all the sheep!'

19 Over the Pampas – Andy

Two days later we were, unexpectedly, invited to stay on an *estancia* far out in the bush. Our host had seen us on television and knew we were British. He stopped and talked to Tim beside the road whilst I was still some way behind. From their brief exchange, Tim felt sure that the chap was okay and was not likely to give us any trouble.

Taking into account our need for rest days and the long slow climb into the Andes, we were in danger of running seriously behind schedule. I protested but Tim insisted that this invitation was too good an opportunity to turn down. With seventeen hundred kilometres in front of us and only twenty-five days to our August deadline, we again abandoned cycling for the day. It was another conflict between the time schedule and the experience. With a moody silence I chucked my bike in the back of his pick-up, 'Tim, do you realise that this really puts the pressure on?', I said.

'We must meet that deadline.' He was silent. We climbed aboard, the pick-up did a U-turn and we headed out onto the pampas.

Juan took us out to the ranch where we met his brother Ramon and Ramon's wife, Elsa. They were very strongly European and lived a comfortable, almost colonial lifestyle. The house was dark and spacious, crammed with heavy wooden furniture and soft curtains. A cool stone floor, scattered with rugs, gave the place the feel of a baronial mansion.

Our host spoke perfect English, was highly educated and had travelled widely, particularly in the United States. He was starting to go bald; his pate shiny and tanned. Juan had a permanent smile and lively blue eyes.

Ramon, seemed to be the one most involved in running the farm. He wore beautifully tailored baggy pants and a short tweed jacket, well suited to life on horseback. Juan, however, wore more European clothes, best suited to the life of thinking, studying and talking, at which he was particularly expert.

'You know what it was like here in the '70s, before we had a democratically elected Government?' Juan asked, 'It was hell. You never knew who anyone was. You could be stopped at a road block and killed because you supported the Government, or killed because you did not. No one dared speak about important issues, not even in your own house; your cook or your farm-hands could inform on you and you would be taken away.

I wanted to know about the *Disappeared Ones,* the thousands of people said to have been murdered by the Government.

'They say now that nine thousand people were killed,' Juan told me.

'That is a lie though. It was more like twenty thousand. They were just ordinary people, murdered by their own Government or by the rebels.' The conversation went on over a sumptuous dinner prepared by a cook. Each time the cook, a chubby half Indian woman, entered our host stopped talking. Clearly it was important that his views did not become common knowledge, even today.

'What about the Falklands War? Why did Argentina invade the Falklands?' asked Tim.

'Galtieri was playing politics. He was a fool,' Juan said, as we helped ourselves to cold cuts of beef and rice salad. 'Before the War his economic policies were reckless. Argentina had never been so badly off. People hated him. He invaded the Malvinas as a diversion, to deflect his political opponents. One day the streets of Buenos Aires were full of people demonstrating and chanting for him to resign, the next day those same people were back in the streets acclaiming him as a hero. The people were brainwashed into believing they must have the Malvinas.' Juan went on, 'Once the fighting started I got tired of listening to Argentine propaganda on the radio, so I used to listen to the BBC World Service to see what was really happening.'

'To listen to British propaganda you mean,' I added and we all laughed. We agreed that the war could have been avoided with more concerted action by the diplomats during the years leading up to it. 'It was a big mistake', said Juan, 'I think there was much stubborn machismo on both sides.'

'I understand that the British Government had been trying to give back the islands for years', I said, 'but the inhabitants would not cooperate.'

'The war for the Malvinas sent a very strong message to the world', said Ramon, 'Don't mess with the British!'.

'Our government' Juan went on, 'still has not released the names of the men who died. They can't even tell us how many died. I don't think they even know who they sent, they don't care. They think, *So what, they were only stupid farm boys and communists'*. That makes people very angry.'

'Times are good now though', said Elsa. 'We are free people. Everything has changed since the War.'

'I did my military service when I was a young man,' Juan went on.

'That was the worst time of my life. They marched us up and down for weeks, they couldn't think of anything else for us to do. Eventually they trained us to shoot a rifle. They had one gun for thirty men. We had to line up and take our turn with it. We were allowed three bullets each which we fired into a target. I fired my three bullets, hit the target and that was it, they said I was trained to fight. I never touched a gun again whilst I was in the army. Of course living on a ranch we were used to shooting things.' He paused for a moment, adding enthusiastically, 'Do you want to try to shoot an eagle tomorrow?'

I was taken aback, 'Oh no. Thank you. I wouldn't want to kill anything, not just for the fun of it.'

The conversation was interrupted by a loud scratching at the door.

'Oh, you must see this,' said Juan. He got up and opened the heavy door to the yard. In walked an armadillo, sniffing around the floor with a long, pointed nose. 'He likes cheese very much,' we were told. We fed him big lumps of hard cheese which he ate noisily. Long bristles sprung from his tough, articulated shell. Juan picked him up by the tail, holding him a few inches off the floor;

little legs ran in mid-air, like a cartoon character. When he was put down he shot off at full speed in search of more cheese.

Tim recalls: 'It was a long evening. At last we had gained a little understanding of this enigmatic country. The best of British men, though, had died storming machine gun nests at Goose Green and foxholes on Mount Longdon, and I still could not see a good reason for it.'

'You two are very brave coming to Argentina alone like this. You are a kind of peace mission I think. Talking to Argentines, promoting understanding, showing that British are ordinary people.' I replied, 'Kind words, Juan, but not true I'm afraid, not while we are pretending to be Ozzies.'

The next morning we rose at dawn and wrapped ourselves in borrowed jumpers and tweed jackets. The ground was frozen, the air bitter. We were given a couple of quiet horses and headed into the bush. With Juan, we followed behind a team of gauchos as they rounded up sleek red cows and young bulls, and drove them back towards a paddock. My horse was unimpressed by his younger, fitter stable-mates, ridden by gauchos. These were speeding off to either side of the herd to cut off break-away bulls. The gauchos expertly turned the frisky bulls back into the herd. With all this excitement going on around us, my horse concentrated on finding long detours around icy puddles to save getting his feet wet.

In a corral the gauchos separated the young bulls from their mothers. Two men caught one bull and threw it to the ground. One man held it by the neck and chest, another opened its legs. The beast was panic stricken but lay still. With a sharp, curved knife Juan's brother, Ramon, slit the scrotum. There was a little blood as the testicles popped up covered in a white membrane. He plucked them out and cast them into a stainless steel bowl at his side; a delicacy to be eaten later. The wound was dusted with a red powder to prevent infection and the animal was allowed to jump to its feet and run back to mother. Ooh, it made your eyes water! Even these hardened gauchos winced for each bull. It goes against the grain, we are all chaps after all!

Gaucho

It was time to be driven back to the point, in the middle of nowhere, where we had abandoned our journey the previous day. On the way we saw more children in white coats. 'Why do they wear those?' asked Tim. We were told that this was their school uniform. The idea was that the children would not wear out their own clothes and that everyone would look the same.

'It is nonsense', Juan said, 'they have to wear their own clothes underneath anyway, so they still wear out and the parents have to pay extra for the white coats.'

Driving past fields of fine horses our host reached into the glove compartment of the pick-up and tossed me a circuit board, about eight inches by six inches. 'What do you think that is?' he asked.

'A circuit board?'

'It's part of a Soviet Space craft,' he said proudly, 'It crashed near here in the '70s. Look closely and you'll see that each connection has been soldered by hand, and numbered with a felt pen. Isn't that amazing! The Americans use microchips. The Soviets can put satellites and men in space with this gigantic, elementary technology. It is incredible!' The maker of this handmade gadget could not have envisaged it ending up here in Juan's pick-up. The felt pen markings made it very personal, connecting that technician to us all.

'The moon is not a satellite you know,' said Juan, as we neared the drop-off point. 'If you looked at us from another solar system you would say we are a double planet.'

'Really,' said Tim.

'Yes, and I'll tell you something else; When we look into the sky, many of the stars we see are not there. They blew up billions of years ago, long before humans walked the earth. It has taken all that time for the light to reach here.

Oh wow! Man can be so parochial.

As soon as we had waved goodbye to Juan we became Australian again. That is not to say we spent all day getting smashed, surfing and swearing at women; just that we thought in an Australian kind of way.

Winter was upon us now. The days were mainly bright and chilly. As we started to head west across the flat, featureless Pampas the winds blew either north-south or south-north, so rarely slowed us down.

The landscape was mildly monotonous; it was so flat that when I stood up out of saddle I could see Canada. The pampas spread out, endless and unchanging. There were few trees, even fewer rivers, no villages and lots of cows. Finding convenient vegetation to squat behind for those precious, daily calls of nature was a problem, and sometimes required a long wait until a bush or a line of trees popped up.

Out there, in that expanse of nothing, I was struck by the enormous amount of wilderness and farmland we had crossed throughout our journey. Across the world the areas of human population are microscopic dots in an overwhelming enormity of open space, containing only plant life and animals. Living, as I had for years, as an inward looking urbanite, I had never realised this happy and reassuring fact. Perhaps there was hope for the world after all. Surely we cannot destroy all of this, there is just too much of it.

I have heard that, given minimum standing room and all infants under five years old carried, it would be possible to fit everyone in the world onto the Isle of Wight, on England's south coast. There are that few of us, but what a mess we cause. Even more startling is the idea that, given obvious organisational headaches and the dilemma of where to send the invitations, you could throw a party for everyone who has ever lived in the history of the world and fit it inside Scotland. Imagine! Mind you, it would be hell once the whisky started flowing and the bagpipes started howling; and you can bet that in the morning all that would be left would be the bottle of Campari and those mushroom vol-au-vents.

'Do you think you'll go back to the M25 life?' Tim mused as we cranked on west into emptiness.

'No, I don't think so', I said. 'We need the M25. We even need some of the M25 tribe to help make the world go round, but the M25 doesn't need me.'

I had been struggling to find some meaning for what we were doing on this journey. How was it going to make a difference to anything? Were we just feeding our egos? What messages could we draw from our experiences? If we stood up in front of school assemblies or spoke on the radio in the future what would we tell them? Would it be just a list of adventures, feats of endurance and funny stories? I quizzed Tim endlessly as we crossed the Pampas, looking for clues and turned everything over in my head again and again.

Tim recalls: 'At first I thought Andy was up in the clouds again. After a while, though, he got me thinking. The closer we came to an ending the more significant the questions became.'

One morning, in grey half light, I was woken by the annoying yapping of a small dog. Recalling the torment of the previous evening, I realised why I was feeling so miserable. We had been riding for three or four hours through the moonless night and were not looking forward to yet another camp in the frost. A village policewoman had told us, whilst it was still daylight, that there was a lodge only eighteen kilometres up the road and we had decided to head for it. After forty kilometres it was clear that the lodge was not going to materialise. In the end, tired, cold and hungry we camped on this grassy patch near a village.

Neither of us had the energy to make tea or cook food, it was too uncomfortable. I crawled into the comparative warmth of my sleeping bag and slept.

I woke after midnight with a rumbling stomach, my tent cold as a tomb. I thought we should eat and decided to knock up a rice and vegetable mess. The ten litres of water in the bag had frozen into one giant ice cube. How we would have welcomed this in Tanzania, but it was not too helpful here. I gave in and we still did not eat. Even when exposed to the sun next morning, strapped to my rear pannier, the water bag did not thaw out until noon.

After months on the road we were supremely fit. Muscles contained unknown reserves of endurance. The intolerable, draining heat of Africa was long gone. The cold of the South American winter, though unpleasant and tiring, did not take us to the edge of exhaustion as had the heat. We felt we always had excess power up our sleeves, or up our shorts. It was still hard though, keeping going.

We had become like brothers. Even after all this time we were able to sit and chat for hours without feeling the need to scream with frustration and boredom. Thoughts were of home and what we would do next. Riding along through the fields one day Tim, who had been worried and lost in his thoughts for ages, suddenly said, 'We're not normal are we?'

'What do you mean?'

'Normal people don't give everything up and cycle round the world, do they?'

'That's only one view point. Today in Telford or Surrey it's not normal I agree, but if people in the past had been as insular and comfortable as they are now, the world would never have been explored or developed. What about the Spaniards here, the British, Romans, Arabs, Portuguese and Vikings, it was certainly normal for them to drop everything and sail off into the unknown.' We pedalled on in silence for a while. 'Perhaps we live in the wrong era', I said. 'I would have loved to have sailed with Sir Walter Raleigh or walked across Africa with Burton and Speke, they were seen as heroes not weirdos. Look at Thomas Stevens. He cycled around the world between 1884 and 1886 on a penny-farthing. He was a hero.'

'Sounds like a weirdo to me.'

'Yeah me too!'

There are few things more frustrating than being within sight of a summit and being forced back without reaching it. If something happened now to stop us finishing we would have to start it all over again, somehow, someday. Incredible as it had all been, that was not such a wonderful thought. Perhaps we had been lucky to come so far unscathed. Often we felt that someone above was looking after us. I carried a St. Christopher, won from my friend Monty, years before. Tim wore his engraved dog- tags and felt they gave him luck. It was probably more the combination of our smiling faces, our outward display of confidence and goodwill which had deterred people from having a go. Someone once gave me the advice: *'Do your work as well as you can and be kind to all things, every moment, this way things will always work out.'* I think also that we were really very happy and happiness is immensely powerful. Some people will wonder how we could be happy in such hardship and with so little money and few possessions. It is because we didn't need anything else. We were deeply in tune with nature, with each other and with ourselves.

Three times over the next few days we were stopped by mobile TV crews, lurking in wait for us beside the road, alerted perhaps, by passing motorists. By now we were able to tell the bones of our story in Spanish. Though greatly improved over the weeks, it was, to be honest, rather approximate Spanish. The viewing public must have sat down to watch the local news those nights and thought, *'Que the hell are those goddamned Australians hablaing about'.*

We edged westwards towards August. At the end of each day, excitedly I told Tim how far we had to go. It was dropping dramatically. 'We've as far to go now as it was from Féderal to here', or, 'It's as far to go now as from Albany to Perth.' Tim called me Stan the Stats man. I remembered the day in Malawi when we had said it was as far to go now as we had come in the last six months from Sydney. How had we managed to keep our heads together with such an immense distance in front of us? Time had moved so slowly for us. It seemed a life time since Sydney and probably was.

The city of Cordoba was bursting with hordes of smart, young people, talking and dancing in cafés and clubs. Cordoba has been a university city for nearly four centuries. More than once, safe in our Ozzie identity, we heard from the students, strong anti-American and anti-British sentiment. 'The British are arrogant thieves,' they said. 'They have spent centuries robbing people all over the world. They think they can continue their colonialism here.'

One group bent our ears for hours one night. 'The Americans are now the real enemy of the Argentine people and the masters of our government', they had said. 'They are supporting our economy. The world press say that President Menem is a genius, that he has turned our economy around. He wins prizes you know. One day it will all collapse. It is not built on anything solid. It is a false economy, fantasy. We are tied into this system of one dollar to one peso; when the dollar changes we change, the problem is the peso isn't worth a dollar. Fantasy!'

Another went on, 'Now the Americans say that our railways are unprofitable and we must close them. So we close them. Argentina was built on railways. The British built them, before we even had roads. How are the farmers supposed to transport their cattle and crops in good condition when there is no railway and only dirt roads through most of the country? And who will pay for extra trucks and buses and maintain the roads? No one, not the Americans that is sure.'

More than ten years after the Falklands War, British newspapers carried revelations of alleged executions of Argentine prisoners by British Paratroopers. Eye witnesses on both sides provided shocking accounts of murder on Mount Longdon. Ironically it was the British Military Police and Scotland Yard who pursued the alleged culprits and the Argentine authorities who said, *The murdered men are dead and gone, why worry now? These things happen in war.*'

We split for the day in Cordoba, walking the streets, dodging great holes in the pavement, looking and listening, each doing our own thing quite happily. Beautiful girls seemed to be everywhere. They wore dark, serious, clothes and straight black hair which flowed and waved as they rushed about the shops.

I found a cheap, dirty café full of scruffy, unemployed men. The food was simple; fried, battered steak and salad. Here the guys could watch subtitled Kung Fu videos whilst they ate and got drunk, anytime day or night.

In the evening Tim and I went for a beer in a trendy wine bar downtown. We sat chatting and watching a video of the rock band *Police* on a big screen. A smartly dressed couple in their late thirties came in, sat at the next table and ordered drinks. I was aware that the guy was watching us but concentrated on the screen. The guy suddenly got up and stood over our table. He leaned down and said into Tim's ear, 'Hey mister, you wanna fucka ma sister?' We just about fell on the floor laughing and he was, somehow, terribly offended.

Most people in Cordoba looked European. Their forefathers came seeking refuge from repression, poverty and disillusion; Germans, Russians, Spaniards, Italians and British.

Cordoba provided an opportunity for a little entertainment and culture at the cinemas and galleries. Magnificent Cathedrals and churches seemed the centre of attraction for locals; all day long men and women popped in for a few minutes of peace before returning to their offices or shopping expeditions. I longed to get back into the country. Wandering those streets I missed the sky.

I went to see the bus station and found it the liveliest place in town. A gigantic modern building on four levels. It was just down the street from our little guest house, *The Residential Lily*. For hours I sat and watched eager families pushing onto row upon row of smart coaches. Lovers hugged and cried when it was time to part. Pick-pockets watched and waited, waltzing unseen through the crowd, stalking their prey, attacking and disappearing with lightning speed. A tired, slightly nervous old couple climbed off a bus and fussed over their bags. How could they find a taxi without leaving the bags open to theft?

Souvenir shops, news stands and bars filled the second and third floors above the bus parking bays and were never quiet. The news stands sold titles like *International BodyBuilder* and *Golf Monthly*. On the first floor hopeful people sat behind the counters in the long line of ticket booths, above each of which was a plastic sign saying the name of the company and where their buses went. As I walked by, I was called by each ticket salesman, trying to persuade me to go to Buenos Aries, Tucuman or Mercedes.

On the ground floor was the Telecom Office from where I phoned my brother, Colin, in England with mind blowing ease and clarity. How do they do that? People sat on soft blue chairs in the office, patiently waiting for their turn. It was all very comforting.

We left Cordoba in high spirits. At last we were on the road to Mendoza, at the base of the Andes. We wound through low mountains and past a sea-like lake, at the head of which tourists inspected a high dam. Again we were in farmland, ranch houses lay far out on the plain. There was no one to talk to and no one to bother us.

The narrow road was rough but just about tarmac. It jinked north and south wastefully, requiring us to battle into the cold southerly wind every hour or so. We stopped for lunch in a ditch beside the road (Tim was in his element), and managed to find shelter from the wind. Sweat cooled quickly, making us shiver uncontrollably. We listened to the radio. It was strange that since we had been in South America we had usually been able to pick up only one programme on the BBC World Service, *Focus on Africa,* reporting an endless succession of coups and riots.

'You know why we can only get this African programme don't you Tim?'

'No why?' He thought I could solve the mystery.

'It's because we bought the radio in Tanzania.' After two hours, four mugs of tea, soup, pasta and corned beef on bread, we roused ourselves. It was hard to get moving again.

By nightfall we had found Alchive, the only village for a hundred kilometres. The hotel was cheap by Argentine standards, $7 each, so we decided to stay for two nights. I was in bed, either sleeping or reading, snuggled, against the cold, for most of the next thirty six hours.

When we woke at dawn on the morning of our planned departure it was snowing heavily. For a moment we debated whether we should hole up for another day, but agreed that we could not spare the time and anyway, it would be really wimpy. 'We're not here to enjoy ourselves,' said Tim, like a born sports teacher.

It was July 31st; at home people would be lying on polluted beaches or sweltering in traffic jams. Tim and I were climbing a steep hill on a dirt track, in driving snow, in the middle of an Argentine winter singing, *'Good King Wenseslas looked out, on the feast of Stephen, where the snow lay round about, deep and crisp and even ...'* Marvellous!

Our minds were very much on the Andes. As we approached we expected to climb through foot hills, but the plains reached right up to Mendoza, at the base of the mountains. On the final night we camped in the scrub, in loose sand and watched the sun set over the peaks, some three hundred kilometres away. The Andes looked far too big to be cycled over. There was magic in the silence of the plains, the sun turning the snowy peaks soft and warm. How many times had we watched the sun set, over how many different scenes?

We eventually made it to Mendoza by mid-afternoon the next day. For once it was warm and sunny. I felt I was in a trance as we celebrated with coffee and chocolate cake on the pavement outside the *Crazy Bar*. Bikes were propped against the curb. We were still in shorts and T-shirts and filthy as usual. Bus loads of people gawped at us as they stopped at the traffic lights. A gang of school girls, naughty sixteen year olds, surrounded Tim as he sat opposite me relaxing. They quite unashamedly chatted him up, one of them actually told him, 'You are very beautiful', but ignored me completely. They have funny tastes, those Argies. Funny tastes.

20 Appointment at the end of the world – Andy

All that we had once looked forward to, we now looked back on. Well almost. I was mixed up. I did not want it to end, but knew it had to. Everything ends.

We had cycled too far to imagine. Vague images of past moments had distracted me over the last few days. The mental torture of the Nullarbor and the Caprivi; the empty expanse of Turkana; the bandits in Zambia and the elephant in Zimbabwe; The Rio street kids, Iguacu Falls and the Féderal Police. Each had led to this. We could not live one special moment without first living every other moment. Nothing exists in isolation.

From here in Mendoza, only three hundred kilometres stood between us and the end of our journey at Valparaiso. There was now just one little barrier to success: The Andes.

If he had still been alive, Schumacher, the founder of Intermediate Technology and author of *Small is Beautiful*, would, I think, have approved. We had transformed the basic action of turning a pedal into a crossing of three continents just by repeating it four million times. Simplicity.

The memory of the sudden death of the plump, white goose in Féderal had stuck with us. One moment you are merrily hanging out doing your thing, the next you are writhing and screaming in desperate final throws. No arguments, everyone is very sorry and all that; but from the moment you are hit you are absolutely not coming back. *'Don't get goosed,'* had become our rallying cry. This was no time to mess up. We had become even more obsessed with safety. As well as the usual trucks, bandits and policemen we now had to think about exposure, hypothermia, ice and snow on the road and altitude sickness.

As I polished the battered paintwork of the bike frame, a vision played in my mind for the hundredth time.

I am walking up the drive of the Garratt's family house in Shropshire. Gravel crunches under my feet. I am wearing good shoes, highly polished, and a suit. The front lawn is beautifully cut, flower beds alive with colour. This is a safe place. I am scared. Ruth Garratt hugs me at the door. For too long I can't speak, ashamed, I blurt out, 'I'm so sorry. It's my fault he's dead. I shouldn't have got him involved.'

I walked into the Argentine Automobile Association, on the bustling Avenue San Martin, to check out the route. The guy just looked at me and said, deliberately, in perfect English, 'Nobody cycles over the Cordillera (Andes) in the middle of winter. This is not Australia you know.' (I had lied again). 'I know it's not', I said. 'If it was Australia I wouldn't be here.' This just confused us both.

He told me that the pass, at twelve thousand feet, may be blocked by snow. If that were the case, we would not get through and might be stranded up there. This was a big worry because we needed to cross in four days to meet our target: to reach Valparaiso within a year of leaving Sydney.

From the AAA office I walked down *Avenue San Martin* to the big modern Post Office and checked out the poste restante desk. There was a letter for Tim and a couple for me. One was from Cassie. It was covered in postmarks and crossings out and had clearly had quite an adventure of its own. Originally posted to Rio it had missed us and been forwarded to Asuncion and missed us again, but here it was. I resisted the temptation to read it right there in the Post Office and tucked it away in my money belt, resolving to save it until we reached the top of the Andes to treat myself. The other letter was from Debbie Smith at I.T. which I ripped open. She told us that over £35,000 had been raised to support the training projects in Turkana. The schemes we had set up had worked.

'To Valparaiso!' we saluted each other in the street outside the dingy hotel. 'Nothing like saving the best till last,' I said, excited at the prospect of the Andes.

I had a fright when I realised what a prospect it was to cycle over the Andes in mid-winter. It is all very well planning it from a comfy sofa in England. Now we were actually about to do it for real.

We threaded our way through a maze of elegant boulevards lined with jacaranda trees. Colourful gardens and elaborate fountains adorned the many plazas where businessmen read newspapers, lovers whispered and fat hookers patrolled in gangs. Chic young women chatted over *espressos* at street cafés. Traffic cruised sedately along the streets and stopped obediently at the lights. Youths wore tartan scarves and leather jackets, while sleek shops sold Reeboks and 'Batman' T-shirts.

Mendoza had been colonized by the Spanish in 1561; subsequently the Indians had just about died out. The people crowding the streets gave the place a European air. Here, as in Cordoba, they were of Italian, German, Spanish and British stock.

As we left the city a thick, yellow gunk hung in the air obscuring the mountains ahead. Hidden among those peaks and valleys lay the route over the Andes. The only other negotiable pass was a thousand miles further north, near La Paz, Bolivia. In 1817 José de San Martin had pioneered the route from Mendoza when he went off to help liberate Chile from the Spaniards with his Army of the Andes. Once in Chile San Martin fought alongside a revolutionary with the intriguing name of Bernado O'Higgins, whose father had been born in Sligo, Ireland and had managed to become Viceroy of Peru. With San Martin's help, O'Higgins junior became President of Chile. This path over the Andes has had immeasurable effect on Chile's economy. It is much appreciated by the odd cyclist too.

Over millions of years the Rio de las Cuevas had furrowed a deep canyon through the mountains. The road now followed the river's course. In the spring thaw the river would become a wide, dangerous torrent. Now it was only twenty metres across, a comparatively tame trickle. To reach the pass we would have to climb for a distance of more than two hundred kilometres.

We had serviced the bikes thoroughly and fitted new brake blocks. The machines were nearly as good as new, smooth, solid and sweet sounding. Minimal supplies had been bought to keep weight down, though we still carried emergency rations. For over four months I had managed to resist two energy bars, bought in Cape Town. Within four days they would be mine. In trying to lighten my load further, all I could safely discard was an ankle support. It had been given to me by a lovely physiotherapist from Birmingham, whom we had met on the steamer on Lake Malawi. So if you should meet a lama with a limp wearing a stretchy bandage, it's Emma's.

Low down the weather was bright and warm. As we climbed slowly, the tussocks of grass gave way to harsh alpine scrub on the wide valley floor and the road blasted through tunnels to negotiate bluffs of rock. In the distance snowy peaks filled the sky.

Rounding one giant outcrop we were punched by a vicious, escaped hurricane. It caught my front panniers with such force that the one remaining bolt lug holding the front rack was snapped off the frame of the bike. Tim skewed towards the wall which protected him from a drop of a hundred feet. Flying sand stung my face and took off three layers of suntan. The bikes were grabbed from beneath us and crashed to the ground. We crouched beside the road, backs to the onslaught, with hands covering eyes and mouths. I turned to peek as a red truck shot round the bend towards us, on the wrong side of the road, barely in control. He missed us by inches.

I improvised a fixing for the rack and together we heaved onwards, bending into the fury. Locals call the wind *la confluencia*. Cold air was being sucked down the valley from the frozen peaks and spat out onto the thirsty plains below. As an experiment I shouted at the top of my voice but could not hear myself over the bedlam.

Several times we were caught by the wind, turned around and zipped across the road, as if by a child playing with toy cars on a kitchen floor.

Reprieve came as the sun began to set behind the mountains and with the shadows, the cold crept in. We pulled on trousers and jackets and looked for somewhere to stop. An old man with a limp and lots of dogs allowed us to bed down for the night in an empty concrete hut. The old man soon jumped into his pick-up, 'It is too bloody cold for me up here,' he told us in Spanish, and headed off for the city sixty-five kilometres away, leaving us to look after the dogs.

The gentle rise continued next day. It took us through moonscape canyons of unbelievable size. Only when we saw minute trucks crawling along the valley floor in the distance could we work out the scale. The contrast between sunlight and shade was incredible: when we slid behind a mountain we froze; in the sunlight we boiled.

The road became much steeper and my breathing started to become laboured. I was struggling as we reached the Argentine border post at dusk. Outside a soldier gave me a rubber stamped piece of paper which I stuffed away. Inside the concrete building we were pushed around from queue to queue. The officials thought we were from this bus or that bus. I insisted, in my version of Spanish, 'We are not with a bus. We are on bicycles.'

The motherly blonde woman behind the desk threw up her hands and exclaimed, *'BICICLETTAS??'*

Once outside again, we had officially left Argentina but the Chilean border was still over thirty kilometres away. Regardless, we proudly pulled out our Union Jacks, hung them once more on the rear panniers and relinquished our Aussie citizenship. We climbed steeply beyond the border post. The bikes were disobedient on the icy road and we fought to stay upright. A dramatic, snow covered valley opened before us. High peaks on either side lead away towards Aconcagua at the head of the valley; the highest peak outside Asia at 22,833 feet. The moonlit scene was literally breathtaking; I needed a squirt of Ventolin, my first since the cold and wet of Victoria, despite living on eight or ten each day in London to control my asthma.

Friendly lights from a distant village beckoned us along the valley floor. We set the tents up in the snow behind a wooden barn, and settled down to a cold night.

This village, Los Penetentes, had once experienced a snowfall of six metres in one night; not this night though. We woke, still tired and jaded, to glorious blue sky and the crisp, stinging air that is reserved for high mountains. The pass, we were told, was not blocked. Half a day's climb would see us at the top.

A car passed us and pulled up a little way ahead. A middle aged couple jumped out into the snow as we approached and insisted we stop for a chat. Calculating that we were slightly ahead of schedule, we gave in. It seemed a mistake, however, for on seeing our Union Jacks they laid into us with mild accusations of colonial exploitation and of stealing the Falklands. Cora was short, with a bob of shining black hair and a cheeky smile. She said, 'In Argentina we say, 'The Englishman is a gentleman on his own island, and a pirate off it'.

Ricardo was a studious looking architect from Mendoza with a solemn disposition. He had travelled to Britain to study English fifteen years before. 'On my first day in England' he told us, 'I hired a car and drove it on the wrong side of the road. I had a crash almost immediately and was in the Mayday Hospital in Croydon for five weeks. I never did go to college.' We laughed, it was a funny story but even after all these years, Ricardo did not see it. Croydon can do that to people.

'Still,' Cora went on, 'you're doing this journey at the best time, right after university, soon you will have jobs and wives to stop you.' God, I liked Cora. What a fabulous woman. Could it be that in cycling we had found the secret of eternal youth? Could it be that The Holy Grail was simply a medieval bicycle. Seeing our amusement she asked what we did.

'I am a teacher, ' said Tim.

'And I used to be an executive in the oil industry but I'm all right now.'

She gave me a patronising look and it was time to go. Cora and Ricardo waved us off with an offer to stay in their holiday apartment near Valparaiso. On we went, the wind howling into our faces, each turn of the pedals took excruciating effort. We stopped at a lonely graveyard which lay on the hill-side beside the road; unfortunate climbers of Aconcagua rested here. I brushed snow from the graves and read each inscription. One girl, Graciela Olivares Rubio, had been born within a few days of myself, and had died, on the mountain, at the age of 28. Her monument was a tree stump carved with her name.

Oxygen was harder to find now, we had to work for it, breathing deeply and deliberately. As the slope increased, we were forced to stand out of the saddle and inch upwards in low gear. Progress was painfully slow and dangerous, streams of thick ice spewed across the zig-zagging road. Only the effort of the climb kept the cold at bay. There was very little traffic up here and, apart from our grunting and the turning of gears, silence ruled.

What might I take from this journey? Could it really be a metaphor for something bigger? On the zig-zagging road of life do we always work out our objectives in advance? Do we follow a map, and do we know where we are at all times? Do we decide what knowledge and skill we need to acquire along the way? And do we take care in selecting our travelling companions and agree our mutual needs? Do we sit comfortably at home waiting for things to happen, or do we venture out and take a look over that first hill? Do we take the highway with the crowds or, instead, take the less travelled road with more bends and more junctions to consider, which offers more challenge but a better view and greater adventure? Do we set a steady pace or do we steam ahead and leave our companions behind, lost in the mist? When we get to a crossroads do we stop for a minute and check the map, reconsidering our objectives, or do we just plough on without thinking? And do we go out in the sun unprepared for the rain and snow which must inevitably come? And when the rain does fall do we meet it with a heavy heart and a scowl or do we meet it laughing and push through to the sun on the other side? And when we meet strangers on the road do we ignore them, or do we shake their hands and try to know their thoughts? And when the tarmac turns to sand and the flat land turns to hills and seemingly unscalable mountains, when the food and water runs out what then? Do we give up and sit beside the road in tears, or throw the bike in the ditch and catch the bus? Or do we push on, no matter what, to reach our objective with strong legs, a strong heart and skin tanned and hard from the storms? And shall we rush straight up the mountain oblivious to all around, or shall we take many zigs and many zags learning something new at every turn? And at the top do we lay down and sleep, or do we scour the horizon, looking for a new mountain to scale? And do we seek still more friends to accompany us on the next journey, to show them wonders previously hidden to them? Are we truly alive? Are we discovering our intellect and using it? Discovering our creativity and using it?

The road started to flatten out. We were at the top of the Andes.

Glorious, snow covered peaks surrounded us, spindrift howling off the tops. Aconcagua rose a little to the north, massive and foreboding. A pair of condors soared, effortlessly, up and down the valley, searching for something tasty to kill. Mother Nature could have spent her time making designer clothes and fast cars but instead she chose to make THIS!

I looked back east, down the valley and beyond, squinting my eyes. Was that a gorilla I could see, crossing the finish line of this year's *City to Surf Run,* fifteen thousand kilometres away?

Cassie and I once saw *Two Way Mirror,* an Arthur Miller play, at the Young Vic in London. The main character talked about reaching thirty as being a crisis: You are standing on a mountain ridge. Looking back you see everything that led you here, the long hard climb. Looking forward all is downward. This point, thirty years old, is as high as you will ever reach.

I had found this idea terribly pessimistic and was determined to prove it wrong. On my thirtieth birthday I had contrived to be on a real mountain ridge; the snow was perfectly formed into a sharp peak. I walked along that ridge of Sonninghorn, one foot in Switzerland one in Italy. This had been a new, and somewhat gripping, experience for me. I was telling myself, symbolically, that reaching thirty was not the end, from where everything went downward, but was rather a chance for a new beginning. This afternoon, two years later, at the top of the Andes, I looked back at all we had done and determined once again to look forward and upward to the future. It was yet another chance for a new beginning.

The journey, though, from here would be mainly downhill. We had managed to fulfil our first two objectives: firstly to cycle up every hill on the route, never getting off to push; and secondly, to take no lifts. All we had to do to meet the third objective, to finish within one year, was to reach the coast of Chile by the following night.

We reached a small village with a shivering soldier, in balaclava and sun-glasses. His mission in life was to take little white slips of stamped paper off everyone that passed.

'*Que?*' we asked.

'The paper you were given at the border post,' he said in Spanish.

Tim liberated his from his passport, like a good boy, and handed it over. Mine had escaped. The stone-faced soldier was insistent. If I did not have it I would not be allowed to leave Argentina. Disaster! We had no time to lose. He turned to attend to a car coming from Chile. An invisible hand in the wind lifted Tim's slip from the top of the pile the guy was holding and flicked it to the floor at my feet. '*Ah, the famous Argentinian 'Hand of God',*' I thought. 'Here it is!' I cried and he let us through.

A sign said '*BIENVENIDO A CHILE*', (Welcome to Chile). This felt unbelievably good *and* we were going DOWN! As we left the pass behind and plummeted towards the Chilean border post I was in severe pain, the cold burning into hands and cheeks.

I shivered for an hour whilst dealing with the immigration officials. We then jumped about in the little café and drank numerous cups of coffee to try to warm up.

'You know Britain's going to be the same don't you?' I said to Tim as we jigged and shivered.

'I know. It's going to be strange, like a time warp,' Tim replied. 'I don't know if you and I have changed though.'

'We won't know 'till we get home.'

'I think I've gained so much in confidence', he said, 'I can do anything now, within reason, it's just a matter of planning and getting on with it.'

'What do you think you'll do?' I asked, not for the first time.

'I'll take things slowly at first. I won't rush anything', he said, 'but I really want go back to teaching, it's what I do.'

'I think I want to teach as well, in some way', I said, 'that might be the compromise that could help me to work things out with Cassie.'

'I can see you as a teacher,' said Tim.

'Trouble is there are so many other things I want to do. But I reckon it is possible to do everything you want in life, but not all at the same time. You have to do them one after the other.'

We chatted with a gang of cheerful soldiers, guarding the road outside the border post. Two or three of them spoke English. They were well kitted out for the cold, with many layers of underclothes and immaculate, green, woollen coats on top. There was a pretty girl in the group, Maria, who did all the paperwork and was the willing butt of most of the jokes. *'Would we like to marry her?'*

When 6.30 came it was obviously time to knock off. 'Give me help,' said one of the soldiers. I took one end of a heavy wooden bench; the sort you see in a school gym. He took the other and we placed it across the road.

'There my friend', he said, 'today you have closed the border between Chile and Argentina.' I was delighted.

'What did you think of Argentina?' the soldier asked me as we walked back to join the group.

'Umm, It's flat, Argentina. Very flat,' I said.

'Do you like the Argentine men?' they asked Tim.

'Some were very good to us', he replied diplomatically. 'Some were not so good.'

A soldier stage-whispered, looking around him for support, 'The Argentine: he drinks too much, talks too loud and eats too much meat!!' Everyone agreed.

There is a great lack of trust between the two nations.

During the Falklands War, Argentina held many of her crack troops in these mountains, defending against an expected invasion by Chile. The Chileans had enjoyed seeing their oldest foes take a beating.

One soldier put his arm around my shoulder and said cooly, 'I want to screw Maggie Thatcher.'

I laughed, 'We'll let her know.'

An old, snow covered lodge stood next to the police post, it had been damaged by fire and lay empty. The soldiers allowed us to use it for the night. My torch cast long eerie shadows across the wet floor as we searched for a bedroom.

Later I lay in the dark, on the top bunk, staring at the ceiling. It felt like Christmas Eve.

'Tim?

'Yeah,' he answered sleepily from below.

'We've nearly cycled around the world.'

Neither of us spoke for a while.

'I know mate,' he said.

I felt awkward but I had to say it, 'I couldn't have done this without you.'

'You too mate,' he mumbled '... Bloody hell it's cold.'

I remembered the letter from Cassie, which I had saved for the top of the Andes. I switched the light on and excitedly retrieved it from my money belt. I lay back in bed and studied the envelope. It felt much thinner than her previous letters which had been full of gossip, questions and funny ramblings. I opened it and read:

Dear AB,

I don't want to hurt you, but I have been thinking about everything and have decided that I am really happy with my life now. I don't believe we can just carry on after all this time. Perhaps I remember it differently. Please let's be friends. As far as I'm concerned the matter is closed.

Cassie

I lay staring at the letter for a long time. It couldn't be true. From below Tim sensed something amiss and asked, 'You alright?'

'Yes, fine,' I lied.

I could not say any more and stay in control. At that moment my heart was breaking.

Dawn. Four pairs of socks, shorts, long trousers, waterproof leggings, four T-shirts, wool shirt, fleece jacket, rain jacket, woolly hat, hood, sleeping bag liner as face mask, gloves, socks on gloves, nylon tent bags on socks on gloves, sunglasses. Not even Kilimanjaro at 19,000 feet had felt so cold. It was not Chile, it was absolutely bloody freezing! The thermometer in the lodge read minus twenty-five degrees Celsius. Outside the wind-chill factor would have taken the temperature far lower. Exposed flesh begins to freeze at minus one degree and eventually the bodily extremities fall off; we were in serious danger of having our assets frozen.

What did she mean *'I remember it differently'*? What else was there? Was I that much of a shit? Things could be better now if we only tried. Maybe all this time on the road, inside my own head, had led me into a fantasy world. Maybe I had been wrong all along; maybe now I should let go of the past. Could it be I had just been using the ghost of Cassie as emotional support to get me through? The hurt and the sense of loss felt real enough. *'As far as I'm concerned the matter's closed.'*

I tried to push the letter from my mind and concentrate on the job in hand. We had misjudged it badly. The wiggles had stretched these final hundred and twenty kilometres on the map to over two hundred kilometres on the ground. We had left Sydney on 11th August. Today was 10th August. If we ran into tomorrow it would, technically, be a year and a day; 367 days with the leap year. For us that would be too late. We had to finish before midnight tonight. Today would have to be the longest day of the entire journey if we were to meet our objective.

I felt the drama of the occasion, 'Tim, today we can become the first people to cycle across the three southern continents in one year.'

'Only because everybody else has had something better to do,' he replied. 'Like jobs and raising babies and running the world.' It was quite a feeling.

Tim recalls: 'We were not athletes or some of these supermen who can pull sledges across the Arctic or climb Everest, just two ordinary blokes who put their minds to muddling their way through to achieve something. This was our challenge. Few people cared about what we were doing, of course not, why should they? Other people's lives and goals were just as important to them as this was to us. But it still meant everything. We had always had a goal: the next town, the next border, the next continent. Always thinking, Chile, Chile, Chile. Now that I was so close I'm not sure I wanted to go to Valparaiso at all.'

We went, Tim in front. The road fell immediately, snaking down the chasm. The steepness caught me by surprise. Switchback bends came too quickly. Hands were clenched, painfully trying to keep the brakes jammed on. Barely aware of the braking, the laden bikes careered into tight corners over streaks of ice. Another bend and another, gathering speed, we zig-zagged back and forth, gradually losing control. Black crag walls closed in above. There was no stopping; the bikes had smelled the salty ocean and were off. They took wide sweeps using the wrong side of the road. Swinging out too far, the tyres followed a tightrope of gravel above the steep drop. Over-correcting, I swerved across the road and glancing up caught a glimpse of a big, black bonnet on collision course. The car was climbing slowly. If I turned I would hit it head-on; if I carried on straight I could avoid it. With a mighty, helpless, 'Whhuuuhhhaaa,' I closed my eyes and the bike left the road, crunching into the steep, soft bank.

The final fling

I found myself lying in the snow. At least I had stopped. The guys in the car laughed and carried on. Probably going home. 'THANKS BIKE!!' I shouted at it, 'For Christ's sake calm down will you"

The deep snow had saved everything from serious damage, so I climbed, once more, aboard the runaway train and went in search of Tim. I caught up with him a little lower down, trying to unfreeze his knuckles. His hands were shoved up into opposite armpits, his face contorted in agony.

In time things mellowed a bit. The angle of descent got itself under control, the Z-bends unfurled and the sun woke up. We belted through a narrow wooded valley.

'I've been thinking,' said Tim pulling up to cycle beside me, 'I don't think this has been about cycling.'

'What do you mean?' I asked, glad to be distracted.

'There's so much more. I can see now that it's about everything.' He paused for a few moments. 'I don't think there is an answer, but it's like we've been digging a small tunnel though a mountain, picking up nuggets here and there, and its only now, at the end of the tunnel, that we've discovered that all along, just above us, ran a great seam of gold.'

'Right on brother.'

'I think, for the first time, I know the difference between what's important and what's trivia. The things that matter to me are my family, friends, my health and getting fulfilment and satisfaction from life. Everything else is peripheral and unimportant'

Before this all started, we were looking for some answers on balancing needs and resources. Were we any closer to understanding?' Well there's no single answer. It comes from within us, from a shift in attitude. The first step is to face reality and attempt to empathise with all groups living lives void of opportunity and dying through injustice. Accept that we are all in this together, we all deserve rights and we all need the same basic things. If I want to see a different world I must first BE different. If I wish others to find a purpose I must first find and follow a noble purpose.

The problems of the world; greed, millions of hopeless dying children and war will not be solved by the giving of a few dollars to charity. These things will only be solved at the level of the human spirit. Our combined spirits.

Travel and experience are wonderful things. They can lead us a little of the way towards wisdom. Perhaps it takes 2042 significantly different experiences to achieve wisdom. Some reach it aged 80 some 18, most barely get started. I'm on about 543. The further I go the more confusion and frustration I find. I wonder what people think when they reach 2042. I suspect there are just more questions. If only I can hold on to the spirit and make the time to keep questioning and learning.

I foresee and promote responsible, humane multinational corporations (the real power in this world), where genuine personal growth and real life experience is championed. Where people who are interested primarily in money have no place. Profits will always be important but will go hand in hand with a balanced understanding and (through action) contribution to employees, other people and the environment. These corporations have the opportunity to rain down hope and choices to the less lucky and give the future world half a chance. We can create a world where all people are discovering their uniqueness and their talents for using these. Living. If for every hundred dollars of profit one dollar went back to educate through first hand experience, all executives and presidents in the laws of nature and the reality of the world, we'd be in fair shape. They all talk about it, very, very few do it.

It starts with the individual. You? In fairy tales there is always a call to action, the hero responds and overcomes all obstacles to bring benefit to him or herself and to the wider community. The dragon is killed, the town is saved, the Princess won.

This is your call to action.

I urge you to get out there in your world. Take responsibility for life. Take action. Have real experiences. Make a lasting difference to at least one person. Create change. Kill the dragon.

The ancient port of Valparaiso, refuge of mariners, adventurers and pirates since the sixteenth century, was still a long way off. Back in shorts and T-shirts we shot through the foot hills and onto the plains, leaving a jagged horizon in our wake.

I imagined a scene: my brothers and my nieces, perhaps my dad, meeting us at Heathrow Airport in a few days, returning triumphant and safe. We would pull out of Heathrow and onto the M25 into a traffic jam. This time I would be penniless, homeless and jobless, but I did not care. I am not turned on by consuming and owning things anymore; doing and contributing is so much more satisfying.

When dusk came we were depressingly short of our goal. A road sign said VALPARAISO 70 KM. We were exhausted and dejected. We were not going to make it after all.

'What do you think?' I asked Tim. We needed to find a field and camp. With an early start we could finish by early afternoon tomorrow. It was so disappointing.

'Let's finish it,' said Tim.

'What TONIGHT!?' I said. I had not even considered this.

Tim recalls:' I remembered my reaction over two years before, when Andy had turned up at the house, out of the blue, and suggested cycling around the world. 'What TONIGHT?' I had said in the Red Lion. It seemed really strange to be so close now. We had to go for it, after all we had been through it was the only way to finish.'

'Yes, TONIGHT'.'

In the dark, we put our heads down and worked through the pain, digging for the last reserves of energy. I led the way as I now had the only head torch and Tim now had the only rear light, the others stolen or broken. Blinded by headlights, we stared down following the verge. When cars came up behind we slid off into the grass. *Don't get knocked off now for God's sake.'* The miles ticked by slowly. We were unbelievably close.

I wondered then if we had seen too much. I didn't see road signs, concrete and petrol stations anymore, I saw shady camping spots and the movement of clouds and the wind in the branches. I didn't see strangers worse than me, I saw fellow travellers on the road, hoping my hopes. I didn't see a river, I saw the source of life, which must be treasured. We had indeed felt too much sun, wind and cold; seen too much sky and wilderness; slept too many nights on rocky ground. We had drunk too much, danced, laughed and shared too much pain and desire.

We'd had too much of everything to let anything be enough again. And it made me smile. I will remember every moment, every single scene is stored away. The challenge now is not how to get new ideas into my head but how to get old ones out. Don't cosume, conserve; don't chase money, chase love; be one with nature, not a user of nature. Can I always live up to these?

Waves of hills greeted us as we neared the coast. When we

reached the VALPARAISO 19 KM sign we were grey-skinned, blank eyed and exhausted. The climbs kept coming. At last the lights of Valparaiso were sprinkled across smooth-domed hills. The Pacific Ocean, last seen as we left Sydney, shimmered in the moonlight. We climbed the very, very last hill and rattled down cobbled streets, past higgledy-piggledy houses, tatty wooden shacks defying gravity and clinging to the muddy hillside. It was after ten o'clock. There, at last, in the city, was the statue of the 'Heroes of Iquique' and the historic harbour, brimming with floodlit ships from Rotterdam and Panama. After one year and fifteen thousand kilometres, we had arrived with an hour and a half to spare.

At the end of the world we sat, numb, on the dock, dangling our feet in the ocean. For many minutes neither of us could speak.

'Have we done it?' said Tim eventually.

'We've done it!' said I.

He put his arms around my shoulders and I around his, the world stopped spinning and we hugged and hugged and hugged.

Have we really done it?

Postscript

On returning from Valparaiso, Tim and Andy spent six months working full-time writing this book, Andy on the remote Inner Hebridean island of Easdale, Tim at home in Shropshire. Since that time they have chosen to follow quite different paths.

Tim has returned to teaching Physical Education in a local secondary school and has shared his experiences with his pupils encouraging them towards open-minded thinking and a spirit of adventure. He has decided to hang up his rugby boots and has become a coach. In his spare time he writes children's fiction and still loves to travel to remote parts of the world.

Andy has chosen to continue on the voyage of self-discovery which originally led him away from a corporate life-style. He has been contributing to the community as an Outward Bound instructor in Scotland and Hong Kong and running his own training business in Beijing, working with children, businessmen, disabled people and university students. He has tried to inspire co-operation, initiative, leadership, team work and respect for the environment, often drawing from personal experience gained from this journey. He now leads a Conservation NGO in Hong Kong which seeks to help people to live in harmony with nature and live sustainable lives for the good of all life present and future.

Suzanne married and had a family with Richard. Tim married Phyl, Andy married Bianca and they all lived peacefully ever after.

Andy's bike retired to a museum on Easdale Island in Scotland and Tim is occasioanlly seen on his in the lanes of Shropshire with a wistful smile on his face.

'What we call the beginning
is often the end,
And to make an end
is to make a beginning.
The end is where we start from.'

T.S Eliot, Little Gidding

Equipment

The total weight of kit excluding bike: 18 kilograms

Clothes – hot weather
Two pairs cycling shorts, one padded
Four T-shirts with expedition logo, one with long-sleeves
Four pairs socks and undies
Bush hat
Rohan lightweight cotton trousers
Sprayway Goretex Spectrum waterproofs plus leggings
Varnay mountain sunglasses
High-Tech boots (Tim's lasted the whole journey)

Clothes – cold weather
Polar-fleece jacket
Full set of thermal underwear
Gloves
Trackie bottoms
Woolly balaclavas

Recording the expedition
Pentax 105 Superzoom 38-105mm (automatic)
Pentax SLR with 28-210mm lens plus polarising filter
Slide, colour and B/W film (kindly donated by Kodak)
Sony professional Walkman (recordings for BBC)

Camping kit
Phoenix Freeranger EB tent (outstanding)
Therm-A-Rest mat (punctured continually)
Snug pack and RAB down 3-season sleeping bags
MSR multi-fuel stove (excellent but didn't like diesel)

Bike gear
Saracen Limited Edition mountain bikes (kindly donated)
Karrimor Kalahari panniers (kindly donated)
Profile bars
Blackburn racks, low-riders on front
Tioga FJN off-road tyres (each set lasted 5,000km)
Semi-slick tyres in Australia
Cat Eye lights
Cat Eye computer
Girvin flexstem
Ultra-light D security lock
12-gauge steel spokes
Deore DX Thumb shifters

Tools and spares
Cool Tool plus add-ons
Sticky tape
Spoke key
Three tubes each
Freewheel remover
Bearings
Teflon, liquid chain lube
One tyre each
Tyre pressure gauge
Ten spokes each
One set of cables
Chain cleaner

Odd nuts and bolts

Also by Eye Books

My Journey with a remarkable tree - Ken Finn
Following a tree from its illegal logging to a piece of furniture
ISBN: 1 903070 384. Price £9.99

Riding the Outlaw Trail - Simon Casson
Following the footsteps of Butch Cassidy and the Sundance Kid, ISBN:
1 903070 228. Price £9.99.

Desert Governess - Phyllis Ellis
A former Benny Hill actress, as governess to the Saudi Arabian Royal
family.
ISBN: 1 903070 015. Price £9.99.

Last of the Nomads - W. J. Peasley
The story of he last desert nomads to live permanently in the
traditional way.
ISBN: 1 903070 325. Price £9.99.

All Will Be Well - Michael Meegan
Stories of love and compassion.
ISBN: 1 903070 279. Price £9.99.

First Contact - Mark Anstice
A 21st Century Discovery of Cannibals + free award winningn DVD
ISBN: 1 903070 260. Price £9.99.

Further Travellers' Tales From Heaven and Hell -
Best entires to a writing competition.
ISBN: 1 903070 112. Price £9.99.

Special Offa - Bob Bibby
A walk along Offa's Dyke looking at the changes over time.
ISBN: 1 903070 287. Price £9.99.

The Good Life - Dorian Amos
A move from Cornwall to the Yukon in search of the good life.
ISBN: 1 903070 309. Price £9.99.

Baghdad Business School - Heyrick Bond Gunning
Setting up a business in the aftermath of conflict.
ISBN: 1 903070 333. Price £9.99.

Green Oranges on Lion Mountain - Emily Joy
An Accidental Optimist working in Sierra Leone.
ISBN: 1 903070 295. Price £9.99.

The Con Artist Handbook - Joel Levy
Get wise with The Con.
ISBN: 1 903070 341. Price £9.99.

The Forensics Handbook - Pete Moore
A clear introduction to the life of Forensics.
ISBN: 1 903070 35X. Price £9.99.

Seeking Sanctuary - Hilda Reilly
Western Muslim converts who have chosen Sudan as their home.
ISBN: 1 903070 392. Price £9.99

Lost Lands Forgotten Stories - Alexandra Pratt
20th Century female explorer follows her 19th Century equivalent
ISBN: 1 903070 368. Price £9.99

Jasmine and Arnica - Nicola Naylor
A blind woman's journey around India.
ISBN: 1 903070 171. Price £9.99.

Touching Tibet - Niema Ash
A journey into the heart of this intriguing forbidden kingdom.
ISBN: 1 903070 18X. Price £9.99.

Behind the Veil - Lydia Laube
A shocking account of a nurse's Arabian nightmare.
ISBN: 1 903070 198. Price £9.99.

Walking Away - Charlotte Metcalf
A well known film makers African journal.
ISBN: 1 903070 201. Price £9.99.

Travels in Outback Australia - Andrew Stevenson
In search of the original Australians - the Aboriginal People.
ISBN: 1 903070 147. Price £9.99

The European Job - Jonathan Booth
10,000 miles around Europe in a 25 year old classic car.
ISBN: 1 903070 252. Price £9.99

Around the World with 1000 Birds - Russell Boyman
An extraordinary answer to a mid-life crisis.
ISBN: 1 903070 163. Price £9.99

Cry from the Highest Mountain - Tess Burrows
A climb to the point furthest from the centre of the earth.
ISBN: 1 903070 120. Price £9.99

Dancing with Sabrina - Bob Bibby
A journey from source to sea of the River Severn.
ISBN: 1 903070 244. Price £9.99

Grey Paes and Bacon - Bob Bibby
A journey around the canals of the Black Country
ISBN: 1 903070 066. Price £7.99

Jungle Janes - Peter Burden
Twelve middle-aged women take on the Jungle. As seen on Ch 4.
ISBN: 1 903070 05 8. Price £7.99

Travels with my Daughter - Niema Ash
Forget convention, follow your instincts.
ISBN: 1 903070 04 X. Price £7.99

Riding with Ghosts - Gwen Maka
One woman's solo cycle ride from Seattle to Mexico.
ISBN: 1 903070 00 7. Price £7.99

Riding with Ghosts: South of the Border - Gwen Maka
The second part of Gwen's epic cycle trip across the Americas.
ISBN: 1 903070 09 0. Price £7.99

Triumph Round the World - Robbie Marshall
He gave up his world for the freedom of the road.
ISBN: 1 903070 08 2. Price £7.99

Fever Trees of Borneo - Mark Eveleigh
A daring expedition through uncharted jungle.
ISBN: 0 953057 56 9. Price £7.99

Frigid Women - Sue and Victoria Riches
The first all-female expedition to the North Pole.
ISBN: 0 953057 52 6. Price £7.99

Jungle Beat - Roy Follows
Fighting Terrorists in Malaya.
ISBN: 0 953057 57 7. Price £7.99

Slow Winter - Alex Hickman
A personal quest against the backdrop of the war-torn Balkans.
ISBN: 0 953057 58 5. Price £7.99

Tea for Two - Polly Benge
She cycled around India to test her love.
ISBN: 0 953057 59 3. Price £7.99

Traveller's Tales from Heaven and Hell - Various
A collection of short stories from a nationwide competition.
ISBN: 0 953057 51 8. Price £6.99

More Traveller's Tales from Heaven and Hell - Various
The second collection of short stories.
ISBN: 1 903070 02 3. Price £6.99

A Trail of Visions: Route 1 - Vicki Couchman
A stunning photographic essay.
ISBN: 1 871349 338. Price £14.99

A Trail of Visions: Route 2 - Vicki Couchman
The second stunning photographic essay.
ISBN: 0 953057 50 X. Price £16.99

About Eye Books

Eye books is a young, dynamic publishing company that likes to break the rules. Our independence allows us to publish books which challenge the way people see things. It also means that we can offer new authors a platform from which they can shine their light and encourage others to do the same.

To date we have published 50 books that cover a number of genres including Travel, Biography, Adventure and History. Many of our books are experience driven. All of them are inspirational and life-affirming.

Frigid Women, for example, tells the story of the world-record making first all female expedition to the North Pole. A fifty year-old mother of three who had recently recovered from a mastectomy, and her daughter are the authors neither had ever written a book before. Sue Riches is now both an author and highly sought after motivational speaker.

We also publish thematic anthologies, such as The Tales from Heaven and Hell series, for those who prefer the short story format. Here everyone has the chance to get their stories published and win prizes such as flights to any destination in the world.

And here's what makes us really different: As well as publishing books, Eye Books has set up a club for like-minded people and is in the process of developing a number of initiatives and services for its community of members. After all, the more you put into life, the more you get out of it.

Please visit www.eye-books.com for further information.

Eye Club Membership

Each month, we receive hundreds of enquiries' from people who have read our books, discovered our website or entered our competitions. All of these people have certain things in common; a desire to achieve, to extend the boundaries of everyday life and to learn from others' experiences.

Eye Books has, therefore, set up a club to unite these like-minded people. It is a community where members can exchange ideas, contact authors, discuss travel, both future and past as well as receive information and offers from ourselves.

Membership is free.

Benefits of the Eye Club

As a member of the Eye Club:

• You are offered the invaluable opportunity to contact our authors directly.
• You will be able to receive a regular newsletter, information on new book releases and company developments as well as discounts on new and past titles.
• You can attend special member events such as book launches, author talks and signings.
• Receive discounts on a variety of travel related products and services from Eye Books partners.
• In addition, you can enjoy entry into Eye Books competitions including the ever popular Heaven and Hell series and our monthly book competition.

To register your membership, simply visit our website and register on our club pages: www.eye-books.com.